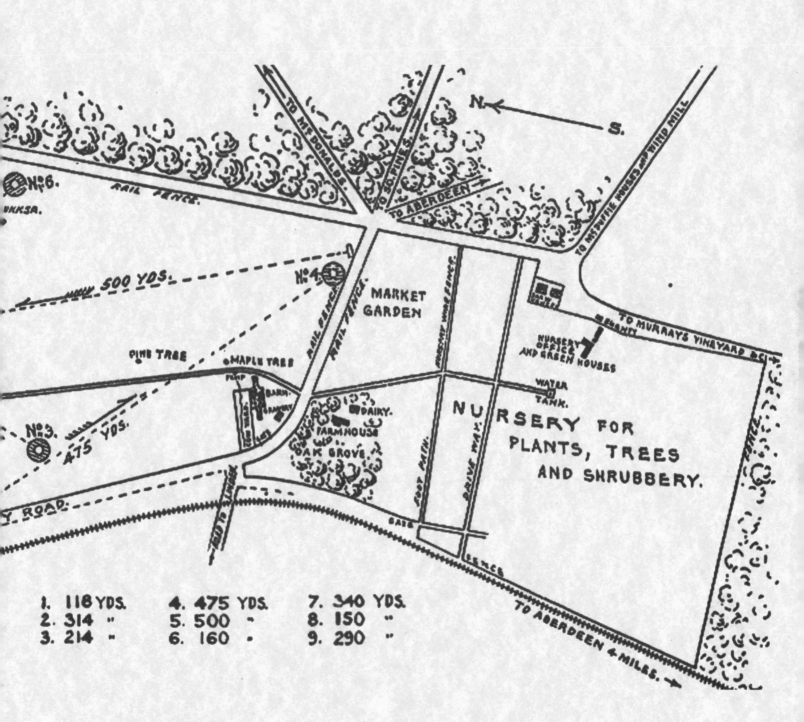

1. 118 YDS.   4. 475 YDS.   7. 340 YDS.
2. 314 "   5. 500 "   8. 150 "
3. 214 "   6. 160 "   9. 290 "

PINEHURST

Home of American Golf
The Evolution of a Legend

Richard Mandell
Golf Course Architect

foreword by
world renowned
golf course architect
Rees Jones

design and layout
by
Jay Bursky

T. Eliot Press
P. O. Box 1119
Pinehurst, North Carolina 28370

First edition published 2007
Printed and bound in the United States of America

10 9 8 7 6 5 4 3 2 1

Library of Congress Control Number: 2007902932
ISBN – 13: 978-0-9794836-0-8
ISBN – 10: 0-9794836-0-3

Book and cover design by Jay Bursky of Studio J (Pinehurst, North Carolina and Upper Nyack, New York)
This book was set in Adobe Garamond Pro and Avenir

To Mary and Thomas

and those who are fascinated by the evolution of a golf course...

THERE IS NO BETTER WAY TO UNDERSTAND WHAT PINEHURST IS ALL ABOUT THAN TO GO BACK TO THE ORIGINAL IDEALS OF ITS FOUNDER. It was the hope of James W. Tufts to establish at Pinehurst a small friendly community where those in need of it could find health-giving relaxation either for their years of retirement or for the purpose of equipping them to perform their daily tasks more efficiently. Through the course of time the fulfillment of this function by Pinehurst has largely been entrusted to the game of golf. The placement of this confidence is fully justified, as there surely is no occupation which can do more for the individual along the lines the founder had in mind.

- Richard Sise Tufts (1962)

TABLE OF CONTENTS

FOREWORD

I HAVE BEEN VISITING PINEHURST SINCE THE 1950'S, WHEN MY FATHER, ROBERT TRENT JONES, WOULD PILE OUR FAMILY INTO OUR STATION WAGON AND DRIVE TO FLORIDA EVERY WINTER. It was a magical place to my father and it has become a magical place to me.

My father loved Pinehurst because the sandy soil, the gently rolling topography, and the way the ground would accept the molding of almost any type of golf course feature made it a natural place for golf. He greatly admired Donald Ross, who lived on the famed Pinehurst Number Two course. These two golf architects knew each other well and along with a handful of other designers, they founded the American Society of Golf Course Architects. Fittingly, their first meeting was held in Pinehurst in 1947.

I guess you could say that I inherited this love for Pinehurst, but I also came to love it in ways my father never experienced. In 1967, while at a friend's wedding reception at The Carolina hotel, I proposed to my wife. She grew up in the area and we have made many trips back to Pinehurst to spend family Thanksgivings and visit friends and relatives.

I also have had the good fortune to be professionally connected to Pinehurst. In 1978, I presided as President of the American Society of Golf Course Architects during our annual meeting in the very same ballroom where my wife accepted my proposal. The sandhills is one of my favorite places to work because the sandy soils are so well-suited for golf. In coordination with my father's design firm (and then on my own) I remodeled The Country Club of North Carolina. Years later, I designed Talamore Golf Resort (in 1991).

One of the highlights of my career was becoming part of the Pinehurst Resort legacy with my design of Pinehurst Number Seven in the mid-1980's. I remember the excitement of the day I got that job as if it were yesterday: I sat at my kitchen table until the wee hours of the morning, working and reworking the routing of what became one of my favorite courses.

Also at the top of my professional resume was being asked to authentically restore the hallowed ground of Pinehurst Number Two, Donald Ross's classic, in preparation for the 1999 United States Open Championship. That Open was one of the most memorable ever, in part because it was the last championship won by Payne Stewart in such an exciting finish. It was hugely successful by USGA standards as well. The event was smoothly organized and easily accessible to the spectators thanks to the remarkable skills of the Pinehurst Resort staff. To that point, the USGA chose to return the championship to Pinehurst Number Two for the 2005 Open, which I again tweaked by adding more length to the course. Certainly more championships are on the horizon.

ONE COULD APPLY THE MAXIM "GEOGRAPHY IS DESTINY" TO PINEHURST. Although James Tufts, who founded Pinehurst, did not come to the Sandhills of North Carolina to create the golf mecca that exists today, he was an astute businessman and recognized an opportunity when he saw it. He soon brought Donald Ross to Pinehurst to implement his vision of a place where Northerners could come for

Rees splits the first fairway on opening day of Pinehurst Number Seven.
(Courtesy: Rees Jones)

good weather, a healthy environment, and recreation. Sandhills recreation by the early 1900's meant the game of golf.

The essence of Tufts's vision of Pinehurst is essentially the same today as it was in 1895 - give people a healthy, beautiful place to be restored. As the focus on Pinehurst increases, the history that Richard Mandell has preserved in his book Pinehurst: Home of American Golf will become increasingly important as well. Richard and I share a passion for the legacy of Pinehurst. He lives in the area and is himself a golf course architect. In this book, his love for golf and his knowledge of Sandhills history is truly displayed.

By writing this text, rich in detail and folklore, Richard allows golfers around the globe to learn about the area's history and the evolution of one of the great golf complexes in the world. Many golf course architects have brought their talent to bear on this sandy land, and their stories are enormously interesting. Although his area of expertise is course architecture (of which he writes very well), the thoroughness of his research goes beyond the famous courses and into the quirks of history. He talks about the land, the early settlers, and the arrival of Mr. Tufts – all with colorful attention to detail.

The winds of change have swept through the Sandhills since Tufts passed away. But cross-currents can be revitalizing, and today, the Pinehurst mystique is stronger than ever. Richard Mandell has been captivated by this mystique and so have I. To this day, the smell of North Carolina Longleaf Pine brings back all those good memories Richard has recounted in Pinehurst ~ Home of American Golf.

- Rees Jones, April 20, 2007

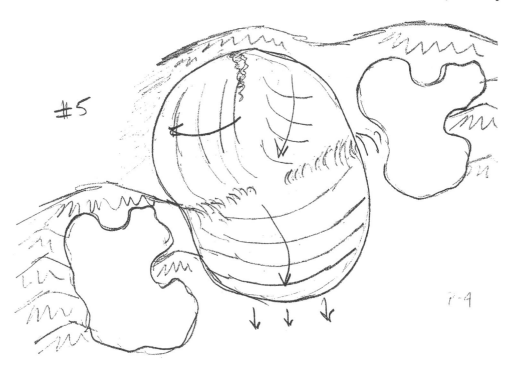

1982 Jones Sketch of Renovations to the Fifth Green of Pinehurst Number Four
(Courtesy: Rees Jones)

PREFACE

I AM SURROUNDED BY GOLF COURSES. Every day I wake up and look out my bedroom window to see the manicured turf and brick wall framing the entrance to a golf course on Midland Road, the main thoroughfare connecting the Village of Pinehurst and the Town of Southern Pines. When I open up my front door to get my newspaper, I am welcomed by one of the most beautiful sights one can possess: The sun coming over the horizon and burning the early morning dew off the green grass of another golf course. The sunlight reflecting on the rolling mounds and hollows create a variety of shadows and hues. This particular course has an old horse track running between my front yard and condominiums in the background. Each morning, the view reminds me of my first trip to Scotland and a little nine-hole golf course outside Edinburgh called Musselburgh Golf Links.

Musselburgh was the site of six British Opens from 1874 to 1889. It, too, has a horse track surrounding its holes and row houses across the street. When I stood on the first tee early one fall morning some years back, I was captivated by how the sunlight played puppeteer to the shadows dancing off the timeworn mounds and hollows and the horse track. I was instantly entranced by the solitude of Links Road and the homes lined up sentinel over the wee links on the other side of the racecourse.

It was in those very row houses where Willie Park introduced the game of golf to his son Willie, Jr. in the mid-1800's. In 1860, Willie captured the first British Open at Prestwick Golf Links to the west. Father

Musselburgh Golf Links in Edinburgh, Scotland
(Courtesy: Richard Mandell)

and son went on to win six British Opens between them. In addition to being a great player, the elder Willie was a club and ball maker as well as a dabbler in golf design. Most importantly, he laid the foundation for his son at Musselburgh, who became one of the true pioneers in the field of course design. My own visual connection to Willie Park Jr. reminds me of ties to another golf architect. Donald Ross and I both share the same home in the middle of nowhere.

The Sandhills of North Carolina does not have the breathtaking views of the Monterey Peninsula in California or golf holes perched precariously on rocky bluffs overlooking the Pacific Ocean. In fact, the closest ocean is more than two hours away. The land here lacks the mountainous topography of Colorado or the daunting scenery found in Monterey and countless other places. One thing the Sandhills does possess is sand (obviously), and lots of it. Sand is the primary element that contributes to the very essence of golf because the game was always meant to be played on firm and fast soils, most typically associated with links land of the British Isles.

It was on links land where the origins of the game promoted the art of shotmaking (adjustment of the golf swing to adapt to various conditions). A golf course that promotes shotmaking must present challenges to the golf ball through deflection, redirection, and defense. Adept golfers observe the way the ball travels along the rolling landscape, knowing the ability to control the bounce of the ball is the key to success. With few vertical elements to rely upon, the golfer must rely on judgement, feel, and memory. It is these skills which distinguish links golf from the modern American game (played through the air) and that is what first made the game so attractive.

Links land is *typically* found in coastal areas throughout the world, including the United States. Yet, there are pockets of sand sprinkled throughout other areas of the country. The most well-known pocket to golfers all over the world is the Carolina Sandhills.

How in the middle of North Carolina, surrounded by seemingly more productive land and natural resources, did such a non-descript land form become a destination all golfers live to make, where the USGA has held numerous championships, where even non-golfers recognize the town names? Conventional wisdom conceded one couldn't grow anything on its useless ground. Years ago, this land could have been purchased for just 25¢ an acre surrounded by more fertile Piedmont clay valued at $10 an acre. The land was left for nothing as lumber magnates stripped it of the only resource it had: pine trees. They were desperate to give it away.

More than one hundred years later, Pinehurst is known as the Home of American Golf. When golfers arrive, a simplicity takes over the landscape. The red clay disappears and in its place a cream-white sand emerges. Slopes along the highways reveal the most interesting rills and ridges, formed by centuries of natural erosion. Towering pine trees frame the horizon. The closer one gets, green brush strokes intermingle with sienna-toned pine needles covering the ground like a carpet. The golfers' senses heighten as these green swaths slowly reveal themselves as golf holes. The peaceful Village of Pinehurst, a New England-like town transplanted to the south, awaits golfers upon their arrival.

An anonymous resident may have best described the character of the Sandhills and what makes it ideal for golf course design: *"The gentle inequalities of the surface are all that relieves the weary eye. You constantly meet with little hills which nature seems to have disunited in a frolic."* The deserted landscape of the Sandhills may be of little value for most endeavors, but the soils and peculiar topography make it gold when it comes to golf course development.

There is only one geographic location in America where golf took hold early, influenced the game consistently over a century's growth, and became a true Mecca for golfers everywhere. Pinehurst, North Carolina, matured into the first golf resort in America and was the first golf destination to have four golf courses, and then five, from one clubhouse. Today, the Sandhills is one of the top three golf destination areas in the world, boasting more than forty golf courses in a fifty-square-mile area.

The story of its evolution is one of dumb luck, ingenuity, and grand visions.

A Sandhills Setting
(Courtesy: Tufts Archives)

THE SPIRIT OF ST. ANDREWS IS ALIVE AND WELL IN PINEHURST.

CHAPTER ONE
LIFE BEFORE TUFTOWN

"Its winter climate is sufficiently mild for a very large class of invalids who now go to Florida or Aiken [South Carolina], because they know of no suitable locality nearer..."

- Washington Carruthers Kerr (North Carolina State Geologist, 1890)

JOHN TYRANT PATRICK WAS A MAN OF VISION. His vision was to transform a piece of land with nothing going for it, not even location, into a health resort that would help mend a country shattered by a debilitating civil war. As one of the country's first true developers, Patrick's plan was to create a destination where the sick could heal their weary bodies from tuberculosis and other ailments. Initially to be known as Vineland, he soon renamed his resort *"Southern Pines."* He decided Southern Pines would more appropriately attract the clientele he sought, much like the quaint village he hoped it would one day emulate.

Patrick's village was to be modeled after the premier resort in the Sandhills of the day. His prototype was a refuge for northerners to escape cold winters and relax among the tall bristling pines. It was a place where visitors embraced an irresistible small town atmosphere. It was a resort with unparalleled service and recreational opportunity. Of course, that resort could only be one place in the New South. Patrick's true inspiration for his own resort was the famed resort in Jackson Springs, North Carolina, twenty miles west of Southern Pines.

At Jackson Springs, a small health resort of ante-bellum years was in the process of revival. Northerners were attracted by the pleasant year-round climate, the simple life in cabins and cottages among the longleaf, the genial southern manners and the tasty southern cooking. According to a New York physician named G. H. Saddleson, who once suffered from tuberculosis and dyspepsia, the springs offered great remedy:

Jackson Springs, North Carolina
(Courtesy: Tufts Archives)

"Where the longleaf pine exists ozone is generated largely and it has been demonstrated that persons suffering with throat and pulmonary diseases are much benefitted when living in an atmosphere impregnated with this gas..."

Jackson Springs Hotel
(Courtesy: Tufts Archives)

THE ROADS JOHN TYRANT PATRICK TRAVELED TO STUDY HIS PROTOTYPE AT JACKSON SPRINGS WERE ONCE ANCIENT TRAILS TREAD BY PREHISTORIC BUFFALO, DEER, AND NOMADIC BANDS OF INDIANS. Long before Midland Road linked Pinehurst and Southern Pines and fourteen golf courses along the way, long before it became the first divided highway in America, it served as a primary ancient Indian trail in the southeastern United States known as the Yadkin Trail.

Toward the end of the ice age, when glacial

ice still covered much of North America, North Carolina was very cold and wet. Mastodon roamed alongside buffalo, deer, and bear. Ancient trails in the Sandhills like the Yadkin (running east-west) and the Pee Dee (running north-south) were first beaten out by buffalo in their annual migrations from the Piedmont to the coastal marshes in autumn and upon their return in spring. The first North Carolina Indians migrated from the west 10,000 years ago, tracking these ancient herds. Known as Paleo-Indians, they lived in bands of no more than fifty people, stayed in one place as long as possible, and moved to better resources only when necessary.

Sioux Indians
(Courtesy: Educational Technology Clearinghouse)

About 8,000 B.C. the Paleo-Indians gave way to the Archaic peoples who were more sedentary than the Paleos and gathered seeds and nuts from the forest floors, fished, and trapped game. Around 500 B.C., the Woodland Indians evolved and hunted with bow and arrow, supplementing their fare with rudimentary agricultural practices. Early in the sixteenth century, various Indian groups developed distinctive cultural traits, yet were still bound by common Woodland Indian languages such as Iroquoian and Algonquin. The Sioux emerged as the dominant tribe of North Carolina and cultivated fields of squash, beans, corn and tobacco in the proximity of springs or water courses, and hunted with finely-made sawtooth-edged arrowheads.

The Indians of the Sandhills first emerged around 500 A.D. About six miles southeast of Mt. Gilead (west of Moore County), archaeologists uncovered what is believed to have been an ancient political, religious, and cultural center of Sioux Indians of the Pee Dee area. The camp and the Sioux were destroyed by Shawnee and Cherokee tribes three or four hundred years ago.

The greatest contribution the Sioux made to the Sandhills was the development of the Yadkin and Pee Dee Trails into genuine thoroughfares. Indian camp sites along the Yadkin were found just east of Pinehurst (between the village and the traffic circle along Midland Road and extending south to the Pinehurst Number Four course). Two Indian camp sites were found along the Pee Dee Road where it once crossed present-day Southern Pines, at the corner of Bennett Street and Illinois Avenue.

Giovanni da Verrazzano
(Courtesy: Comune di Prato)

THE FIRST EUROPEAN EXPLORER TO REACH NORTH CAROLINA WAS ITALIAN GIOVANNI DA VERRAZZANO IN 1524, HIRED BY THE FRENCH TO FIND A NORTHERLY ROUTE TO CHINA. When he stumbled upon the Pamlico Sound, Verrazzano mistakenly assumed it was the Pacific Ocean. For years, maps showed "*The Sea of Verrazzano*" stretching from the Carolina Coast to southern California. In 1583, the first English exploration of North Carolina was attempted. Five others followed. All failed to establish a settlement as ships were lost at sea, bad weather killed off settlers, and bands of Indians murdered any remaining English. After these failed expeditions, North Carolina Indians remained undisturbed for decades.

The first successful North Carolina settlers came not from the Atlantic Ocean, but from the Virginia territory in search of income-producing commodities. In February 1622, John Pory, former secretary of the Virginia colony, set out for the Chowan River. It was reported that Pory had passed through a "*great forest of Pynes 15 or 16 myle broad and above 60 myle long. The pines would serve well for Masts for Shipping, and for pitch and tarre.*" The land Pory found was described as "*a fruitful Countrie blessed with abundance of Corne, reaped twise a yeere.*"

By 1655, in the area east of the Chowan River and south of the Great Dismal Swamp, North Carolina had its first permanent settlement. This began an exodus south as Englishmen from Virginia found acres of arable land. The land was sometimes acquired for "*a valuable consideration of satisfaction.*" Other times they paid nothing at all and risked the consequences. Indian land was in high demand and land-hungry settlers continued to stream into North Carolina from Virginia.

Collecting Pine Pitch
(Courtesy: Tufts Archives)

Tar Kiln
(Courtesy: Tufts Archives)

THE NAVAL STORES ACT OF 1705 WAS SOON PASSED BY THE ENGLISH PARLIAMENT TO PROVIDE A STIMULUS TO THE DEVELOPING NORTH CAROLINA ECONOMY. English mercantilists hoped the Act would wean the British shipbuilding industry from its dependence on products made in such countries as Sweden and Finland. The Act encouraged production in North America by offering subsidies for tar, pitch, and hemp (essential materials for the construction and maintenance of wooden sailing ships).

For North Carolina merchants and planters, the Naval Stores Act subsidies meant the trade in tar and pitch was suddenly profitable, especially for those among the Longleaf Pine stands in the Cape Fear region. Longleaf yielded tremendous amounts of resin, the raw material necessary for production of turpentine. *"The Planters make their Servants cut large cavities on each side of the Pitch-Pine tree wherein the turpentine* [resin] *runs,"* explained North Carolina naturalist John Brickell. The resin drained into containers near the bottom of the tree where servants ladled it into barrels. Every few weeks it was taken to a distillery and

Turpentiner
(Courtesy: Tufts Archives)

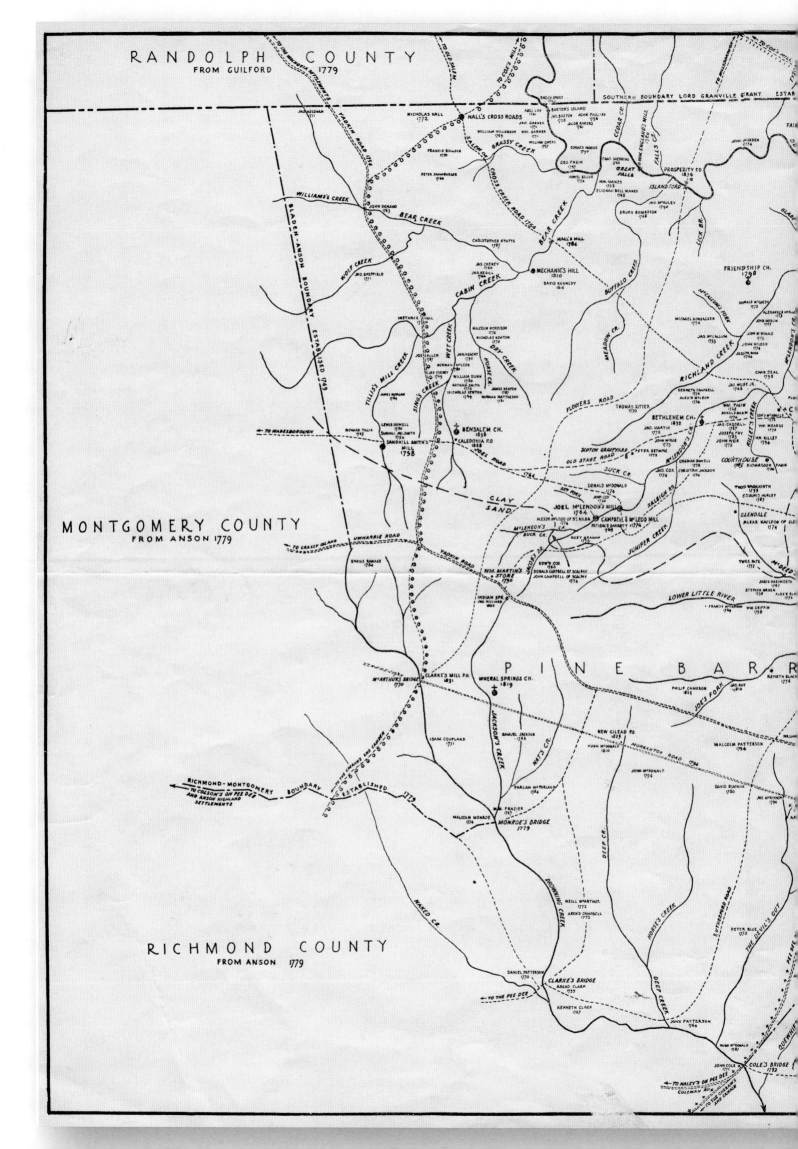

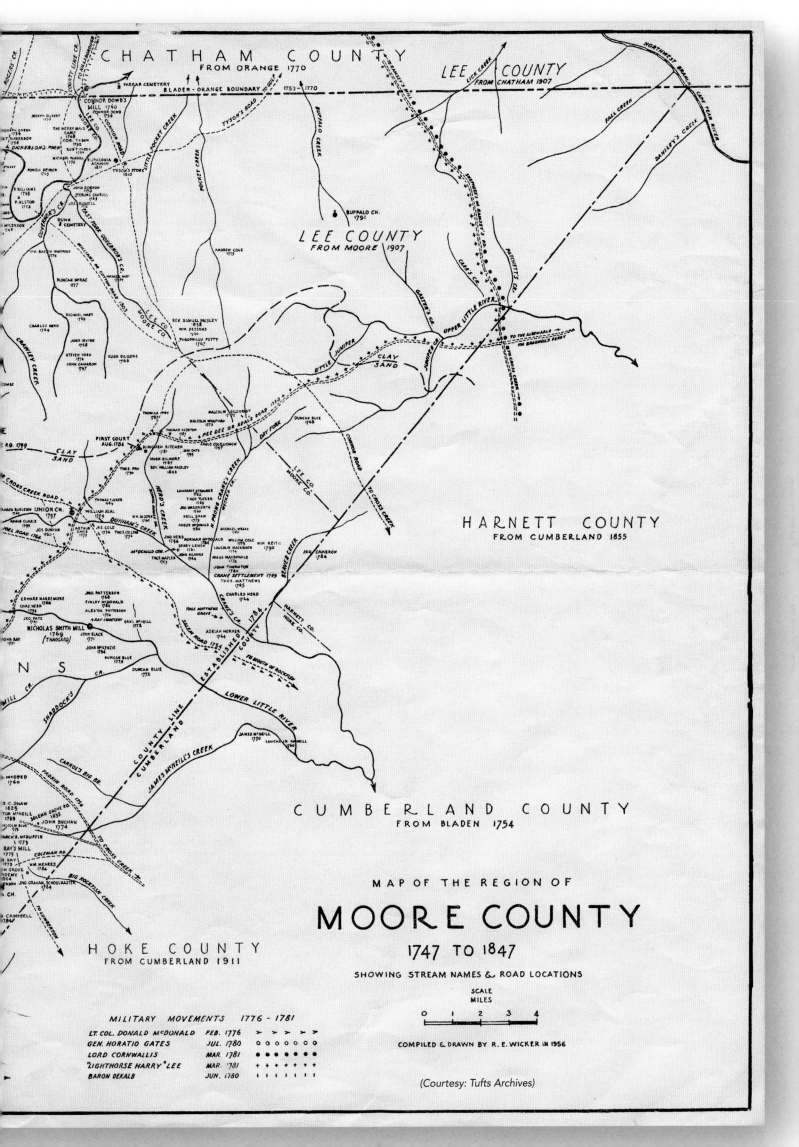

MAP OF THE REGION OF

MOORE COUNTY
1747 TO 1847

SHOWING STREAM NAMES & ROAD LOCATIONS

SCALE
MILES
0 1 2 3 4

COMPILED & DRAWN BY R. E. WICKER IN 1956

(Courtesy: Tufts Archives)

CHATHAM COUNTY
FROM ORANGE 1770

LEE COUNTY
FROM CHATHAM 1907

LEE COUNTY
FROM MOORE 1907

HARNETT COUNTY
FROM CUMBERLAND 1855

CUMBERLAND COUNTY
FROM BLADEN 1754

HOKE COUNTY
FROM CUMBERLAND 1911

MILITARY MOVEMENTS 1776 - 1781

LT. COL. DONALD McDONALD	FEB. 1776	> > > > >
GEN. HORATIO GATES	JUL. 1780	o o o o o o
LORD CORNWALLIS	MAR. 1781	• • • • • •
"LIGHTHORSE HARRY" LEE	MAR. 1781	+ + + + + +
BARON DEKALB	JUN. 1780	ı ı ı ı ı ı ı

separated into the clear turpentine and a darker solid called rosin, scraped from the residue left in the cauldrons after the distillation process. An observer in 1765 claimed one slave would tend three thousand boxed trees to produce about one hundred barrels of turpentine.

Each tree ran resin for about three years before dying and falling to the ground. The wood of these pines, referred to as "*lightwood*", was then burned to make tar. Slaves would select a site, usually on top of a small rise, and fashion a concave floor. They would then cover the lightwood with "*clay earth or sods*" and set it on fire through holes opened in the turf. The wood burned continuously for several days and generally produced 160 to 180 barrels of tar. Sailors would then patch leaks with the tar and coated a ship's rigging to protect the ropes from the salty air. Workers also boiled tar into a more concentrated form called "*pitch*." For thousands of years, boat makers used pine pitch to waterproof the seams between the planks of their ships.

WITH THE EVENTUAL DISAPPEARANCE OF THE INDIANS AROUND 1725, NEWCOMERS OF WELSH DESCENT SETTLED ALONG THE NORTHEAST CAPE FEAR RIVER IN 1730. Starting in 1732, Scottish Highlanders emigrated from Argyle, Inverness, Moray, Ross, Sutherland, Islay, the Orkneys and the Shetlands into the Cape Fear back country. Later on, Scotch-Irish and German immigrants from Pennsylvania, Maryland, and Virginia traveled down the Great Wagon Road to the North Carolina Piedmont, seeking better religious and political conditions. The first permanent residents of the area were John and Thomas Richardson, who settled on Deep River some time prior to 1747.

The first Highland Scots arrived in the Sandhills around 1754. They simply moved upriver along the Cape Fear to settle what land remained available, disregarding soil composition. In 1769, a settler named Hector McNeill located to the southeastern section of Moore County on land now occupied by Southern Pines Country Club. Prominent among the first Highland families to settle in Moore were the Camerons, Blues, Curries, Rays, McDonalds, McQueens, and Campbells. The overwhelming majority of these highlanders were desperately poor and illiterate, but they quickly displayed a native ability that led them to develop a hardworking, self-educated community.

Just as these early settlers were adjusting to their new lives, they were faced with the choice of loyalty to the King who gave them their land or freedom as part of an independent nation. No great battles of the Revolutionary War were fought in Moore County, but its roads were tread by Lord Cornwallis on his march from Guilford Courthouse. In 1780, the Foxfire area was the site of a skirmish between Tory and Whig forces. Tory forces led a surprise attack on a camp of Whigs, massacring several American patriots.

UNTIL THE LATTER PART OF THE 1800's THE NORTH CAROLINA SANDHILLS REMAINED SPARSELY SETTLED, MOSTLY BY CATTLEMEN WHO LET THEIR COWS AND HOGS FREELY ROAM THE WOODS. A harsh frontier life lingered in the Sandhills. The farmer hoed a corn patch and tended a pig pen, making his own bread and raising his own meat. His family spun wool, cotton, and flax into thread to make cloth for garments. Such a farm produced little more than life's necessities. A small surplus of cotton, grain, wool, or tobacco went to the crossroads store in exchange for salt, gunpowder, iron nails, and liquor. By 1847, the Sandhills' dunes and bottoms became so densely forested with the tall Longleaf Pine that relatively little naturally open ground existed. The forest floor was covered inches deep with pine straw; animals struggled to find pastureland.

But hope ran high that America would discover Moore County and its resources, bringing economic prosperity. Due to the proximity of the Yadkin and Pee Dee Roads (as well as a burgeoning timber business), the Sandhills benefitted from major transportation advances in North Carolina. The new Fayetteville and Western Plank Road was planned for freight wagons and coaches. Paved with thick wooden planks, the road was to run northwest from the head of the Cape Fear River in Fayetteville to Salem, 129 miles away in Forsyth County. Toll houses were set up at intervals of ten to twelve miles to supervise traffic and collect fees. The pine forests of the Sandhills, previously only slightly exploited for lumber and naval stores, appealed to a new breed of entrepreneur traveling the Plank Road. The first rush for land occurred in the fall of 1851 when the State sold vast stretches of longleaf pine for a few pennies per acre.

The Western North Carolina Railroad was chartered in December 1852, built to connect Fayetteville with the recently-discovered coal region of Moore and Chatham Counties. Unfortunately, the civil war slowed work on the railroad. Consequently, the Plank Road did not become the commercial artery locals hoped for because there was no commerce to pass over it during the conflict between the states.

Transporting Pine to the Mill
(Courtesy: Sandhills Area Land Trust)

Working the Lumber Yard
(Courtesy: Tufts Archives)

Moore County sent fifteen hundred soldiers into the Confederate Army, representing virtually all of the county's white men capable of bearing arms. A few miles from where Southern Pines Country Club sits today, near the Connecticut Avenue extension, random fighting took place. Thankfully, little damage was caused by the few brief marches through Moore County by both armies. By the end of the war, however, the locals were without money, prospects, and almost without food. Sandhills residents on the whole did not rely on slave labor, but reconstruction after the war affected the residents of the area as poverty and discouragement crept into daily lives.

Hopes rose again when railroad construction resumed after the war. As important as the Plank Road was to Moore County development before the war, the emerging railroad industry after the war literally put the area on the map. In 1874, the Raleigh and Augusta Air Line Railroad reached the Sandhills. Three years later, it linked Raleigh to Hamlet (the line later merged with others to become the Seaboard Airline Railroad). Freight stations were established every ten miles to handle pitch, tar, turpentine, and timber of the Sandhills. By 1880, Moore County had no less than twenty-two distilling operations with twenty-six sawmills and twenty-two cooperages (barrel makers) for the burgeoning barrel-making industry.

Suddenly, the Sandhills was a prosperous place for business. A man named M. J. Blue established a turpentine distillery at a freight station called Blue's Crossing. When the

Allison Francis Page
(Courtesy: Tufts Archives)

The Aberdeen & Rockfish Railroad
(Courtesy: Tufts Archives)

Seaboard Airline Railroad reached Blue's Crossing in 1876, a depot for the shipment of lumber was immediately established. Lumber operators were able to transport their products anywhere in the world via hundreds of ships anchored in Wilmington and Charleston.

ALLISON FRANCIS PAGE HAD BEEN BORN IN WAKE COUNTY, NORTH CAROLINA IN 1824.

As a youth, he had become a pioneer in the production of lumber by use of the steam mill and had contracted

Charles Shaw
(Courtesy: Moore County Historical Association)

with North Carolina's early railroads to provide crossties. But the civil war destroyed Page's fortune and he was forced to scout for new frontiers. Fifty-five years old and $10,000 in debt, Page and his son Robert arrived at Blue's Crossing in 1879 hoping to rebound. By June of the following year he was able to buy 1,660 acres of timber for $3.50 each. Once again he became a highly successful lumberman. By 1882, Page built the first lumber mill at Blue's Crossing and several miles of tramway across Moore County to haul timber to the mill. Tram cars trundled back and forth upon wooden rails, dragging tremendous freights of logs that would have sunk wagons hub-deep in the soft sand. By the 1890's, dozens of tramways twisted through the forests, hauling out millions of board feet of timber.

Page then decided to build a true railroad, with iron tracks and a steam locomotive along a new line to the western boundary of Moore County and beyond to Asheboro. It was called the Aberdeen and West End Railroad. In 1892, the Aberdeen and Rockfish Railroad began operating in the opposite direction. That same year Blue's Crossing officially became the Town of Aberdeen. Francis' son Robert was the town's first Mayor.

THE ARRIVAL OF RAIL BROUGHT ABOUT A PERIOD OF FEVERISH AND WANTON DESTRUCTION OF THE LONGLEAF PINE FOREST. When the trees gave out in the pursuit of naval stores, lumbermen came in, the forests were stripped clean, and the tramways were abandoned when the timber cutters moved to the next area. One such lumberman was named Charles Shaw. Back in 1821, Shaw had begun purchasing land in Moore County, thinking it would be a good investment for naval stores and lumber. He bought over 2500 acres extending from a freight station called Manly south to Blue's Crossing. In less than ten years, the timber was depleted. Shaw and his wife built a house at the crossroads of Morganton and Pee Dee Roads. Their barren acreage was named Shaw's Ridge.

In 1884, John Tyrant Patrick acquired 675 acres of land from the Shaw family for $1,265. At the time, Patrick was the State Commissioner of Immigration. His charge was to create ways to attract people to North Carolina. He focused his attention on the Sandhills' empty countryside and superb climate. His personal motivation, however, was to champion towns along the Seaboard Airline Railroad. Traveling from town to town, he bought up as much land as possible until he was one of the largest landowners in the state. He stayed at each site long enough to see the settlement off to a good start, then moved his tent to the next spot.

Southern Pines Train Depot
(Courtesy: Moore County Historical Association)

Upon Patrick's purchase from the Shaws, he established the New England Manufacturing, Mining, and Estate Company. He hoped the name would attract prospective settlers from New England and brought in engineers to help lay out a new town he called *"Vineland."* Patrick soon decided the name Southern Pines was more appropriate for his plan to create a health resort for northerners suffering from consumption (tuberculosis, or the Great White Plague). At the time, the only treatment was fresh air, sunshine, and mineral water.

North Carolina's State Geologist at the time, Washington Carruthers Kerr, endorsed Patrick's town based upon his expert opinion of the desirable qualities of the Sandhills. These qualities included a *"sufficiently mild"* climate, *"the most perfect drainage possible"*, an elevation of 600 feet, and *"that it is within twenty hours of New York; so that a multitude of people can easily reach it."*

Despite the strong support, the fledgling resort experienced difficult times in the early 1890's. In order to stay afloat, Patrick and the town commissioners shifted their business strategy from a refuge for consumptives to a *"winter resort for all who wished to enjoy a temperate climate during the cold months."* Within three years of the market shift, the town grew from *"a half-dozen pretty cottages, one hotel, another in construction, and a railroad depot,"* to almost one thousand residents, two-thirds of which were winter visitors from New England. One of those New England guests went by the name of James Walker Tufts. Every bit the salesman Patrick was, Tufts saw the same value in Southern Pines and decided to create his own health resort for consumptives.

*The corner of Broad Street and New York Avenue in downtown
Southern Pines. The Piney Woods Inn sits on the hill to the far right.*
(Courtesy: Moore County Historical Association)

CHAPTER TWO
THE PINEHURST IDEAL

"There is an old chap up in Boston who I fear has more money than good common sense, and he has a wild scheme in the back of his head that he can make a resort up here in these barren sand wastes."

- Walter Hines Page

IT WAS CLEARLY HIGHWAY ROBBERY. Highway robbery by whom was the issue. The salesman or the purchaser? On the surface, it seemed as if the seller had pulled a fast one, or so the locals thought. Sandhills resident Neil Shaw certainly was convinced the asking price was inflated by at least twenty-five percent.

Looking back on this particular transaction, however, it very well could be that the buyer was the culprit. This miscreant was the new owner of more than five thousand barren acres of sand. So barren was this land that when it rained an attentive listener could detect the sizzling rain as it must have clearly struck the depths of hell. So barren that crows would find their own food before flying over this wasteland. The land was so devoid of life that the buyer's son thought it only existed to bind the rest of the world together.

Once home to the most beautiful Longleaf Pine forest in the world, lumbermen came, made their fortunes, and then left this desolate land for dead. Anyone with the gusto to buy some of this land – much less 5,000 acres of it – must not be worried about going hungry, or thirsty for that matter. Luckily so, the buyer was a person well versed in satisfying people's thirst. He was the inventor of the Famous Arctic Soda Fountain: Mr. James Walker Tufts of Boston, Massachusetts.

"I have had an amusing experience. There is an old chap up in Boston who I fear has more money than good common sense, and he has a wild scheme in the back of his head that he

can make a resort up here in these barren sand wastes. We have just finished extracting the turpentine from a large number of pines on a big acreage and then cut them up for lumber. There are about ten thousand acres in all. I asked him to make me an offer and he suggested that it might be worth $1.00 an acre, but I closed the deal by selling it to him for $7,500. He gave me his check for $500 to bind the bargain, but I am afraid that I will never see him once he gets home and thinks it over."

- Walter Hines Page to Frank Presbrey (1895)

Page did indeed hear again from the "*old chap*", but it was nip and tuck while Tufts surveyed nearby sites before settling on what was referred to as the "*JR McDuffie, 4,800 acre tract*." The land had been purchased by the Page family from the McDuffie brothers, who operated a turpentine distillery just beyond the two lower ponds on where the Pinehurst Number One course sits today (in front of the eleventh and twelfth tees).

James Walker Tufts
(Courtesy: Tufts Archives)

James's grandson Richard recounted early negotiations:

"*Grandfather had looked over the tract and left to look at other sites, I believe at Hoffman and perhaps the Overhills tract near Fayetteville. Mr. Page had given up hope of making a sale when on Sunday a colored boy appeared at his house and said there was a gentleman waiting at his office...*"

The gentleman was Tufts and after meeting with Page, he agreed to purchase more than 5,000 acres for the astronomical sum of $1.02 per acre. There was nothing on the property except a few blackjack oaks and scattered patches of wire grass.

The natives thought Tufts was clearly boondoggled and robbed blind by Page. That old Shaw fellow was convinced the land could only be worth eighty-five cents an acre and this Yankee was swindled. It was indeed Shaw's humble opinion, but who really swindled whom? By many accounts these holdings as they sit today are valued at $150,000 an acre.

JAMES TUFTS WASN'T THE TYPICAL LAND DEVELOPER. He

certainly wasn't the typical golf course builder so common today, one who pores over feasibility studies and runs numerous spreadsheets and proformas to develop the best business plan for golf. In fact, there is ample evidence from his family members that James Tufts never heard of the game of golf when he made his purchase in June of 1895.

He was born on February 11th, 1835, in Charlestown, Massachusetts, to Leonard and Hepzibah Tufts. One of his first work experiences was as a sixteen-year-old apprentice in an apothecary store owned by Samuel Kidder in Charlestown. At twenty-one, he opened his own store and soon expanded to a chain of three apothecary shops in Medford, Massachusetts. After becoming fascinated with the mechanics and creativity of

(Courtesy: Library Of Philadelphia)

soda fountains, he moved away from the pharmacy business toward the development of syrups and fountain apparatus.

His venture was named the Tufts Soda Fountain Company and it produced and distributed an ornate Italian marble soda fountain in England and the United States. His company also specialized in manufacturing an extensive line of silver-plated items such as pitchers, dishes and vases. Tufts was one of the first to develop a carbon dioxide cartridge that gave soda its fizz.

Tufts's business exploded after he gained exclusive rights to sell ice cream sodas at the Philadelphia Centennial Exposition of 1876. His advertising included a thirty foot fountain, statues, and his trademark *"Arctic Soda"* banner. In 1891, his company merged with other soda fountain companies to become the American Soda Fountain Company. By the age of sixty, James Tufts was a millionaire. He built his success on quality products of the most modern design, sold at a fair price. It was a policy that would guide the development of his next enterprise, a small health resort in the Sandhills of North Carolina.

After making his fortune, Tufts turned to philanthropy. He assisted in the establishment of an

FACTORIES:

Bowker, Chardon, and Portland Streets, BOSTON,

OFFICE, 33 BOWKER ST., BOSTON.

WAREROOMS, 96 PORTLAND ST.

(Courtesy: Tufts Archives)

apprentice school for the plumbing and printing trades in the North End of Boston and started a savings bank to protect the earnings of immigrant Italians. A close friend was Edward Everett Hale, a well known minister who was involved with Tufts in various altruistic projects around Boston, including the Lend A Hand Society and the Invalid Aid Society. Together they became interested in helping ailing people of modest means who sought a warmer climate during the cold New England winters.

Tufts and Hale formulated the idea of a new community dedicated to health restoration under modest living standards. Tufts also considered the development of a place where an invalid's family could find gainful employment until the consumptive's health was restored. The interest in health restoration wasn't all philanthropic, though. Tufts himself suffered from poor health and frequently took respites to Florida and elsewhere.

Tufts intended to establish his health resort in Florida but was persuaded to consider the Sandhills by Hale and his friends the Goodridges. While a committee member of Hale's Lend A Hand Society, Tufts had met the wife of Reverend Dr. Benjamin Asbury Goodridge of Dorchester, Massachusetts. Not only did the two share committee duties, they endured similar health problems. Mrs. Goodridge had been strongly advised by her doctor that the only chance for recovery was to take up residence for several years in a healthy Southern locale. In 1885, Reverend Goodridge took his wife to a new health resort named Southern Pines to remedy her condition. Within five years she returned to Massachusetts fully cured. Mrs. Goodridge told Tufts about this magical health resort where she recovered from an "*incipient phthisis* [pulmonary tuberculosis]."

There is no evidence that Tufts ever visited Moore County before June of 1895. On one of his return trips from Florida, he left the Seaboard Air Line train at Southern Pines to inquire about and inspect a Sandhills site. He had previously conferred with officials at North Carolina State University who reassured him the Sandhills offered a healthful climate. They spoke of many tuberculosis patients who recovered from their ailments quickly.

Great entrepreneurial instinct led Tufts to make the plunge. As John Patrick was influenced by his visits to Jackson Springs years before, Tufts was equally convinced of his success upon visiting Patrick's Southern Pines town. On June 28, 1895, a contract of sale and purchase of 5,200 acres of cut-over timber land was executed for $5,300. Immediately after closing the sale, Tufts asked a surveyor named Francis Deaton to accompany him to a spot on the property (it was just west of the present Given Memorial Library and across from the Holly Inn) and told him to "*Drive a stake here.*" That spot became the center of the resort with boundaries extending out one mile in all directions.

The first parcel of land - 400 acres - came from Lewis Page,

Francis Deaton, Civil Engineer
(Courtesy: Tufts Archives)

GENERAL PLAN

FOR THE VILLAGE OF

PINEHURST

MOORE CO. N C

SCALES

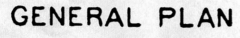

OLMSTED OLMSTED & ELIOT
LANDSCAPE ARCHITECTS, BROOKLINE, MASS.
WARREN H. MANNING, LANDSCAPE ARCHITECT IN CHARGE.

KEY SHOWING LOCATION OF PRINCIPAL BUILDINGS.

1. HOLLY INN.
2. CASINO.
3. VILLAGE HALL.
4. THE MAGNOLIA.
5. PINE GROVE HOUSE.
6. SCHOOL HOUSE.
7. GENERAL STORE AND OFFICES.
8. PINE REST.
9. THE CEDARS.
10. THE PALMETTO.
11. THE OAKS.
12. THE HANOVER.
13. THE BEACON.
14. THE TREMONT.
15. THE MARLBOROUGH.
16. THE DARTMOUTH.

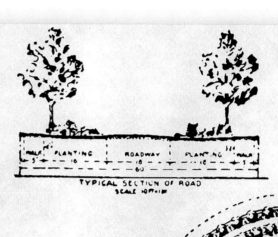

TYPICAL SECTION OF ROAD
SCALE 10FT = 1IN

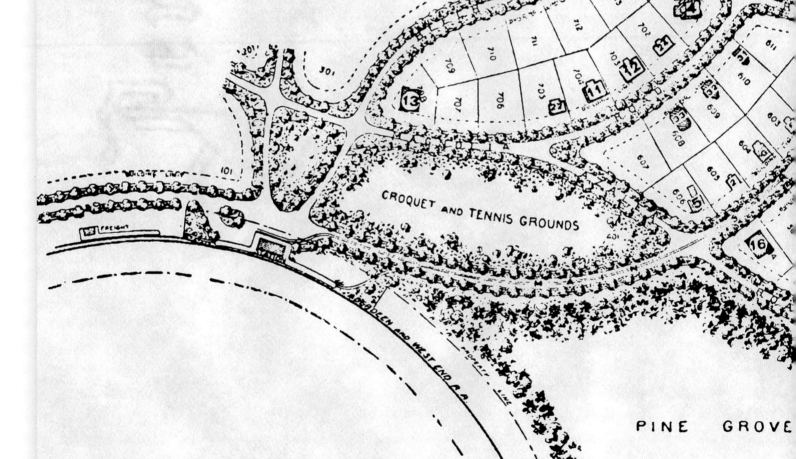

CROQUET AND TENNIS GROUNDS

PINE GROVE

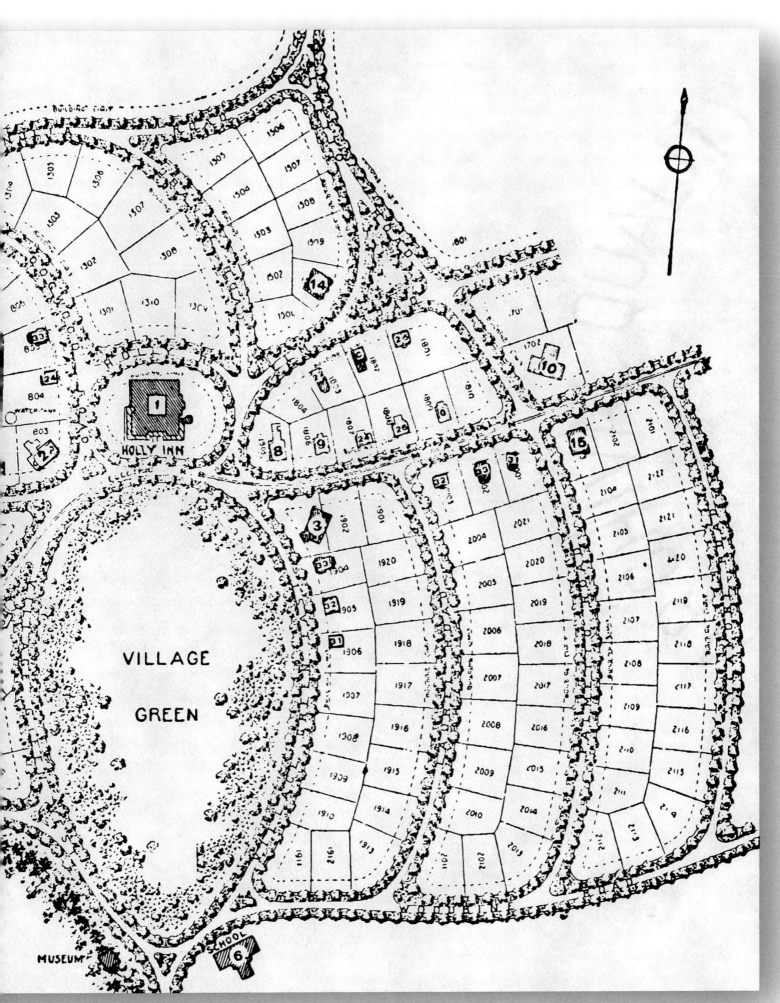

VILLAGE GREEN

HOLLY INN

MUSEUM

SCHOOL 6

(Courtesy: Tufts Archives)

25

Casino Building in 1895
(Courtesy: Tufts Archives)

Walter Page's uncle. A second Page tract of 4,800 acres soon followed under contract through Walter's brothers, Henry and Junius, who ran the Page Trust Company for their father, Allison Francis Page. An additional tract east of the second Page tract was bought from a Mrs. Thorne and included property surrounding the MacDonald place and along Devil's Gut waterway (near the Country Club of North Carolina).

A week before closing, Tufts asked John Charles Olmsted what his landscape architectural firm, Olmsted, Olmsted, and Eliot, would charge for the design of a new village. The fee was $300, which included the supervision of all necessary planting for the year. On July 3, 1895, Tufts called to accept the proposal. He wanted the sites for six houses determined and a well location by the following Monday.

Olmsted, Olmsted, and Eliot, formerly known as F. L. Olmsted & Company, was still led by John's Uncle, Frederick Law Olmsted, known as the father of landscape architecture in America (it was he who first coined the term "*landscape architecture*"). Tuft's new village would possess a character that was very much Frederick Law Olmsted although he wasn't involved in the detailed design. For the most part, his leadership was just in spirit because the great landscape architect's mind had slowly been slipping.

With the Olmsted firm working feverishly on design plans and Francis Deaton plotting out the village boundaries, Tufts devoted his financial and physical resources exclusively to the resort, turning over management of the soda fountain company to his son Leonard. A. C. Campbell was the contractor engaged to begin work on the village buildings. Twenty-three were completed that first year, none of which were probably started before the first of August. One building, known as "*The Casino*", was built to provide a place for town meetings, social events, religious services, and boarding rooms. A general store was built with space for a post office and library. A power plant provided lighting for the buildings and steam to heat them. There were also employee shelters, a small livery stable, pump houses for the wells and many other subsidiary buildings. Tufts's new hotel was the thirty-room Holly Inn.

At the peak of construction in late November, Campbell's crew consisted of one hundred seventy-four men. There were another two hundred seventy-five men engaged in related village business on a part- or full-time basis. Workers were paid at a rate of sixty-five cents per ten-hour day. By December, the streets of the new town were graded in sculptured curves and circles. Once a telephone system was installed, the Holly Inn was open for business.

STRUGGLING TO FIND THE RIGHT NAME FOR HIS NEW TOWN, JAMES TUFTS KICKED AROUND MANY IDEAS. He referred to the resort as Pinalia and Sunalia in early letters to his wife, sometimes in the same letter. The locals nicknamed the venture "*Tuftown*", but a more appropriate variation would have been "*ToughTown*", due to the demanding production schedule Tufts had presented the workmen. Eventually, Tufts remembered a contest to name a new community on Martha's Vineyard. Among the list of losing entries was the name "*Pinehurst.*" It meant "*Pine trees on a piece of rising, sandy ground.*"

The next challenge for James was transportation. It's not hard to imagine what it must have been like for resort guests trying to reach Pinehurst in 1895. Although well established train lines ran through Southern Pines, it was only half the battle. The matter of traversing the Sandhills from the Southern Pines depot to the new village was a six-hour horse and buggy ride. To provide a more comfortable and speedy route, Tufts built a trolley line with iron rails covering the six miles to Pinehurst. Traveling at four miles an hour, the trolley followed Rail Road to Wisconsin Avenue and through peach orchards (along

Schooners pass by the Department Store Building.
(*Courtesy: Tufts Archives*)

The trolley train in front of the Department Store and Casino buildings
on the way to Southern Pines.
(Courtesy: Tufts Archives)

Original train track from Pinehurst to Aberdeen. This section is across Highway 5
Just south of the train trestle. The Village of Pinehurst is in the background.
(Courtesy: Tufts Archives)

Midland Road roughly from the corner of Pee Dee Road to the Mid South Club). From the orchard, the line ran west along Midland, stopped at the Holly Inn and continued down Main Street (Cherokee Street today).

THE EARLY VILLAGE WAS A BARREN PLACE. One could stand where the present Carolina Hotel is located and have an unobstructed view for a mile past today's main clubhouse. Warren Manning, the lead landscape architect for the Olmsted firm, suggested Tufts hire Otto Katzenstein to grow all the necessary plant material for the village. Kazenstein, an expert nurseryman, immediately set to work clearing a nine-acre nursery just east of the village (where the horse track and fair barn sit at the corner of Morganton Road and Highway Five). By Christmas, 226,000 plants from Europe (including 47,250 plants and shrubs from France) and elsewhere in the United States had arrived. Primary trees included pines, spruce, cedar, magnolia, holly, and pin oak. Crepe myrtles, dogwood, azalea, camellia, and numerous fruit trees also helped create charm and a sense of serenity within the village.

By the summer of 1896, additional water was needed for the survival of the growing plants. An abandoned pond, previously the site of the McDuffie's turpentine still, served as the source of irrigation. A large wheel pumped the water through pipes to a storage tank at the nursery. Initially, the water wheel generated too much pressure, so a windmill on a steel tower was installed. Much of the early history of Moore County revolves around the area between this old pond and the grove of old sycamore trees located at today's entrance to the Pinehurst Country Club. The *"Sandhills Fair"* horse races were held through the sycamores. The area was

Village of Pinehurst Trolley Tracks 1895 - 1906 (service stopped to Southern Pines in 1906)

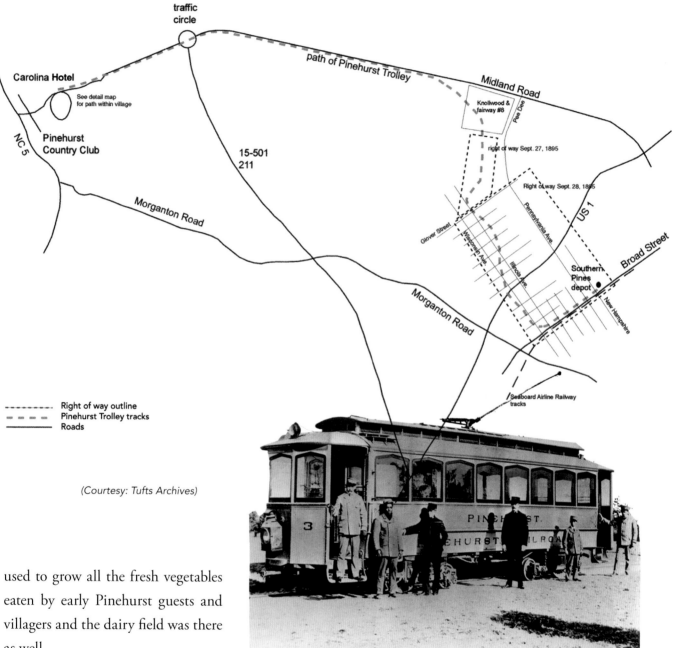

- - - - - - - - Right of way outline
- - - - - - Pinehurst Trolley tracks
——————— Roads

(Courtesy: Tufts Archives)

used to grow all the fresh vegetables eaten by early Pinehurst guests and villagers and the dairy field was there as well.

For the first two seasons, Tufts solicited business from his many friends. No other effort was made through mailings or magazine and newspaper advertisements to promote the venture. The only other effort he made was an open letter to physicians in which he related specific guidelines for guests:

> *"My choice of a location in North Carolina was made after careful consideration, and the evidence appears conclusive that the place selected is eminently adapted to benefit invalids. While it will be evident that my work is of semi-philanthropic character, yet I desire it*

to appear in the light of a business enterprise, also that it may attract only a refined and intelligent class of people. Physicians are best qualified to judge not only of the physical condition, but also of the financial status of those who require a change of climate. If the usefulness of the work meets my anticipations, I intend to continue building and thus have many more houses ready for another year."

Although Tuft's original intent was to attract people seeking relief of pulmonary troubles, the presence of visitors in the early stages of consumption cast a depressing atmosphere and those who enjoyed good health were understandably inclined to stay away. At about this time, medical authorities discarded the old belief that tuberculosis was an inherited ailment. In 1926, Leonard Tufts recounted the quick lessons his father learned:

"Outdoor Sport and Diversion"
(Courtesy: Tufts Archives)

"After he built the Holly Inn and a lot of cottages he discovered three things: Consumption was a contagious disease; there were not enough winter vacationists to go around even if tubercular people were debarred; and no one would hire a cottage for their two weeks vacation, which was a typical time frame for vacations of the time."

James Tufts decided to exclude tubercular patients after the first winter and inaugurated an absolutely new idea: *"outdoor sport and diversion (variety) rather than vacation (emptiness)."* According to Leonard, it took twelve years of hard work to impress the public enough to make a profit of $2,118.38. Leonard recalled:

"It took years more before it would pay more than a gross rental of five percent on the cost of a cheap cottage. The people who could afford it went to the hotels. Those who hired the cottages were mostly those of more modest means."

To aid in marketing his new concept, James hired summer resort operators from the North to manage Pinehurst during the winter season. These operators were happy to make arrangements for jobs on a basis that would be attractive to Tufts, but more importantly they also had an established guest list they were willing to share. Those guests had the desire and financial resources to visit Pinehurst during the winter.

Tufts's next goal was to provide visitors with entertainment. Outdoor sports were to become a big feature of the new resort. During the first few years, tennis was the primary sport. Other activities included archery and bowling in an open patch bisected by today's Carolina Vista Road and bordered by Shaw, Azalea, and Magnolia roads. A hunting and trapshooting club was located where the second hole of Pinehurst Number Two sits today. Guests entertained themselves with more passive activities as well. They gave recitals, played cards, danced, took carriage trips, rode horses, and played Roque (a form of croquet).

EVERYTHING IN PINEHURST WAS OWNED AND OPERATED BY TUFTS. The sale of beer and liquor within the village was prohibited. Those who came to Pinehurst for work or play had to do so with Tufts's approval. But Tufts also had a great sense of humor and indeed wanted to foster a sense of relaxation at his new venture. He was known to express his humor in devious ways.

For example, an "*Iron Spring*" was built by Tufts at the edge of Muster Branch to the right of the fourth hole of the present Number Two course. New arrivals to the village were encouraged to visit the spring to enjoy its beneficial waters. Upon reaching their destination, picking up the chained dipper and lifting the cover of the spring, their thirst was hardly quenched when, instead of a flow of cool water, they found the box to contain only a coiled steel spring.

The new venture was also not without its controversies and challenges. Tufts took on the roles of both politician and circus ringleader of everything from jealous neighbors to unwanted four-legged visitors. Almost immediately, Tufts's trolley line from Southern Pines became a point of contention. Local merchants were not happy to watch guests leaving town to spend their money in Pinehurst. Tufts was equally unhappy about having to spend thousands to advertise the resort throughout the North with the constant reminder to have train tickets stamped "*Destination: Southern Pines.*"

Village Gate Crashers
(Courtesy: Tufts Archives)

In order for Pinehurst to be listed on the timetable of the Seaboard Airline Railroad, the company insisted that a sign labeled "*Pinehurst Junction*" be plainly visible on the grounds of the Southern Pines station. When a sign was erected, the Southern Pines townsfolk reacted angrily, concerned that visitors would mistake their town for Pinehurst Junction. Pinehurst's manager at the time, C. W. Cotter, added to the animosity by

*A seven foot fence was erected to keep the native razorbacks
out of the village and away from the resort guests.*
(Courtesy: Tufts Archives)

ignoring the concerns. Tufts finally cleared the air by changing the sign to read "*Trolley Track Junction to Pinehurst*." Cotter quit a year later.

IN THOSE EARLY DAYS, THE RAZORBACK HOG WAS AN UNWANTED VISITOR AT THE RESORT. A herd of razorbacks in search of their daily bread operated with the efficiency and swiftness of a fleet of bulldozers. They could also be quite dangerous if someone got in their way.

Not surprisingly, the new shrubs and flowers of the village became a favorite feeding ground for the razorbacks. The succulent roots of the young plants were popular items on the razorback's menu and a hungry family would plow along with a deliberate and focused crawl, leaving stumps and branches in their wake. Deer and cattle were additional guests without dinner reservations. Protection was essential, so the entire village was enclosed by a seven-foot-high wire fence in December 1896. According to Leonard Tufts, the fence was also necessary to prevent the razorbacks from going under the cottages at night (most were built up on pillars) and scratching their backs on the underpinnings, disturbing the guests.

The somewhat pentagonal fence started at a point several hundred feet south of the railroad station (on Highway 5 near the railroad overpass) and went through the southern edge of Marshall Park to a corner near the present second green of the Number Two course. From there it moved to a corner behind the Manor Hotel. From the Manor it went past the present entrance to the Carolina Hotel to the railroad tracks back to the station (eventually the Number One course was also inside the fence). There were five fence gates around the perimeter of the village.

Tufts established a $50 fine for anyone leaving a fence gate open, although few were ever collected. When a gate was left open, the ever-hungry razorbacks took quick and full advantage. The only way to remove them was to gather a large group of quick-moving, strong-willed villagers and chase them through the streets and out the nearest gate. The village workforce had to respond to emergency hog-rooting calls as often as they

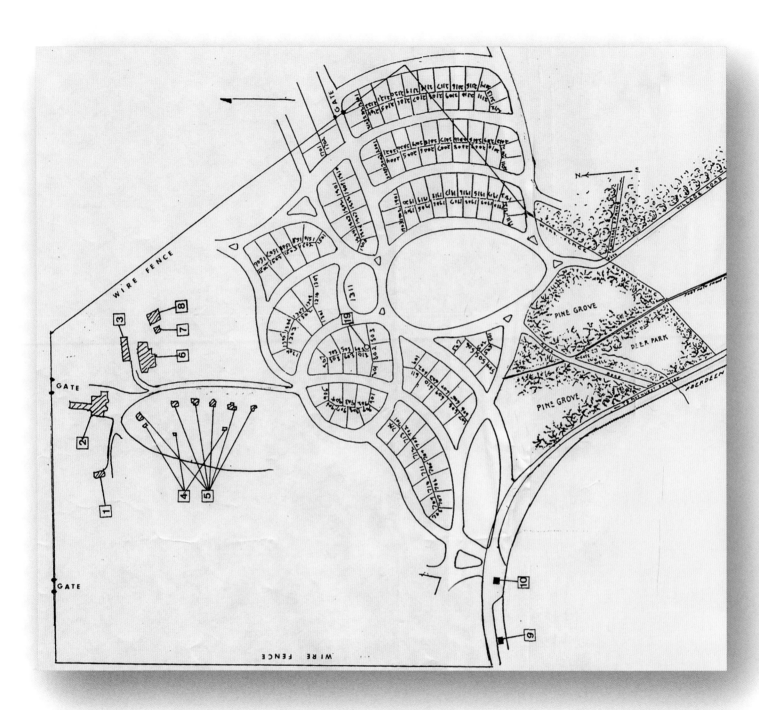

Map of the Village Fence
(Courtesy: Tufts Archives)

Peach Orchards in the Springtime   Pinehurst, N. C.

Horseback Through the Peach Orchards
(Courtesy: Tufts Archives)

would have to respond to forest fires. When the razorbacks eventually settled in the swamps along the streams and rivers, the fence gradually fell to the ground and rusted away.

IN 1891, FOUR YEARS PRIOR TO TUFTS'S ARRIVAL, J. VAN LINDLEY PURCHASED 1,800 ACRES OF PEACH, PEAR, AND PLUM TREES ALONG THE OLD YADKIN TRAIL. By 1898, the first crops were ready. In 1902, 8,000 crates of pears, 7,500 crates of peaches, and 4,000 crates of dewberries were exported throughout the Southeast.

Following the business plan that he and Edward Hale had developed long before, Tufts planned to take advantage of the peach orchards. Tufts decided to clear land for his own orchard in the vicinity of the present race track and fair barn. The cultivation of peaches would provide a source of income for those obliged to spend a full year in Pinehurst. Unfortunately, a blight called the San Jose Scale destroyed the peach industry in Moore County before Tufts ever had a chance to plant a single tree.

The blight did great damage to a Moore County economy trying to replace a dried up lumber and naval stores industry of the past century. But their fortunes would soon change when a new economy for the Sandhills would emerge on the same land. On January 1, 1901, Tufts opened the Carolina Hotel doors to ten guests. By the end of the year, the Carolina swelled to three-hundred fifty visitors and was the largest wood-frame hotel in the state.

CHAPTER THREE
THE FIRST GOLF COURSE

"Everybody can play it - some excellently, others indifferently, still others very badly, but all enjoyably. It keeps the player out in the open air; it keeps him moving over wide spaces; it exercises all his muscles and all his wits. It is an ideal sport for the maintenance of bodily and mental health. Golf experts and all those who cherish the hope of becoming such will find excellent opportunity to indulge in the game at Pinehurst."

- James Walker Tufts, Fall of 1898

WHEN IT WAS APPARENT HIS RESORT FOR CONSUMPTIVES WAS ILL-CONCEIVED, AND WHEN THE SAN JOSE BLIGHT ELIMINATED THE MOORE COUNTY PEACH INDUSTRY, PROSPECTS FOR TUFTS'S RESORT BUSINESS SEEMED JUST AS BLEAK. There was hope, however, that a resort built on recreational pursuits could be a success (although few in the United States had attempted such an endeavor). He needed that special hook to establish Pinehurst. The hook was unwittingly provided when a few Pinehurst visitors were observed playing a game near the Carolina Hotel. Golf was new in America and very much a mystery to the general public.

Tufts's local newspaper, The *Pinehurst Outlook*, reported that by the fall of 1897, people were knocking balls around the dairy fields disturbing the cows. Golf was about to explode on the American scene and Tufts saw an opportunity to put Pinehurst on the map. His timing was dead on. By 1900, there were 982 courses in 45 states, including one in Pinehurst.

Since few Americans knew how to play the game, even fewer knew how to create layouts on which to play the game. Tufts turned to the only person he knew who had visited the golf courses of the British Isles (and specifically the Old Course at St. Andrews). Dr. Leroy Culver, the former medical chief of the Department of Public Charts of New York City, was now the resident physician at the Piney Woods Inn in Southern Pines. He was a natural to assist Tufts in capitalizing on the few Pinehurst visitors who played the game.

Village Dairy Herd
(Courtesy: Tufts Archives)

Perhaps because many of the early designers of America's first courses looked to St. Andrews and the old world for influence, so did Dr. Culver. The *Yankee Settler* of January 26, 1897 described Dr. Culver's simple mission to *"bring about a course similar to the famous St. Andrews Golf Links."* It is most likely that these early holes were simply no more than a built-up tee and a few feet of rolled ground around the hole. The land upon which it sat was relatively flat and easily adaptable for a utilitarian layout. Like others of this period, it was a sufficient beginning. The investment was minor and Tufts took quick advantage of his resources by calling on Dr. Culver, likely the only one around who knew enough to direct construction. The first nine holes were ready for play in February of 1898:

"A nine hole course has been laid out after the famous St. Andrews, near the foot of the Village Green. Mr. Tufts is giving his personal attention to the construction. Grounds cover 60 acres of thoroughly cleared land, well fenced in, and covered with a thick growth of Rye, which will be kept short by a flock of more than 100 sheep. A large force of men have been at work on the links, which are now in good condition."

- Pinehurst Outlook, January 18, 1898

Dr. Culver felt his design at Pinehurst was far superior to the courses found up north because his layout more resembled the great links of Scotland mainly due to the lack of trees, which he saw as a huge advantage:

"Resorts of the North can boast of grass covered meadows, dotted here and there with trees. To be sure groves of trees beautify the landscape, but mar the joy of the game for him whose ill-directed drive has landed his ball in the midst of the foliage. This lack of appreciation of the beautiful in nature is a feature of golf. No matter how artistic or picturesque with woods and ravines may be the course, the golfer only sees in them so many more or less insurmountable 'hazards' and 'bunkers'. We are happy to say that there are no obstructions other than those placed there in connection with the few hills met with on our course, and those lend interest to the game. There are no links in the South to be compared with those at Pinehurst, and they will prove the great magnet of attraction to lovers of the game."

No. 8

No. 2

No. 7

Red Centerlines Depict the Original Nine Holes of
Pinehurst Number One (1898) Overlaid on Present Resort

Willie Dunn (Third from Left)
(Old Tom and Young Tom Morris - Fifth and Sixth from Left)
(Courtesy: Ron Whitten)

Early returns showed Tufts's gamble was a success and he saw an opportunity to create a truly different resort never before attempted in the States. He immediately brought it upon himself to improve on the basic Culver design and incorporate a more sporting layout, again following the lead of St. Andrews. Tufts went about construction of the new course in the summer of 1898. This time around he turned to Scottish import John Dunn Tucker for design expertise.

Tucker was a member of one of the early pioneering families of golf course architecture: the Dunns of Musselburgh, Scotland. They were led by Willie Dunn Sr., a greenskeeper and professional at various clubs in Great Britain, including Royal Blackheath, Leith, Musselburgh, and North Berwick. His son, also named Willie, was the first in the family to come to America. He secured a position as greenskeeper of Shinnecock Hills Golf Club on Long Island and was instrumental in expanding that layout.

Young Willie's brother, Tom, was the most prolific architect of the family, with most of his work in England. Tom's children, John Duncan and Seymour, traveled to America in 1894 to work for their uncle

Willie at New York's Ardsley Country Club. John Duncan went on to plan, build, and operate golf courses for the Florida West Coast Railroad. Tufts hired their cousin, John Dunn Tucker, as the first Pinehurst golf professional.

The revamped Pinehurst Number One course was truly a team effort as Tufts surrounded himself with able associates. Although his health was in decline, Tufts was kept informed on a daily basis by his General Manager, Charles Benbow, through letters and drawings (Benbow served as Pinehurst's Manager from 1897 to 1900, when he returned to his hometown of Greensboro to open a new hotel). Through these early letters, it is apparent that Benbow acted as project manager. Francis Deaton and a second surveyor named Pritchett laid out the first holes and kept Tufts informed by letter throughout the process. Tucker communicated by letter and advised the team on items such as bunker locations prior to his arrival. Even Leonard Tufts sent along encouragement throughout the development process. The following is part of a letter from Benbow to the elder Tufts dated August 8, 1898:

> *"Suggestions by Leonard Tufts will be an improvement on the grounds. You can get distance in every instance suggested by the red lines without any serious obstacles. There will be very little expense as it will be necessary to go over nearly all the course and put it in shape again.* [One of Leonard's proposals was to add land from the] *eastern point in the field up to and near teeing ground #3. It looks well on the grounds. This will give you a course of at least 300 yards in a straight line and if distances add anything to the value of the game, I should advise the adoption of the new change."*

As FAR BACK AS 1898, A DESIGN TREND WHICH TODAY RENDERS MANY VINTAGE COURSES PRACTICALLY OBSOLETE WAS CLEARLY A FOCUS WITH EARLY BUILDERS. In the above letter, Benbow questioned the value of distance to design and conservatively concluded length was a driving force in the game. Team Tufts made it a priority to add yardage to attract golfers.

By the end of 1898, the new and improved nine holes were completed. Ever the marketer, James Tufts made sure the public knew it was designed by an *"expert"*, promoting his Scottish professional, John Dunn Tucker. Tucker officially arrived in Pinehurst on December 15th of that year as head professional and greenskeeper. His first priority was to fine-tune the new greens and tees:

> *"During the 1897-98 season, a field comprising 60 acres of cleared ground, located near the foot of the Village Green and about two minutes' walk from the center of the village, was taken for this purpose and courses were laid out under the direction of an expert. The sod was turned under and the courses rolled and sown to grass, a handsome new clubhouse was erected and many little conveniences added.*

"The links are laid out on rolling ground and no two holes are alike, affording a great variety of play for the golfer. The bushes have been removed and there is but one tree in the whole field. There is absolutely no cross on the courses, nor any place where there is any danger whatsoever. A horse roller is frequently run over the fair green, keeping it hard and smooth. The soil is almost pure sand many feet deep and quickly absorbs all moisture, so that there is no surface water even after the heaviest rain, and the links are in condition for play at any time when rain is not falling."

- Pinehurst Outlook, February 24, 1899

Taking a Break Between Holes
(Courtesy: Tufts Archives)

Once Tucker was firmly entrenched in the daily operations and the tees and greens were up to his standards, he turned his attention to the sand bunkers. By the first week of May, all the bunkers were completely remodeled. The primary change from the Culver bunkers was deepening the cavity and building up the faces just enough to make recovery from the hazards more challenging. Previously, poor shots were not punished because even the novice found recovery a simple task.

Site specifics and a lack of construction expertise were the driving forces determining the forms of course features in those early days. For instance, the tee boxes at Pinehurst were very small. Only one golfer at a time could stand on the entire tee box. Each hole had only one tee with a clay surface that was slightly raised above the surrounding ground. Because there was only one tee from which to play, each hole always played the same length.

IN THOSE DAYS THERE WAS NO SUCH THING AS A WOODEN PEG FOR TEEING UP A BALL. Golfers instead formed a tee out of wet sand. Each hole's teeing ground had wooden boxes that were 30" long by 14" wide by 12" high. A partition divided the boxes into compartments of sand and water for forming the tee. The hole number and yardage were painted on the side of each box, with a towel attached at one end.

Pinehurst fairways were short of a decent stand of turf to say the least. As great as the sandy soil was for drainage, it was a deterrent to growing grass in

Harry Vardon Tees Off on Number One Course
(Courtesy: Tufts Archives)

Pinehurst. The inability to grow grass in the Sandhills due to a lack of water and organic material forced those at Pinehurst to build and maintain their golf courses in native conditions.

The absence of grass created challenging playing situations as golfers had a different lie with almost every shot. The challenge for the golfer was to perfect one of two plays: off sand or from a very thin patch of grass. A more frustrating challenge was losing well-struck balls in the fairway because the native sand camouflaged golf balls effectively and regularly. A small steam roller kept the sand smooth. The grass was cut by a single-unit reel mower drawn by one mule, eventually replaced by two mules drawing a three-unit reel mower.

Through the guidance of the *"experts"*, the need to have proper putting surfaces was quickly recognized. Since a sufficient stand of grass was not achievable due to the heat of the summer, the putting greens were built of a clay and sand blend. The first Pinehurst greens were not the inverted

Rolling the Green Before the Day's Play
(Courtesy: Tufts Archives)

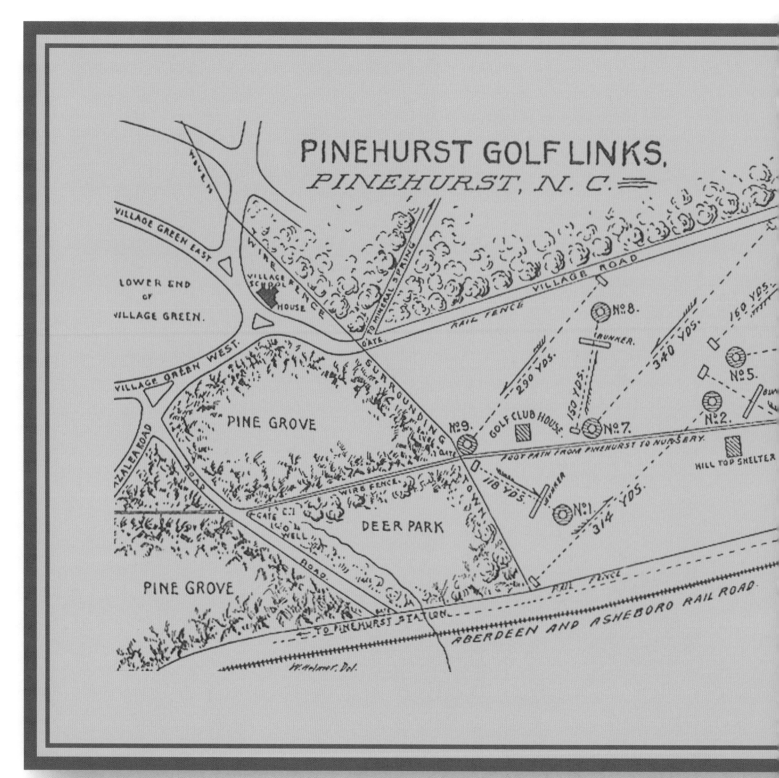

Original Nine Holes of Pinehurst Number One (1898)
(Courtesy: Tufts Archives)

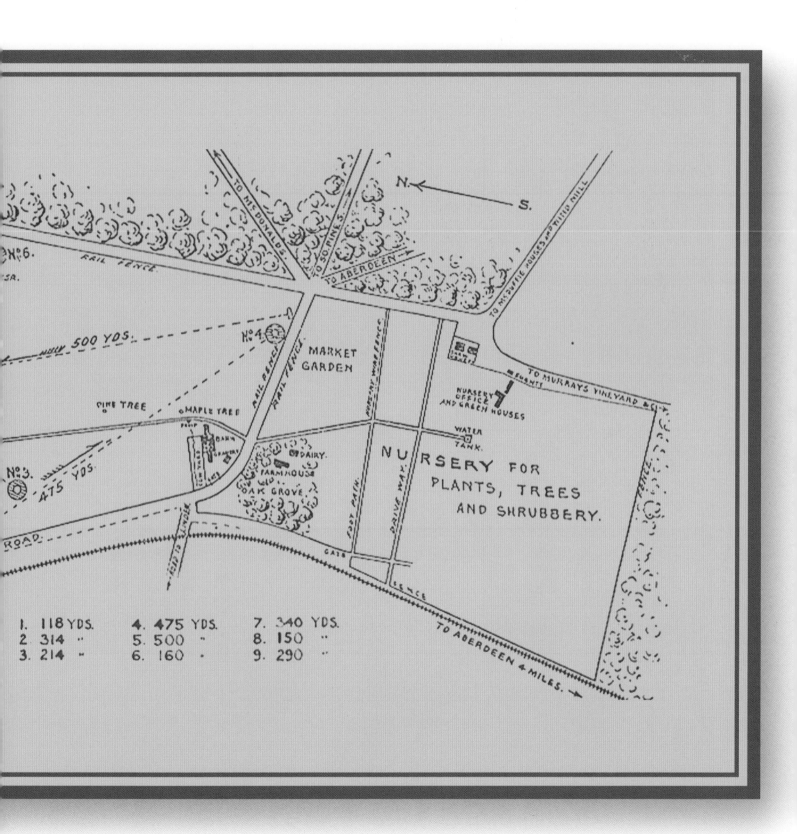

Eighteenth Green of Course Number One
(This photo is taken from upstairs in the clubhouse.)
(Courtesy: Tufts Archives)

bowls of later years but very flat, sixty-foot-by-sixty-foot squares.

The greens were flat because conditions couldn't allow any contour for fear of washouts and the inherent difficulty in spreading sand evenly through daily maintenance practices. Because the greens were flat the surfaces could not be seen from the fairway. From a playability standpoint, approaches that landed just short of a green would not roll onto the putting surface. To make matters more frustrating, approaches landing directly on the green would ricochet over the back. Successful shots were achieved with a knockdown half-swing using a stronger club than needed in order to keep the ball low enough to run onto the green and stay. Because the putting surface would not hold most shots, sand bunkers were rarely placed directly in front of the green. Bunkers of this era, and well into the 1930's and 1940's, were usually placed twenty to thirty yards in front of the green to challenge low running shots.

One can argue that the maintenance of those sand greens was more involved than the practices for today's grass greens. The main challenges were player's footprints, sand blown by the wind, and the aforementioned washouts. Daily maintenance consisted of a morning roll with a barrel to eliminate the prints and putting tracks. To smooth the putting surface, a two-foot-by-four foot piece of carpet was dragged around the green. This is the same technique many golf course builders use today in *"floating out"* (smoothing) a green before seeding. But it makes most sense because it is essentially a sand green at that stage of construction.

To keep the greens in optimal shape, oil barrels were sunk in the ground and kept full of water supplied by a mule-drawn cart to minimize sand displacement. There was also a small pile of sand next to each green to replace sand lost from the clay surfaces. The sand was spread with a shovel and then worked into place by a wooden board four inches wide by three feet long. To slow the speed of the putting surfaces, additional sand was sprinkled on top. They were a bit slower than a grass green, especially around the hole due to watering and the hole never changed locations. One worker for every three greens was needed to maintain a top quality surface.

While players of less ability found the challenges of the greens and bunkers frustrating, the resultant *"sporty"* shot making was what attracted many players to the game. Early Pinehurst conditions were standard practice of the times and did not affect the growing popularity of the resort. The golf presented to the eager Pinehurst visitor inspired the rest of the world to take notice and the Tufts family to continue moving forward.

Ready to Smooth the Sand Green
(Courtesy: Tufts Archives)

CHAPTER FOUR
PINEHURST GOES NATIONAL

"Donald Ross came here as a club professional and not as an architect or a green superintendent. I am sure he took some interest in the maintenance of the course but sand-clay greens and Bermuda fairways were both new to him at first. He did play in exhibition matches but surely had nothing to do with the design of the original Number One course, which was built before he came to Pinehurst."

- Richard Tufts

IN THE SPRING OF 1899, JAMES TUFTS CONSULTED ALLEN T. TREADWAY, ASSOCIATE MANAGER OF THE HOLLY INN, REGARDING THE FEASIBILITY OF BUILDING A SECOND NINE HOLES. Treadway advised Tufts that golf was a fad that would not last. Nine more holes would be a waste of money. Cherishing Treadway's sage advice, James Tufts began construction of the second nine holes at Pinehurst.

The success of the first nine holes at Pinehurst convinced Tufts that golf was the shot in the arm his resort needed. Though in failing health, he was again consulted on a daily basis through letters from Charles Benbow: *"Mr. Deaton is at work on the golf ground survey and I hope to be able to send it to you within a day or two. We are locating the holes, the greens, and will have all information that will be necessary to give you a complete knowledge of the course. We think it is getting in a pretty nice fix."* [May 1899]

Although the new layout was more involved than Culver's original design, construction was still very rudimentary, in keeping with typical practices of the day. Part of a letter from Benbow to Tufts illustrates the focus of construction as being a rather utilitarian process:

"The workmen are now on the last course of the new ground plowing. The grubbing and clearing force is working all the time. They are pretty nearly together [June 6, 1899]*."* It is interesting to note that early discourses between the parties referred to a golf hole as a "course", rather than the more accepted term 'hole'.

The more common references to golf holes and golf courses were relied upon throughout the States, but Team Tufts adopted its own nomenclature, which may just provide a hint of naivete about the game. Thanks in part to the *Pinehurst Outlook*, his goal of creating the first true golf resort in America was well on its way:

> *"Well may Pinehurst boast of having the best 18-hole course in the South. It is safe to say that Pinehurst will become, if that distinction has not already been gained, the Winter Mecca of golfers, for such a course as we now have here is bound to add in a very large measure to the popularity of this delightful winter home."*
>
> *- Pinehurst Outlook,* December 8, 1899

THE EXACT DATE PINEHURST OFFICIALLY BECAME AN 18-HOLE FACILITY IS NOT WELL DOCUMENTED. What is known is that discussion of more than nine holes did not ensue until Spring of 1899. However, the first description of the new layout appeared in the *Pinehurst Outlook* on November 9, 1900:

> *"Golf links now covers 150 acres, surrounded by a woven wire fence. There are three courses of 6, 9, and 18 holes. The links are laid out on rolling ground, from which all bushes have been removed. The new addition provides a great natural variety of hill and dale, and of level and gully, thus affording a most interesting course for experts. Fairgreen is 50 yards wide, frequently rolled and grass closely cropped."*

What's interesting is that the article (above) refers to three courses, although there were only 18 holes. This reveals a deliberate and innovative way to provide the choice of playing six, nine, or 18 holes. The

First Hole of Number One Course (1903)
(This shot is taken from where Highway 5 passes the club today.)
(Courtesy: Tufts Archives)

50

*The original second hole of Pinehurst Number One. In 1900, it
became hole four and by 1907 it was the sixth hole.*
(Courtesy: Tufts Archives)

Tufts were ahead of the curve when it came to customer service and promotion because it allowed players to decide how much time to spend on the links. James correctly anticipated that many first timers could only dedicate a limited number of hours to this pursuit and if provided the opportunity to experience the game, they would graduate to 18 holes and become "*lifers.*" Team Tufts also recognized the importance of using natural topography to create variety in design, yet still produced a playable layout for beginners concerned with keeping the ball in play.

The first official greenskeeper of the Pinehurst course was Edwin R. Sheak. John Dunn Tucker and Lloyd B. Hallock were the professional instructors in the Spring of 1900. Throughout the summer the holes were rolled, cut, and fertilized in an effort to enhance what little grass that existed. Six new bunkers were added to the layout at the suggestion of some better players who had visited Pinehurst the previous season. The suggestions did not stop there as top golfers from across the country provided critical opinions on the design.

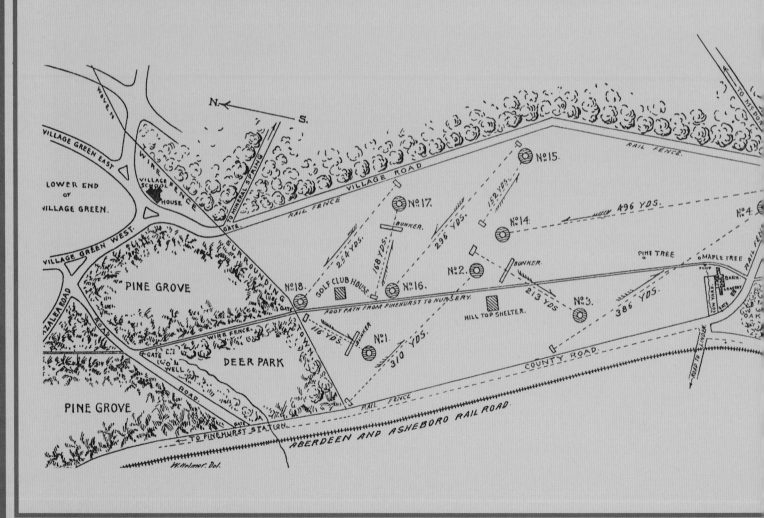

PINEHURST GOLF LINKS,
PINEHURST, N. C.

1. SHORT ONE,	116 YDS.	5. NURSERY,	437 YDS	9. GHOST WALK,	153 YDS.	13. CROSS ROADS,	257 YDS.
2. DEER PARK,	310 "	6. PUNCH BOWL,	213 "	10. BUCHANS BRANCH,	317 "	14. LONG ONE,	496 "
3. RIDGE,	213 "	7. WIND MILL,	355 "	11. WESTWARD HO,	258 "	15. EASY ONE,	152 "
4. BARN,	386 "	8. DAM,	311 "	12. WILDERNESS,	484 "	16. HOME,	296 "
		17. GROVE, 168 YARDS.			18. CLUB HOUSE, 254 YARDS.		

TOTAL 5166 YARDS   NEARLY 3 MILES.

Original Eighteen Holes of Pinehurst Number One (1900)
(Redrawn By Walt Young)

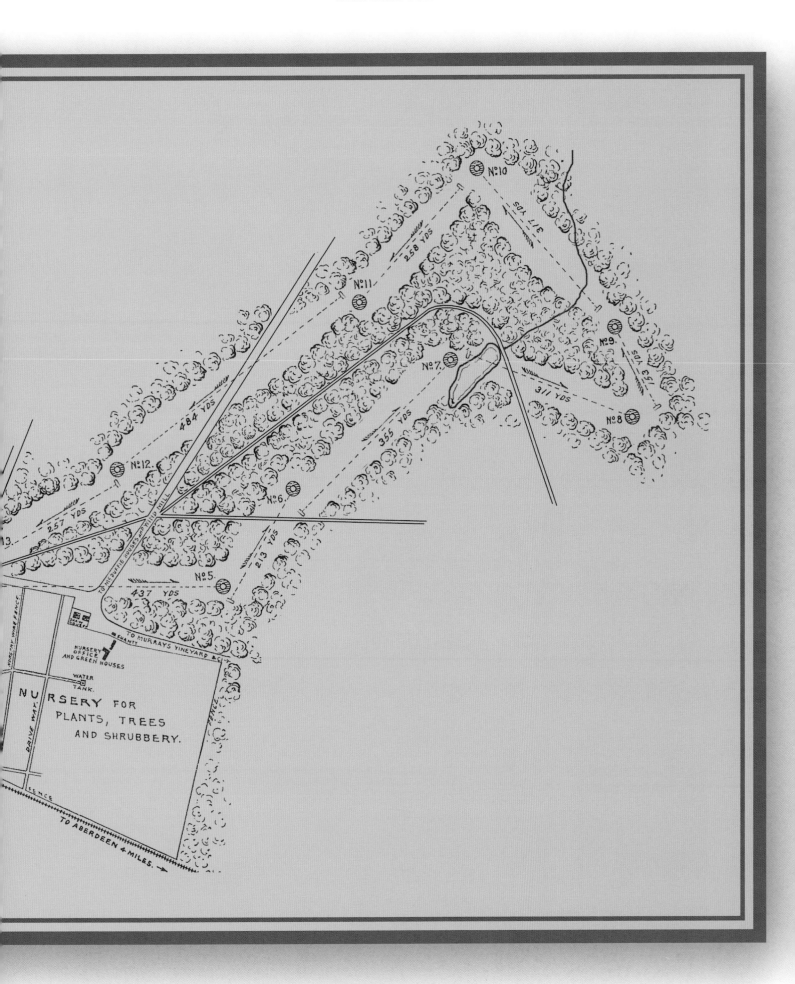

Red Centerlines Depict the Original Eighteen Holes of Pinehurst
Number One in 1900 Overlaid on Present Resort

DONALD ROSS BEGAN A CAREER AS AN APPRENTICE IN HIS HOMETOWN OF DORNOCH, SCOTLAND UNDER A LOCAL CARPENTER NAMED PETER MURRAY. Several locals, recognizing his golfing ability and easy personality, decided to send him to apprentice under Old Tom Morris at St. Andrews, figuring his future would be brighter if he crafted golf clubs made of wood rather than furniture made of wood. They turned out to be right. Ross's primary study was in how Old Tom manufactured club heads, shafts, and grips. Along the way he learned how a green should be made to properly drain and how a bunker should be placed so that it would be fair yet challenging.

The Ross Family in Scotland
Donald is third from the left in the back row.
His brother Alec is fourth from the left.
(Courtesy: Tufts Archives)

The second green at Royal Dornoch Golf Club in Dornoch, Scotland
(Courtesy: Richard Mandell)

It was at St. Andrews where Ross first met another young Scot named Robert White. White emigrated to America in 1894 from his hometown of St. Andrews to study agronomy. Ross then returned to his hometown to become the first professional and greenskeeper of the Dornoch Golf Club. According to Rod Innes (whose father was a schoolmate of Ross's in Dornoch), Donald soon made improvements to Dornoch Golf Club.

Upon White's arrival in the United States, he became pro-greenkeeper at Myopia Hunt Club in Hamilton, Massachusetts. It was there he first met Leonard Tufts. In a letter dated December 7, 1900, White shared with Leonard what the Pinehurst Number One course lacked:

> *My Dear Leonard,*
> *To my mind its chief fault is in the absence of any long and difficult carries, but I suppose that would not do for the class of players who will mostly use it. Still it seems to me that one or two bunkers at 125 yards from the tee would improve it immensely. I think that the hole on this old course that especially needs some bunkers is the fifth; which needs something to break up the monotony of the 485 yards of playing distance.*
> *- yours truly, Robert White*

Robert White
(Courtesy: Ron Whitten)

Ross followed White to America in 1899 at the urging of Dr. Robert Wilson, a Harvard professor who had spent summers in Dornoch. He spent his life savings on the voyage overseas and arrived with just seven dollars and no idea of where he might find a job. With the help of his friend Dr. Wilson, Donald quickly found employment as golf professional at Oakley Country Club in Watertown, Massachusetts, where he first met James Tufts and learned of Pinehurst, North Carolina. Mutual friend Robert White may very well have been the bridge between Ross and Tufts.

Ross got his first official taste of golf course design at Oakley. On his first day he immediately began an ambitious plan to overhaul the golf course. The challenge was immense as the site had little space for a course over 6,000 yards. Working with a large contingent of workers, Ross fashioned a new layout that was typical of the era: punch bowl greens, blind shots, and rudimentary mounding. The new layout was completed in time for the 1901 season.

That summer, James Tufts asked Donald Ross to come to his home in Medford, Massachusetts to

A golfer gains a view high on a 1903 tee box.
(Courtesy: Tufts Archives)

One of Donald Ross's first tasks was to purchase a steam roller to maintain Pinehurst's sand greens.
(Courtesy: Tufts Archives)

interview for the position of golf professional at Pinehurst. By then, John Dunn Tucker had moved on to the Onondoga Golf & Country Club in Syracuse, New York. At the meeting, a gentleman's understanding was reached on terms of employment for Donald and his brother Alec, who had recently arrived from Dornoch. The agreement would result in bountiful results for Ross, the Tufts family, and the landscape of American golf forever. Even though a course was in place when Ross arrived, it didn't stop him from making his mark and earning his keep immediately. His very first design task was to lower some of the tees, which were then accessible only with a stepladder. His first purchase was a steam-roller, which caused great local excitement as it stormed about the course: *"A new steam roller has been purchased for the course and is expected to be here in a week or so. The impression of the roller will make it as smooth as a billiard table"* (*Pinehurst Outlook*, January 11, 1901). Part of a November 21, 1977 letter from Richard Tufts (James Tufts's grandson) to Herb Graffis (a founder of the National Golf Foundation, *Golfdom Magazine*, and the Golf Writers Association of America) recounted Donald Ross's early role in the family business:

"Donald Ross came here as a club professional and not as an architect or a green superintendent. He had plenty to do making clubs in his shop, supervising the caddies and perhaps giving a

few lessons. I never had one from him and do not recall seeing him give any lessons. I am sure he took some interest in the maintenance of the course but sand-clay greens and Bermuda fairways were both new to him at first. He did play in exhibition matches but surely had nothing to do with the design of the original #1 course, which was built before he came to Pinehurst. In 1901, nine holes of Number Two were built and their total length was 1,275 yards. In 1903, this nine was extended to 2,750 yards, but I even wonder whether Donald had any part in their design."

Harry Vardon
(Courtesy: Tufts Archives)

IN MARCH OF 1900, ENGLISH GOLFING GREAT HARRY VARDON PLAYED FOUR EXHIBITION ROUNDS AT PINEHURST. Vardon's visit was part of a barnstorming tour of 65

UNDERSTANDING BETWEEN DONALD J. ROSS, ALEC. ROSS AND LEONARD TUFTS.

The Ross Brothers agree to take position at Pinehurst, N. C. as Golf Instructors. They are to have general supervision of the Links under the Greens Committee upon the following terms:

Mr. Tufts is to furnish them with board at the Pinehurst Casino and one room in the Franklin Flats without charge.

The Ross Brothers are to depend for further remuneration upon fees paid them for teaching and from sales of clubs and golf supplies of which Mr. Donald Ross is to have the exclusive authorized sale.

This agreement as to time shall be togo into affect not later than December 5th, 1902 for Mr. Donald Ross, and continue until April 15th,)1903 unless sooner relieved from service by Mr. Tufts. The term of service for Mr. Alec Ross shall be December 5th, 1902 until until May 1903.

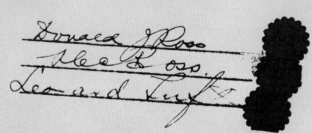

(Courtesy: Tufts Archives)

matches from California to Florida promoted by A. G. Spalding and Company. The impact of Vardon's trip showed American players that they had far to go to match the skills of British golfers. It cemented Spalding at the top of the golf equipment business and fueled the fire of American enthusiasm for the game across the country. Vardon had particularly high praise for the facilities in Pinehurst.

Nonetheless, it was too soon to create a *"field of dreams"* where golfers from all over the world would find this sandy plain in the middle of nowhere. There was no *Golf Digest, Travel + Leisure Magazine*, television, travel agents, commercial aircraft or the internet to promote this new *"golfing resort."* But luckily for James Tufts, there was a man named Frank Presbrey. Presbrey was that same man in whom Walter Hines Page confided concerns about a land deal with that *"old chap up in Boston"* back in 1895. Presbrey may have kept tabs on Tufts's land deal, hoping opportunity would one day come knocking.

Alec Ross
(Courtesy: Tufts Archives)

Tufts did indeed knock. In 1901, he hired Presbrey as head of advertising for Pinehurst. The specific charge was to promote the resort to the world (no easy task considering its remote setting and lack of identity). Further building on Vardon's endorsement the previous season, Presbrey sought to publicize Pinehurst through the creation of tournaments to attract more top golfers. Competition was very popular at the time and the many tournaments played at Pinehurst not only served to attract players but also gave the new destination invaluable publicity. The inaugural United North and South Amateur Championship was played in 1901, and both men and women participated. Presbrey went on to create additional United North and South events, including an Open Tournament (won by Donald Ross in the spring of 1903) and a Women's United North and South.

PRESBREY FOUNDED THE AMERICAN GOLF ASSOCIATION OF ADVERTISING INTERESTS IN 1905. Through years of annual meetings, the group had the resources to generate publicity for Pinehurst across the country. The *Pinehurst Outlook* resembled more of a travel magazine than a source for news with entries such as the following:

*The seventh hole, nicknamed "The Windmill", played 355 yards long
in 1899. By 1901 the hole was renumbered as the ninth below.*
(Courtesy: Tufts Archives)

COURSE 1.   NINTH GREEN AND TENTH WATER HAZARD.   PINEHURST, N. C.

Henry Clay Fownes
(Courtesy: Tufts Archives)

"There is something in the air of Pinehurst that makes it insidiously attractive; all who breath it want more of it. Here, golf is the sport of sports; experts are counted by the dozens and enthusiasts of all kinds by hundreds. Every weekday on the links may be seen by many parties of players of both sexes and all ages, oblivious to everything but the fascination and charm of this most healthful and invigorating of all sports. Golf is popular everywhere, but particularly so at Pinehurst, where climatic conditions are ideal for the game and where players have the advantage of a course that is unquestionably the finest in the south, and which compares favorably with, if it does not surpass, any other in the United States."

- November 15, 1901

IT WASN'T LONG BEFORE OTHER EARLY GOLFING LEGENDS MADE PINEHURST A COG ON THEIR TOURING SCHEDULE AND IT CONTRIBUTED TO THE RESORT'S GROWING REPUTATION. Three particular players, Henry Clay Fownes, his son William Clarke Fownes Jr., and Walter Travis were frequent guests of the Tufts family. They would later make their mark as designers, perhaps partly influenced by their affection for the Pinehurst links.

Henry Fownes began playing golf in 1898 and shortly after 1900 first came to Pinehurst, spending six months of the year there as one of the early village settlers. He established a permanent home in the heart of the village by 1914. William won the U. S. Amateur in 1910, became President of the USGA in 1926 and moved to the area permanently two years later.

In 1903, the Fownes opened Oakmont Country Club, outside Pittsburgh, Pennsylvania. Like Leroy Culver and Team Tufts, the Fownes looked to Scotland for inspiration. But their goal had been to create a British moorland layout that would be the hardest course in the world. The site was just like the ground at Pinehurst – raw, flat, and devoid of all trees, partially because Henry cut down the few trees that did exist.

When it opened, Oakmont Country Club was the pinnacle of penal design in America. Over the years, William constantly tinkered with the course. Whenever he saw a player successfully negotiate a bunker, he would build a more difficult bunker. At one point, Oakmont overflowed with 350 of these hazards.

The Pinehurst courses provided the relief the Fownes sought from their own demonic creation because the Tufts family didn't prescribe to their sandy formula for infamy. However, William was so influenced by his Sandhills experiences that he remodeled the first green at Oakmont after those at Pinehurst. He also removed many bunkers when he saw how a correctly-placed hazard at Pinehurst effectively challenged the right type of golfer. Because of Pinehurst's influence, Fownes incorporated more thoughtful decision-making at Oakmont instead of continuing the survival strategy he had previously promoted.

Walter Travis first visited Pinehurst in 1904 and spent parts of subsequent winters there playing golf. Travis was one of the top golfers in America at the time. He won three U. S. Amateurs, three North and South Tournaments, and finished second in the 1902 U. S. Open. He became interested in the Sandhills at the suggestion of Presbrey, who told him Leonard Tufts had a comprehensive list of names and addresses of golfers throughout the country. Travis wanted this list to promote his *American Golfer* magazine, to be released in October 1908.

Travis later became a top golf course architect and the early Pinehurst courses helped shape his golf course design philosophies. Travis' designs took on a more functional – some may even say penal –

Walter Travis
(Courtesy: Tufts Archives)

The Carolina Hotel
(with the Music Hall to the right)
(Courtesy: Tufts Archives)

appearance. Similar to the hazards utilized by Tucker and the Tufts's, Travis utilized flat sand bunkers, pot bunkers, and cops (a type of cross bunker that was a staple of early Pinehurst courses). Travis also closely followed the contours of the land in routing golf holes. The gentle rolls of the Pinehurst courses and fond memories of his successes there stayed with him throughout his design career.

JAMES WALKER TUFTS PASSED AWAY IN HIS CAROLINA HOTEL ON JANUARY 2, 1902, HIGH ABOVE AN ODD EXPANSE OF GROUND WITH A FAR OFF VIEW OF GOLFERS PURSUING A LITTLE WHITE BALL. Upon his death, he bequeathed the entire village and every structure to his son Leonard, who intended to continue the same program and policies. James was not only a visionary, but also a smart businessman who never sought out bank loans, issued stock, had investment partners, or required a bond issue for any part of the venture. He left Leonard with zero debt and $100,000 cash with which to carry on the Pinehurst dream.

After many attempts to develop an identity for Tufts's village (and a profit), it took an ancient game from across the Atlantic Ocean to save his investment in a deserted landscape of sand and scrub. For someone who knew absolutely nothing about golf, it was his ability to see the game's future and ability to pull together the right people at the right time that secured a recipe for success that would become an American icon.

James Walker Tufts
(Courtesy: Tufts Archives)

CHAPTER FIVE
EXPANSION IN AND OUT OF PINEHURST

"It's a freak course. A bunch of experts had simply turned themselves loose and tried to see just what they could do."

- 1908 *Pinehurst Outlook* (regarding Number Two)

ONE OF THE LAST CHARGES SET FORTH BY JAMES TUFTS BEFORE HE DIED WAS EXPANDING GOLF OPERATIONS AT PINEHURST. The first course had exceeded expectations, and before it got too crowded a large tract of land northeast of that layout was *"cleared, plowed, harrowed, rolled, seeded, and generally put in suitable condition for golfing purposes"* (*Pinehurst Outlook*, November 15, 1901). The standard construction practices of the day produced a nine-hole course of 1,275 yards that started and ended at the clubhouse.

As the marketing arm of Team Tufts hit full stride, it was apparent to Leonard that expansion was more about opportunity than necessity. So in 1903, the new course was expanded to 2,750 yards. To create a variety of options for his clientele, Leonard envisioned Number Two as an alternative to those who did not want to commit the time necessary to play a full 18 holes. He also saw a marketing opportunity in labeling the new course specifically as a beginner's course. The land chosen for the new nine (northeast of the Number One course) was relatively flat, lending itself to simple play. According to the February 1903 *USGA Golf Bulletin*, *"The nine hole course (Number Two) is intended for beginners. It is easier than the 18 hole course (Number One) and more level."*

The USGA's opinion that the new course was easier was based primarily upon Number Two's length. Way back in 1903, when club manufacturing wasn't the economic juggernaut it is today, golfer's perceptions

Original Nine Holes of Pinehurst Number Two in 1901
[Overlaid On Present Course]

were based upon yardage. The length factor in determining the popularity or difficulty of a golf course has plagued the game ever since. A 1905 issue of the *Pinehurst Outlook* defends this view: *"The smaller nine hole course, which was lengthened last season, is now in excellent condition and will prove most attractive for many who do not desire as strenuous a game as the championship course (Number One) provides."*

The architecture of the twenty-seven Pinehurst holes in 1903 was more functional than Leroy Culver's original utilitarian design. Between John Dunn Tucker, James Tuft's friends, and Ross, the holes took on a more thought-out purpose as cross-hazards and protective sand bunkers around greens were added. Leonard shared the discovery of a layout of these early holes in a letter to *Pinehurst Outlook* Editor Frederick Severance:

> *Dear Mr. Severance:*
>
> *"I am sending you under another cover a tracing that just came to hand showing the conditions at Pinehurst some years ago. This shows a nine hole and an eighteen hole golf course and dates back to approximately 1900. Evidently the black portions indicate pits and the raised portions indicate bunkers. The old cross bunker and trap were evidently the standard of the time altho [sic] on the nine hole course you will notice a couple of pits near the greens of #4, #5, and #6 holes - also #7, that are not directly in the line of play. I believe these were rather experimental things."*
>
> - Leonard Tufts, December 20, 1926

IN 1906, THE DECISION WAS MADE TO EXPAND THE NUMBER TWO COURSE TO A FULL 18 HOLES, BECAUSE IN THREE YEARS' TIME THE OVERFLOW NINE HAD ALREADY REACHED CAPACITY. More than a thousand guests a season created congestion and delays from the first tee to the ninth green. The need to create safer playing conditions was additional impetus as many of the new holes were partially blind. According to Richard Tufts, Ross took complete control of design and construction of the expansion.

Ross's original plan was to use six or seven of the existing holes and incorporate trap shooting fields and rolling countryside beyond the village fence to create the new holes. But by the time the new 18 was completed, only the first hole of the original nine remained intact. According to Leonard, construction of the entire Number Two course was undertaken by a man named Orin Morrison, born to an Englishman father and a Native American mother in 1865. Morrison cleared and plowed all 18 holes with a pair of black mules. Construction began in the summer of 1906 and the new course opened 12 months later, measuring 5,680 yards.

The turf conditions that Ross faced were unlike most other course designer's challenges of the day, expert opinion being that favorable turf was more easily produced in areas of greater rainfall and humidity. Through careful study and use of the sandy soils, Ross created a low maintenance layout with innovative

The Fourth Hole of Pinehurst Number Two, circa 1907 - 1913
(Courtesy: Tufts Archives)

placement of hazards to challenge the golfer's decision-making ability. Features such as naturally rolling mounding and sand bunkers compensated in part for the lack of turf and introduced the element of strategy.

Before Ross's involvement, there was no way of varying the hole lengths from day to day (because of the permanent location of the tee boxes), nor did the design of the first courses demand any strategic decisions from the golfer. Besides the rough conditions (lack of turf), the only problems presented to the golfer were created by a series of sand bunkers extending across the fairways perpendicular to the golfer's line of play. In 1913, Ross presented his view of these rudimentary holes:

> *"The design of early No. 1 did not demand any strategy or alertness on the part of the golfer.*
> *Each hole went straight from tee to green and, aside from the thin fairway conditions and*
> *the play to the hard clay greens the only problems presented to the golfer were created by a*
> *series of cross bunkers extending all the way across the fairways at right angles to the line of*

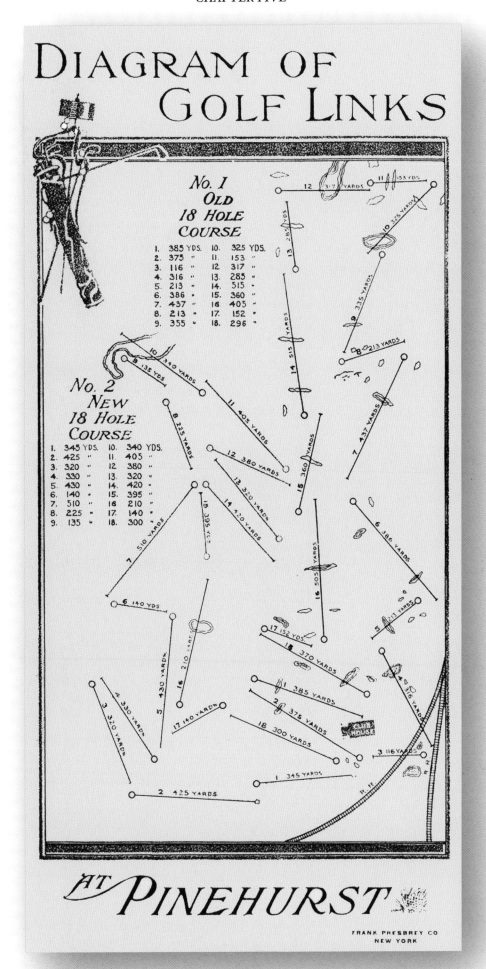

DIAGRAM OF GOLF LINKS

No. 1 OLD 18 HOLE COURSE

1.	385 YDS.	10.	325 YDS.
2.	375 "	11.	153 "
3.	116 "	12.	317 "
4.	316 "	13.	285 "
5.	213 "	14.	515 "
6.	386 "	15.	360 "
7.	437 "	16.	405 "
8.	213 "	17.	152 "
9.	355 "	18.	296 "

No. 2 NEW 18 HOLE COURSE

1.	345 YDS.	10.	340 YDS.
2.	425 "	11.	405 "
3.	320 "	12.	380 "
4.	330 "	13.	320 "
5.	430 "	14.	420 "
6.	140 "	15.	395 "
7.	510 "	16.	210 "
8.	225 "	17.	140 "
9.	135 "	18.	300 "

AT PINEHURST

FRANK PRESBREY CO
NEW YORK

1907 Layout of Pinehurst Number One and Number Two Courses
(Courtesy: Tufts Archives)

play. There were no elbow holes, no bunkers, no mounds placed so that the ambitious golfer could gain some advantage by accepting the risk of playing over them, but which would be avoided by the shorter player by going around them. There was no particular advantage to be gained for the shot to the hole by the skillful placement of the preceding shot nor could the challenge of the shot to the green be varied by changing the location of the cups. One got the impression that he was starting on a steeplechase with certain fixed hurdles which had to be cleared. The prospect was not inspiring and the test of the golfer's skill was limited."

*Before Donald Ross arrived in Pinehurst, artificial
hazards such as this berm dominated the golfscape.*
(Courtesy: Tufts Archives)

Without hazards and elbow holes, the aggressive golfer had no advantage over a player who may have chosen to play around the hazards except length. Ross had a more penal design tendency in his early days, demonstrated by prolific use of sand and long grass completely surrounding many greens. The new layout had numerous forced carries, three water hazards, and many of Ross's traps and pits (scooped out sand bunkers either on the face of slopes or built on flat land with a raised face), which demanded accuracy from the golfer.

It is in this early iteration of the course one begins to see Ross's use of high points in his routing, especially for plateau green sites. In deciphering early *Outlook* descriptions, it is apparent Ross also put a premium on straight and long play. The 345-yard first hole started to the left of the clubhouse and required a drive to a wide landing area, a prototype for many future Ross starting holes such as those at Mid Pines and Southern Pines Country Club. Ross relied on long grass to protect the green. The second hole required two wood shots to reach the green. Here Ross punished the golfer down the entire left side of the hole, intending for the longer player to attack all 425 yards from the opposite side. These holes are part of today's layout.

Instead of continuing east as it plays today, the third hole (320 yards) went from the edge of Midland Road due south, crossed over today's second green through the front of seven fairway and straightaway into the woods. The tee shot required a carry of 145 yards to a plateau landing area followed by an iron approach to a punch bowl green. Number four played 330 yards straight out of the woods to today's number seven green site. Ross once again put a premium on a well hit tee shot in order to reach a well guarded green with the approach.

In 1907, the fifth, sixth, and seventh holes played within the golf course corridors for the current eighth, ninth, and tenth holes. Although Ross tended toward a proliferation of sandy hazards at the time, he began to incorporate the more strategic (and prudent) use of undulation to create strategy on these holes. On five, the use of rolling ground placed importance on two long, straight shots to reach a thoroughly guarded putting green. The sixth hole required a precise tee shot to another plateau green with a forced carry of *"rough ground lying between."* The seventh required three shots straightaway downhill, over *"undulating fair green"* to the putting surface.

The next three holes of the 1907 layout were among the most exciting on the course and with the most elevation change. The eighth hole played 225 yards downhill from below today's fourteenth green across ten green to a punch bowl on a knoll just above the fifth hole of today's Number Four course. The *Outlook* referred to the ninth hole as an *"Island Hole"* putting green being entirely surrounded by water. Only 135 yards long, it continued eastward across Number Four's fifth hole to where that course's thirteen green sits today. Number ten was 340 yards long and also utilized a water hazard. The tee sat on the far side of a dam at the base of today's four tees of the Number Four course and played over the same pond that fronts the fourth green. It continued uphill across number five fairway and finished at the top of the hill just before eleven fairway of today's Number Two Course.

The 1907 layout then returned to the same corridors in use today with holes eleven through fourteen playing basically over the same ground. This stretch displays an early example of Ross's desire to weave rhythm into his design. The ability to alternate a variety of hole distances and play requirements is a hallmark of Ross's routings and the back nine of Number Two is a textbook example. Eleven played 405 yards and required two good long shots to reach the green. A simple drive and iron twelfth hole followed on level ground over 380 yards. Thirteen was a drive and pitch of 320 yards to a green on a natural rise guarded by a Ross pit. After

Original Eighteen Holes of Pinehurst Number Two in 1907
[Overlaid on Present Course]

these two relatively short plays, the fourteenth again demanded two wood shots to reach a green located on the brow of a small hill 420 yards away.

Numbers fifteen and sixteen are the only holes of the 1907 back nine which vary greatly from today's back nine. Fifteen was a 395 yard hole with the same tee as the existing par three, but required a long shot to clear a pond that guarded the original fairway. That pond sits benignly between the tees and the fairway of the par-five sixteenth today. In 1907, sixteen was a 210 yarder that began about 45 yards beyond the left fairway bunker of today's hole. The hole played downhill to a green built into the slope leading to the present sixteenth green.

Number seventeen was a short, 140-yard downhill hole which was well guarded by sand on all sides. The hole began in front of today's tees and played directly over the existing green to a target left of today's eighteenth fairway, about 70 yards in front of the championship tee box.

A staple of many Ross layouts was a demanding two-shotter best negotiated by a fairly long carry to a flat area. Its genesis can be found in the original eighteenth. Without a long tee shot, a golfer would be unable to see the final green for the approach. The same slope that penalizes a sliced ball today also served that

Course No. 2, 18th Green   Pinehurst, N. C.

(Courtesy: Moore County Historical Association)

purpose one hundred years ago. The green sat about 40 yards behind today's green complex and was guarded by a deep trap.

Ross's expansion and redesign of Number Two transformed him from a jack of all trades to a full-fledged golf course architect, able to create attractive playing conditions and challenge in a variety of situations.

Upon completion of Pinehurst Number Two, golf was clearly the foundation of the Sandhills. Presbrey and Team Tufts set about establishing Pinehurst as the premier golf resort in the country and the editors of the *Outlook* equated it to the center of the golf world much like Paris was the focus of the fashion world. Frank Presbrey's tournaments attracted an annual assembly of experts, drawn by the excellence of the courses and unrivaled equipment. They all agreed Pinehurst was the most complete facility in America. Pinehurst was declared the complete representation of the game and did more to perpetuate golf as a national sport than the rest of the clubs in America combined.

The rest of the golfing world agreed as Leonard Tufts found a great ally for spreading the virtues of Pinehurst: The USGA and its *Golf Record*. Presbrey, with an office in Manhattan, advertised the resort through the USGA on a regular basis (the organization was also located in New York City at the time).

THE FOLLOWING SUMMER (1908) BEGAN A FORTY YEAR QUEST BY ROSS TO PERFECT PINEHURST NUMBER TWO. He refined his infant layout with routing adjustments and more strategic options for the player than the penal demands that previously characterized the course. The construction practices of the era allowed Ross to experiment on a temporary basis with very little investment.

An example of the elasticity of an early twentieth century golf course is shown in the *Official Golf Record* of 1908. A layout of Course Number Two shows holes fifteen through seventeen as

1908 Changes to Pinehurst Number Two
[Overlaid on Present Resort]
Blue: 1907; Red: Early 1908; Green: Late 1908

a two-shotter followed by back-to-back one-shotters. By 1908, number fifteen was changed to a 220-yard hole, sixteen became a 400-yard straightaway hole playing over the small pond in front of the tees, and the seventeenth hole was lengthened from 140 to 300 yards. Yet by the end of the 1908 season, seventeen reverted

Pinehurst's New Golf Course

from *The Official Golf Record* (1908)

With two complete 18-hole courses, the old course of 5,900 yards in length and the new course of 6,076 yards in length - Pinehurst will be the Mecca of golf next season. For the past seven years the club has had a nine hole course to relieve the strain upon their sporty 18 hole course, which is considered to be the most complete 18 hole course in the South. The new 18 hole course, when completed, will, if anything, be superior to the famous old 18 hole course.

The Sixteenth Fairway of Course Number Two
(Courtesy: Tufts Archives)

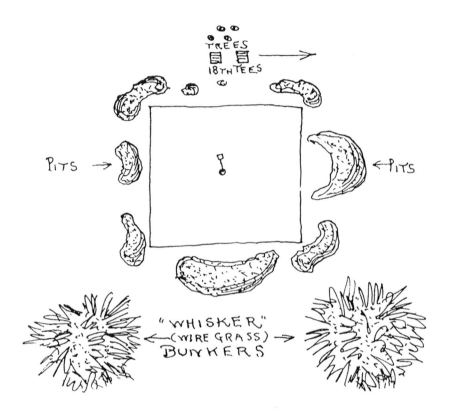

Ross's 1907 Design for Number Two's Seventeenth Green
(Courtesy: Tufts Archives)

back to a one-shotter, this time playing 165 yards long. The green was a perfect square and completely surrounded by nine sand pits. Two "*whisker*" (wire-grass covered) bunkers were set in front of the pits to further protect the green at the approach.

Criticism from all sides abounded upon Ross's completion of Number Two. The 1908 *Outlook* went as far as to call it a "*freak course*" with a bunch of so called experts running around haphazardly. Ross explained the resistance in his memoir, *Golf Has Never Failed Me*:

> *"During the construction and bunkering of the Number Two Course, a large number of our very best golfing friends complained bitterly about what seemed to them very radical steps that we were taking. They predicted that it would be a course very little used. At the time, our Number One Course was rather easy and quite free from bunkers, and was not comparable in difficulty or as a test of golf. Before Number Two was open many days, we were confronted with the problem of what regulations we could make to relieve the congestion resulting from the desertion of Number One. This difficulty has been confronting us ever since. Those men who were so skeptical are now Number Two's strongest admirers."*

Although some considered Number Two freaky, there was also great praise from the golf industry. Walter Travis gave high marks to Ross's talent and the course:

Donald Ross's Description of Number Two in 1908

Following is a hole by hole description by Donald Ross upon his improvements (first published in the Early Times edition of the *Pinehurst Outlook* of 1908). The narrative gives the best insight into Ross's design philosophy of the time in his own words:

#1 From the tee the player has the choice of carrying a bunker and having a clear second to the hole, or playing to the right, with a trap to carry on the second. Traps catch pulled and sliced tee shots, and a trap guards the green. A fine two-shot hole - 430 yards.

#2 Two long shots are required to make the green, a pulled ball landing in the railroad track. To get a clear line for the second, a trap 140 yards from the tee, must be carried. Playing the tee shot to the left of the trap, makes a long carry over the trap on the second necessary. This hole is a splendid test of the long game - 430 yards.

#3 A drive and an iron should make the green, which is situated in a hollow. A poor tee shot makes the second shot a difficult one, as the green is well guarded - 360 yards.

#4 A drive and a mashie should make the green. Distance is essential on the tee shot, as the approach must be a high pitch, the green being closely guarded - 325 yards.

#5 The placing of a tee shot on this hole is most important, as the fair green is undulating and a good lie is necessary for the brassie second, which should make the green. Traps at the left catch pulled or topped seconds - 427 yards.

#6 A mashie shot should make the green which is situated on a knoll, guarded on all sides. Between the tee and green is a deep gully which severely penalizes a topped ball - 145 yards.

#7 The long hole, three shots being necessary to make the green. The tee shot calls for a carry 150 yards over the brow of a hill, and throughout accurate long play is required; the feature of the hole being the carry on the second, over a deep pit - 460 yards.

#8 A 225 yard straight downhill tee shot, with a bunker to be carried at a distance of 150 yards, will make the green. Traps gather in any balls off the line - 225 yards.

#9   A mashie shot from the tee which is on a hill and overlooks the green which rests on a narrow strip of fair green and is partly surrounded by water. To avoid trouble, the tee shot must be dropped within a few feet of the green, making accurate play essential. This is the most unique and attractive hole on the course - 140 yards

#10   A drive and an iron, with a water hazard fifty yards away, to be carried from the tee. The fair green is slightly uphill and traps catch sliced or pulled tee shots. The green on the brow of the hill is well guarded, and the approach shot must be played accurately - 321 yards.

#11   Two long shots should make the green and carrying a trap from the tee makes the second clear. Playing to the right of the trap, brings the second shot very close to the bunkers guarding the green - 415 yards.

#12   A drive and a cleek should make the green, the feature of this hole being placing of the tee shot; the player having the choice of playing to the left of the trap, 185 yards distant from the tee, and having a clear line to the green, or playing short of the trap, with a long second to the green - 375 yards.

#13   An elbow hole, calling for a drive and mashie, with both distance and line on the tee shot. The green is on a plateau, making it necessary to pitch the approach shot - 318 yards.

#14   A splendid two shot hole with the tee shot slightly downhill, a sliced ball severely penalized, but comparatively easy with straight play - 425 yards.

#15   A clean cut tee shot 210 yards, makes the green; but traps lie in wait for poor plays - 225 yards.

#16   A drive and a cleek required to make the green, a water hazard, 140 yards away, to be carried from the tee; the fair green slightly uphill for 185 yards, making a long drive a decided advantage. A closely trapped green makes the second shot a difficult one - 385 yards.

#17   An accurate mid-iron shot is necessary here; the green being entirely surrounded by traps - 165 yards.

#18   A splendid hole and an excellent finish; a long straight drive over the brow of the hill, finding a good lie for a cleek to the green. Woods catch a pulled ball, and long grass a slice at the foot of the slope; accuracy on the second being required as the green is guarded on all sides - 380 yards.

"Maintenance upon the highest lines, combined attractiveness and variety, place it among the very few famous courses of the world. It is absolutely unique in this country, a modern course for the modern ball; a distinct value being given to a particular shot on each hole - a course which makes you think. Certain holes will be quoted from one end of the country to the other, just as the half dozen famous holes of the world are quoted as really first class."

LEONARD WAS RIGHT ON TARGET WITH HIS EXPANSION PLANS BECAUSE BOTH COURSES QUICKLY FILLED TO CAPACITY AND THE TUFTS DID NOT STAND PAT FOR LONG. The family's philosophy of creating supply to attract more demand necessitated plans for a third layout to preserve early Pinehurst's new popularity. This meant avoiding crowded courses that may lead to dissatisfaction. In turn, it meant planning the first nine of the Number Three course. The first step was to clear land near the Pinehurst dairy for the holes beginning in the Winter of 1907:

"More than eight miles of golf links!" Three distinct and separate courses, two of them recognized championship length and a long new nine hole course made in anticipation of the increasing demand. The new nine hole course, laid out during the summer, is complete and seeded to Rye and arctic grasses. This course, however, is largely a wise provision for

COURSE 3. A BUNKER—FIRST FAIRWAY. PINEHURST, N. C.

(Courtesy: Tufts Archives)

the future, to keep a good cap ahead of demands which even now prophesy the time when it will become a third 18-hole course."

-Pinehurst Outlook, 1907

Just as the *Outlook* predicted, Pinehurst Number Three was expanded to eighteen holes in 1910. Rave reviews followed that as well, mostly because the course traversed the severest terrain in Pinehurst. The choice of land quickly paid dividends as Number Three's popularity quickly trumped her older siblings. Many felt Ross's work here was his best yet. His success with Pinehurst Number Three primarily came from the great topography, but may also be attributed to the timely addition of a key player for Team Tufts. The year that clearing began for Pinehurst Number Three (1907), Frank Maples took a position with Pinehurst as greens keeper, beginning a four-decade partnership with Donald Ross.

The new layout was the first course that Ross had begun from the ground up and according to Leonard, his foresight and routing ingenuity related directly to increased play: *"Number Three course is so popular nine out of ten people seem to want to play it or at least write asking if it is to be open."* The *Pinehurst Outlook* was also convinced it would outdo Number Two:

> *"Almost as popular as the Number Two course, and in another year or so it will be the finest course at Pinehurst. The general topo of the ground is decidedly of a more rolling character than the other two courses, and Donald Ross has shown excellent judgement in laying out the holes."*

BECAUSE OF HIS WORK ON PINEHURST NUMBER THREE, ROSS BEGAN TO TRULY APPRECIATE THE UNIQUE CONDITIONS HE FACED IN THE SANDHILLS. The soil characteristics reminded him of his home course in Dornoch and the Old Course at St. Andrews. Ross recognized the drainage advantages that sand allowed in building golf course features. The ability to drain areas quickly afforded him the opportunity to introduce low profile golf course features which were less like the artificial chocolate drops and coffin bunkers of the past.

But he also understood the need for more variety and challenge to the layouts. In 1910, for example, there were 115 sand hazards on Pinehurst Number Two. In Ross's estimation, however, only through poor play or absence of judgement was a golfer penalized. With a lack of reward for inspired play, the golf courses were destined for monotony.

In an effort to remedy this situation, Ross and Maples set out to rectify the bland features of the golf courses. Ross built mounds and hollows to present the golfer *"with an infinite variety of nasty short shots that no other form of hazard could provide."* He considered inventiveness a vital aspect of an accomplished player's repertoire. To Ross, mounds forced the aggressive golfer to make up strokes as the occasion demanded or

Original tenth hole of Pinehurst Number Three. Today it is the third hole.
(Courtesy: Tufts Archives)

Original tenth of Pinehurst Number Three prior to construction.
(Courtesy: Tufts Archives)

Eighteenth Green of Pinehurst Number Three
(Courtesy: Tufts Archives)

Looking from the green toward the tee of hole eighteenth following tree clearing.
(Courtesy: Tufts Archives)

suffer the consequences. Mounds served as uncomfortable barriers to par, leaving the player no alternative but to use one's imagination. He also began to develop undulating "*fairgreen*" (fairway) that contrasted with long, level stretches. Negotiating undulation rewarded those looking to gain an advantage. Other hazards incorporated by Ross and Maples were their "*deadly whisker*" bunkers, traps and mounded sand pits.

SANDHILLS GOLF WASN'T JUST CONFINED TO PINEHURST. While its 54 holes dominated the early American golf scene, Leonard's neighbors made sure they were not left behind. A few miles southwest of Pinehurst, in a town called Pinebluff, a nine-hole course popped up adjacent to the Pine Bluff Inn (built in 1903 as an apartment building on the east side of Currant Street between New England and Philadelphia

THE FIRST GREEN, NUMBER THREE COURSE   PINEHURST, N. C.

(Courtesy: Moore County Historical Association)

Avenues). No physical evidence of this golf course exists other than a few photographs and postcards that refer to a course in Pinebluff.

An early brochure for the Pine Bluff Inn includes the same photographs, but with a caption that simply reads, "*area golf courses.*" There is no mention of the Inn's own course anywhere in the brochure, only an invitation to come visit the Inn and play those area golf courses. This is where the mystery lies. If the Inn actually had its own course, the owners would have certainly urged visitors to play their golf course and not the "*area golf courses.*"

But according to ninety-year old Cecilia Troutman, who has lived in Pinebluff her entire life, she was about twenty when she accompanied her grandfather as he played the course. "*There was a golf course there. Now, it wasn't much of a course, but there was one there,*" she remembered in 2005.

THE PINEBLUFF COURSE WASN'T THE FIRST LAYOUT OUTSIDE OF PINEHURST TO CAPITALIZE ON JAMES TUFTS'S NEW MONEYMAKER. In fact, speculation for this fascinating new game was so rampant that another golf course shrouded in mystery, Southern Pines Country Club, was just about traded for a suitcase of grape vines, peaches, and dewberries.

As early as 1897, a rudimentary golf course surrounded the Piney Woods Inn in Southern Pines. The Inn sat on a bluff overlooking a swamp on the corner of where South Bennett Street and West Illinois Avenue lie today and the same spot two Indian camps were established along the old Pee Dee Trail thousands of years before. Sitting on four acres, the golf course was the centerpiece of the Inn much like Pinehurst Number One was for James Tufts' resort:

Original hole number ten of Pinehurst Number Three, circa 1910.
Today this is hole number four of Course Number Three.
(Courtesy: Tufts Archives)

"Piney Woods Inn, at Southern Pines, North Carolina reached via Seaboard Air Line, not being surpassed by summer resorts of the North in other respects, is now apace in golf attractions. A club has been formed, including many of the prominent society townspeople of Southern Pines, and no doubt there will be many interesting match games. Many inquires from persons contemplating spending their winter in the south make it a special point to ask

if golf links are in connection with this noted resort, and we are happy to reply that there is and one of the finest."

- The Yankee Settler, January 26, 1897

(Courtesy: Moore County Historical Association)

There is no architect of record, yet it seems logical that Leroy Culver could have had a part in its inception since he was the resident doctor for the Inn while he oversaw construction of the first nine holes at Pinehurst. It is not known what happened to the Piney Woods course nor when it ceased operations.

THE DISAPPEARANCE OF THAT GOLF COURSE IS JUST AS ODD AS THE MYSTERIOUS APPEARANCE OF ANOTHER GOLF COURSE IN SOUTHERN PINES WITH MANY UNANSWERED QUESTIONS. The question of its name was easy to answer: Southern Pines Country Club. But the when, where, by whom, and how Southern Pines Country Club started are difficult questions to answer. The first question, when, begins on April 4th, 1906. That day, the Town of Southern Pines Board of Commissioners moved to appoint three commissioners to study a potential location and establishment of a "*free*" golf course. This town amenity would be under the control of the Board and be used by citizens and visitors. The town leaders may have hoped to take some of the Tufts family business, especially since the expansion of Pinehurst Number Two was well underway. Any opportunity to keep visitors from boarding the trolley to Pinehurst was worth pursuing. So the following week, on April 11th, a motion was carried that a report of the golf committee to pursue the "*free*" golf course be accepted, and that a location be secured (provided that said land

View of Southern Pines from Piney Woods Inn
(Courtesy: Moore County Historical Association)

could be leased at a nominal figure for a term of five years). The Board of Commissioners would have control of all funds contributed and expended for construction and upon completion, would be under the Board's supervision and control as well.

There is no record of the golf committee's report nor is there any mention again of this golf course in the Town Board minutes. A review of the Town of Southern Pines Statement of Indebtedness from April 25, 1907 mentions nothing about a golf course. In addition, there was not one bill paid from 1907 to 1910 in relation to any golf course. Yet at a Board of Commissioners meeting on July 24, 1907, it was voted that an order for $25 on the general fund be drawn for *"claying the road between Broad Street and the Country Club grounds"*.

A 1912 Town marketing brochure makes reference to a nine-hole golf course built in 1906 that sat on 365 acres along with a more recent nine-hole addition, one that seems very favorable in the Town's eyes: *"Another nine-hole course has been constructed recently. It is pronounced by golfers better, in every way, than the old course. The two may be played separately or as on eighteen-hole course."* There is no mention of ownership by the Town or anyone else. At this point our second question, by whom, becomes the focus.

Town lore gives credence to a meeting in 1909 of a group of men at a Nicholas F. Wilson's home to found Southern Pines Country Club. Wilson was voted the first President of the club and was one of the prime movers in the development, along with James Boyd and his son John. James was a retired coal merchant from Harrisburg, Pennsylvania, who settled in Southern Pines in 1903. He bought 2,000 acres on Southern

Highland Pines Inn
(Courtesy: Moore County Historical Association)

Pines' eastern edge and named his estate "*Weymouth.*" Many people believe this golf course was built as part of the Highland Pines Inn. But Weymouth was too far from the Inn, making access unrealistic. What also must be pointed out is that the Highland Pines Inn opened its doors in 1912, meaning that whether Southern Pines Country Club was built in 1906 or 1909, it was well before the debut of the Inn.

We are now deep into the question of where. The 1907 reference to the *"claying of the road between Broad Street and the Country Club grounds"* is consistent with today's location of Southern Pines Country Club and this property was the very land settled in 1769 by the first resident of Moore County, Highlander Hector McNeill. In 1881,

(Courtesy: Moore County Historical Association)

Eleventh Putting Green, The Country Club.   SOUTHERN PINES, N. C.

(Courtesy: Moore County Historical Association)

a nurseryman from New Jersey named Henry Bilyeu offered the owner of record a suitcase of grape vines, peaches, and dewberries in exchange for this land, which he turned into one of the area's first nurseries.   In 1906, the land was primarily owned by a D. J. Blue and J. H. Bowers.

Whether the first nine holes of the country club was built in 1906 of 1909, there is little argument the second nine holes was built in 1912. According to Moore County tax records, Southern Pines Country Club officially became a corporation that year as well. The Bilyeu home was first utilized as a temporary clubhouse. When the second nine was built, a new clubhouse incorporated it as the kitchen.

The final question is who designed Southern Pines Country Club? Local knowledge points to the most logical possibility: Donald Ross. By 1910, Ross had terminated all of his professional connections with the exception of Pinehurst to focus on a burgeoning design career. The architectural features developed by Ross and Maples proved so popular with locals and guests that he soon had numerous offers to build courses across the country. The time frame for Ross's career move might suggest a possible association with Southern Pines Country Club. However, no one truly can say for sure without concrete documentation. There are no drawings of Southern Pines Country Club, nor any references to the project in any of Ross's writings.

Nonetheless, his new career as a golf course architect showed the far-reaching influence Pinehurst had on American golf development in the early years, if not directly from the Pinehurst courses and their design features, then certainly because of the experience that Ross took to other locales. The Tufts's resort positioned itself as a major influence in the golf world at a time when other developments sought much-needed direction.

THE MIDLAND ROAD, SOUTHERN PINES TO PINEHURST, N. C.

CHAPTER SIX
THE AGE OF THE GOLDEN PINECONE

"I believe we are strong enough now and firmly enough established so that we can move quite a way out from this section in the establishment of a resort. I believe with our present organization we could build, for example, down below Pine Bluff or even up towards Eagle Springs."

- Leonard Tufts (March 29, 1928)

THE PERIOD FROM 1910 TO 1935 WAS AN AGE IN GOLF COURSE ARCHITECTURE MANY CALL THE HEIGHT OF THE ART FORM. It was a time when Ross and his contemporaries – Albert Tillinghast, Alister Mackenzie, George Thomas and others – were on the top of their game in the United States. This era was known as the *"Golden Age of Golf Course Architecture"* and it began with the opening of Charles Blair MacDonald's National Golf Links of America on Long Island. The evolution of golf course design made great strides for internal reasons as well as external factors which led to prosperous growth in the game.

The biggest contributor to the golden age was simply design experience. The profession had been in North America since the 1880's. Designers began to have a larger and larger breadth of reference to draw upon for inspiration, both in what to do and what not to do. Advances to the game contributed to the desire to build upon a foundation of design bound together by the bricks and mortar of utility and function. It was only natural that the aesthetic would become an aspect of new design in the teens and twenties.

The whole was far greater than the sum of its parts as architects used the very basic principles of design to improve the scenery and make golf course features appear as if they were always part of nature. Gone were the days of following the flat contour of the ground in the construction of putting greens with little or no embellishment. Eliminated were the straight line artificial *"rampart"* bunkers and other stark features. Any elements that distracted one from the general scenery, regardless of their use as function or ornament, were erased as well. All this was done while developing hole-by-hole strategies derived from the natural contours architects included in their work.

All these factors were instrumental to the success of golf development and the art of golf architecture. But without growing popularity of the game itself, a golden age would not have existed. For the first time, American players made statements with their game on a national and international stage, finally challenging their British counterparts. The press took notice and exposed the game to the public.

Francis Ouimet
(Courtesy of Tufts Archives)

In 1908, Walter Travis ingeniously promoted his new *American Golfer* magazine when he claimed medalist honors at the U.S. Amateur. Johnny McDermott was the first American to win the U.S. Open, taking the title in 1911 and 1912. The following year, Francis Ouimet's historic Open victory over Englishmen Ted Ray and Harry Vardon made front page headlines from coast to coast. Such a stunning David over Goliath win inspired many to try their hand at the game and participation levels spiked. William Howard Taft became the first sitting U.S. President to play golf. In office, he encouraged Americans to learn the game and praised its merits. This added greatly to golf's popularity in America.

COURSE 2. NINTH HOLE. PINEHURST, N. C.

Original Ninth Green of Course Number Two until 1935
(Courtesy of Tufts Archives)

THE TRANSFORMATION OF THE PINEHURST COURSES FROM FUNCTIONAL TO CHALLENGING CAME PRIMARILY AS ROSS AND MAPLES WORKED TO DEVELOP A GRASSING SOLUTION IN THE SANDHILLS. Team Tufts struggled for many years to establish any sort of acceptable turfgrass on its playing surfaces. Ross was not familiar with the sand greens and the fifty-fifty sand-to-grass ratio in the fairways. The inconsistent playing conditions made bounce and roll too unpredictable and a true ground game could not be developed.

Without suitable playing conditions it was impossible to replicate the firm, yet spongy conditions of Ross's homeland. Although the sandy soils were relatively the same as in the British Isles, the differences in temperatures and rainfall prevented the lush fescue and bent grasses of Scotland from thriving in North Carolina. He soon concluded alternative solutions would be necessary if Pinehurst was ever going to develop proper golfing grounds. Irrigation became a top priority.

In 1911, Ross made some minor strategic modifications and lengthened a few holes on Pinehurst Number Two. In addition to lengthening the eleventh hole, he added sand bunkers right of the landing area to create an elbow hole, and three more bunkers in front of the green on that side to catch a sliced approach. Both the first tee and eighteenth green were moved closer to the clubhouse.

The most significant improvement of 1911 was the installation of a more permanent irrigation system at many of the more *"central greens and various rain shelters."* The rudimentary pipe system was much more effective than the original oil barrel cistern system first incorporated at Pinehurst. By the following summer, water was piped to all eighteen greens.

WHILE TURF STUDIES OCCUPIED MUCH OF TEAM TUFTS'S TIME, ADVANCES IN THE GAME REQUIRED OTHER INNOVATIONS. Previously, practicing one's game was an incomprehensible idea. A golfer may have played an occasional round strictly for practice, but never took steps beyond the course to hone one's skills. The only teaching came in the form of playing lessons or informal instruction on a vacant fairway.

This mind set changed as the game became an opportunity for some to make a decent living. Perhaps the first golfer to practice away from the golf course was Walter Travis. He always practiced chip shots, putts, and even full shots whenever an empty Pinehurst hole was available. Leonard Tufts took note of Travis's new habit.

So by the fall of 1913, Pinehurst established an area solely for the purpose of practice. The first, second, third and fourth holes of the Number One course were utilized for this activity. By the following summer, seventeen and eighteen were also incorporated. The second and eighteenth greens were converted to practice putting greens. This new facility was dubbed Maniac Hill for, obviously, the maniacs who planned to use it. It was the first of its kind in America, replacing the centuries-old Scottish playing lesson with a new alternative.

TURFGRASS EXPERIMENTS STARTED IN 1913 AND CONTINUED FOR MORE THAN TWENTY YEARS. One of the experimental plots Ross and Maples tried that year was of Bermuda grass. Bermuda was

Maniac Hill
(Courtesy of Tufts Archives)

usually propagated from roots and made little progress where other grasses appeared to thrive. But by the fall, all the other grasses died out and the Bermuda was discovered growing fairly well. A carload of roots was obtained from Georgia and planted on the Number One course.

Quoted in the 1913 *Outlook*, Ross was less than thrilled with the progress his irrigated grasses made that first growing season on either course. Although he had his share of successful experiments, *"The Fairgreen on one and eighteen are not good enough to permit making the contemplated changes."* But the following year, growing conditions on Number Two improved enough that Ross expanded one fairway and opened eighteen green for play. In addition, hole four (today's sixth hole) was greatly improved and *"twelve and fourteen landing points have been perfected with grass."* Progress was finally made:

> *"For 17 years, I have been trying to learn how to make a satisfactory stand of grass on the golf links. During that period, the well-known expert, Katzenstein, experimented with a large number of plots, testing soils, varieties of grasses, fertilizers, etc. We even shipped in soil by the car load and dug up and brought in swamp muck by the ton, but we were unable to arrive at definite conclusions as to definite results. The past summer, however, demonstrates conclusively that through careful study by club superintendent Ross and greenskeeper Maples, we have arrived. The expense has been enormous, but the experience was valuable and the returns are, at last, definite"*
>
> - Leonard Tufts, *Pinehurst Outlook*, early 1914-15

The answer that summer was simple organic fertilizer in the form of cow manure. All the experimentation Ross and Maples undertook and all of Leonard's investment in the finest authorities on the subject gave way to good old-fashioned observation and blind luck. Leonard recalled the fateful day when he realized grass at Pinehurst could be achieved:

"I shall never forget the thrill I got when in looking out of the car window coming up from Florida, I saw several real sods of Bermuda, ten feet square or more in a sandy, dusty, mule pen, where the mules were turned out on Sundays and when not being worked. From this glimpse I knew with plenty of animal manure we could make a sod. That spring and summer we manured heavily and reset spots to Bermuda and it worked but we had to feed several carloads of cattle every winter for the manure and we had to manure and reset such holes every three or fours years."

From that point on, the goal for everyone was the further cultivation of Bermuda grass and its establishment throughout the courses. As grass took hold, so did the golden age details of Ross's imagination.

As more grass took hold, Ross slowly introduced the famous swales and ridges that are the trademarks of Pinehurst golf today. By 1915, he decided that the utilitarian style typical of Tom Bendelow and Alexander Findlay - *"beautifully square and flat and large - the joy of the casual approacher and the pendulum putter"* was altogether too easy. Thus began the gradual conversion of the old greens to the inverted saucer-shaped style that most critics have pigeon-holed him into to this day. He created putting surfaces with irregular shapes and mildly undulating rolls running into surrounding peaks and valleys. The green approaches were transformed from a dead flat fairway to an undulating surface which never produced the same shot twice. Similar to the strategic development of the Old Course at St. Andrews, Ross widened landing areas to provide a balance of safe and daring alternative lines of play. For example, sixteen was widened to the right for the player who elected to play safe and not attempt to carry the sand trap on the opposite side.

Ross continued to overhaul Number Two the next year, further challenging the golfer with more difficult choices but also demanded a wide variety of shots in the golfer's repertoire, focusing on *"an even greater science of the stroke."* His efforts were shown in the remodel of the ninth hole (no longer in existence). Previously a penal oasis in a swamp, the green and its surroundings used to slope away from the drive. Ross changed the approach so that a small depression on the near side of the hole could *"hold a good mashie"* (five-iron). Yet an aggressive drive based purely on strength was penalized more than before after he created small valleys and hills behind the green to punish the careless.

Ross also exhibited strategic flair by the simple relocation of the thirteenth green to the left of its original home and directly behind a well. The golfer who drove anywhere except down the right side of the hole (skirting the bunkers on that side) was obligated to approach the green directly over the well.

When Ross changed holes fifteen and sixteen to create better rhythm among golf holes in 1908, he created two blind holes. He resolved the issue in 1916 by relocating fifteen tee on a rise and cutting down the hill that separated the tee and the green. Ross then moved sixteen green out from a hollow and 35 yards further uphill, making it visible from the tee.

Fifteen illustrates very well Ross's ambition for the Number Two course: To make the penalty fit

As early as 1915, Ross began to incorporate swales and mounds around his greens. He also added a good percentage of slope to the putting surfaces as shown on the eighteenth green of Course Number Two (above) and the fifteenth hole of Course Number One (below).
(Courtesy of Tufts Archives)

the shot (the further off line, the greater the penalty). Although he improved the playability of the hole by eliminating the ridge, he countered this kind gesture with a complete line of defense established on every side of the green. To the left he placed mounds and enormous sand pits, placing a premium upon a straight approach. In place of the hill in front of the green, he carved out a significant trench to ensure only truly struck tee balls reached the putting surface. Two more bunkers protected the right side.

The Carry From the Sixteenth Tee, circa 1916
(Courtesy of Tufts Archives)

The evolution to undulating ground brought about criticism that Ross's philosophies were too penal. On the surface it certainly appeared that way. The changes of 1915-16 meant that green approaches were narrowed, sand bunkers moved closer to the line of play, and the surroundings more rolling and dangerous. Ross also started to dig deeper bunkers so a golfer couldn't just chip out. *"A bunker must be a real hazard not an apparent one,"* he said. Ross determined that for the average golfer with a tendency to slice or pull, the course was four or five strokes more difficult.

To the unsophisticated, deeper bunkers and smaller targets could easily be construed as more penal, even by today's standards. But in reality, Ross was trying to bring thoughtful decision-making into the game when previously only brute strength distinguished one player from the next. The architectural advances Ross introduced did more to equalize the game than the critics realized. By providing alternative routes and choices, he put the focus on more than just pure ability. Ross put it succinctly:

> *"To play well a man must have a wide variety of shots. More and more he will be forced to use his head as well as his hands and arms. More and more the golfer will have to have control over the club to insure direction or meet certain trouble."*

Gene Sarazen negotiates one of Ross's deep bunkers.
(Courtesy: Tufts Archives)

THE PHILOSOPHY OF CREATING STRATEGIC OPTIONS TO FORCE A PLAYER TO THINK WAS BASICALLY UNHEARD OF IN 1916. Although Charles Blair MacDonald's National Golf Links of America ushered in the Golden Age of golf architecture and its emphasis on strategy, few golfers had been exposed to this philosophy. Ross certainly was a pioneer in this field, along with MacDonald and other contemporaries. Although the full strategic revolution wouldn't get into full gear for another few years, Ross planted some of the first seeds in Pinehurst. It should also be noted that the seeds were pretty inexpensive. The cost of golf course construction on Pinehurst Number Two from January 1906 until May of 1921 totaled $13,703.09. This included two complete reconstructions, countless other small projects and numerous efforts to grow grass.

As grassing advanced the architecture and popularity of the Pinehurst courses, the Tufts unknowingly marched toward the creation of the Home of American Golf. Fifty-four holes were not enough for Pinehurst. In fact, clearing for a fourth course commenced just as Number Three opened in 1910. Six holes were ready for play by 1912 and another three in 1916. The *Outlook* declared the new nine as "*the prize of the whole lot as far as condition of the fairways and greens is concerned. It has no bunkers or pitfalls to discourage the novice or interfere with the progress of instruction.*" The full 18-hole Pinehurst Number Four course debuted in 1919. Total construction cost came in at $12,138.20, a significant increase from the $8,242.75 spent to build Number Three a decade earlier.

Fifth Green of Course Number One. Today it is the fourth green.
(Courtesy: Tufts Archives)

Eleventh Green of Course Number One.
(Courtesy: Tufts Archives)

Pinehurst Number One Course in 1922
[Overlaid on Present Resort]

Pinehurst Number Two Course in 1922
[Overlaid on Present Resort]

Pinehurst Number Three Course in 1922
[Overlaid on Present Resort]

Pinehurst Number Four Course in 1922
[Overlaid on Present Resort]

THE 1923 SEASON BROUGHT THE MOST SIGNIFICANT ROUTING CHANGES TO NUMBER TWO IN SIXTEEN YEARS. In one of the earliest efforts of residential golf course development, Ross extended the course farther east along Midland Road by replacing the old third hole with a slightly longer version (playing 330 yards) that elbowed to the right. Ross owned the first two lots along Midland Road and may have seen it advantageous to extend Number Two behind his real estate holdings, foreshadowing the future for Pinehurst, Inc and its successors. A new fourth hole (210 yards long) returned the routing back in the other direction.

To minimize further disturbance, Ross built a new fifth tee and fairway within the confines of the old third fairway. He then retrofitted the last 175 yards of the old fourth hole to create the new 380 yard fifth hole. The result was a severe dogleg-right hole, a forced attempt at cost control, and one of the few Ross holes which doesn't properly follow the lay of the land because he never intended for the golf hole to play in that direction.

Once Ross's re-routing was complete, the net result meant one hole had to be discarded. With the original third and fourth hole no longer intact, Ross made the most logical and least disruptive modification. He combined the original eighth hole (220 yards) and ninth hole (140 yards) to make a new ninth hole that played 385 yards downhill. It is not clear if a new green was built as part of this work.

The total sum of Ross's modifications netted an additional 353 yards to Number Two bringing the total length to 6,479 yards, considered quite long for 1923 (in fact, some of the holes played longer than they did for the 2005 U. S. Open). In addition to the first hole (ten yards longer), thirteen (twelve yards) and fifteen (nine yards) played longer.

At the time, Pinehurst Number Two had close to one-hundred and fifty sand bunkers strewn throughout the layout. Many of these bunkers were tiny pots or ragged hazards that would make Pete Dye shake his head in wonder. Of those, about fourteen could be considered cross bunkers, many of which were positioned to suggest the shorter route off the tee in order to gain an advantage. The total number of bunkers was less than a routing from 1918, which showed more than one-hundred and sixty bunkers. This reduction was most likely attributed to the fact that many of Ross's bunkers were similar to a modern waste bunker. As grassing improvements were made, these areas were replaced with turf.

In 1923, Ross combined the original eighth and ninth holes of Course Number Two into the new 385-yard par four ninth hole.
(Courtesy: Tufts Archives)

Before grass took hold in Pinehurst, many of Ross's bunkers were unkempt waste areas cut randomly into mounds, far from the grassy slopes most people attribute to a Ross bunker.
(Courtesy: Tufts Archives)

IN AN EFFORT TO CONTINUE DEVELOPING GRASS AND FIRM PLAYING CONDITIONS ROSS AND MAPLES STARTED A LITTLE EXPERIMENTAL PLOT NEAR THE FIRST TEE OF NUMBER TWO IN 1924. The goal was to find exactly the right mix of seed, soil and fertilizer at an expense that would not be prohibitive. They continued experimenting with Bermuda, yet also introduced cool season alternatives like Red Top Fescue, Meadow Fescue, and Italian Rye grasses.

Slowly, Ross continued to develop the characteristic plateau greens and severe slopes Number Two is famous for today. Vintage photos show a clear elevation in the putting surface of two to three feet above the fairway on many holes. In 1925, Ross moved the seventh green back twenty feet and reworked the approach to give the appearance of a raised putting surface. Each greenside bunker's face was raised for visibility and to divert water. He then converted two bunkers behind the green into grass hollows and incorporated a series of undulations. The eleventh and fourteenth greens were raised considerably as well. Eleven was raised one foot in the front and two feet in the rear; fourteen was raised enough to ensure visibility from at least 250 yards away.

As the tinkering continued into 1927, Ross filled in portions of some bunkers but raised faces on others to ensure that more and more sand was visible. Bunkers were added at the dogleg beyond existing sand in the fifth fairway (today's seven) to catch any tee shots cutting the corner. On number twelve, to pinch the corner, he added a row of sand bunkers on the left in the 180 - to 250 - yard range from the tee.

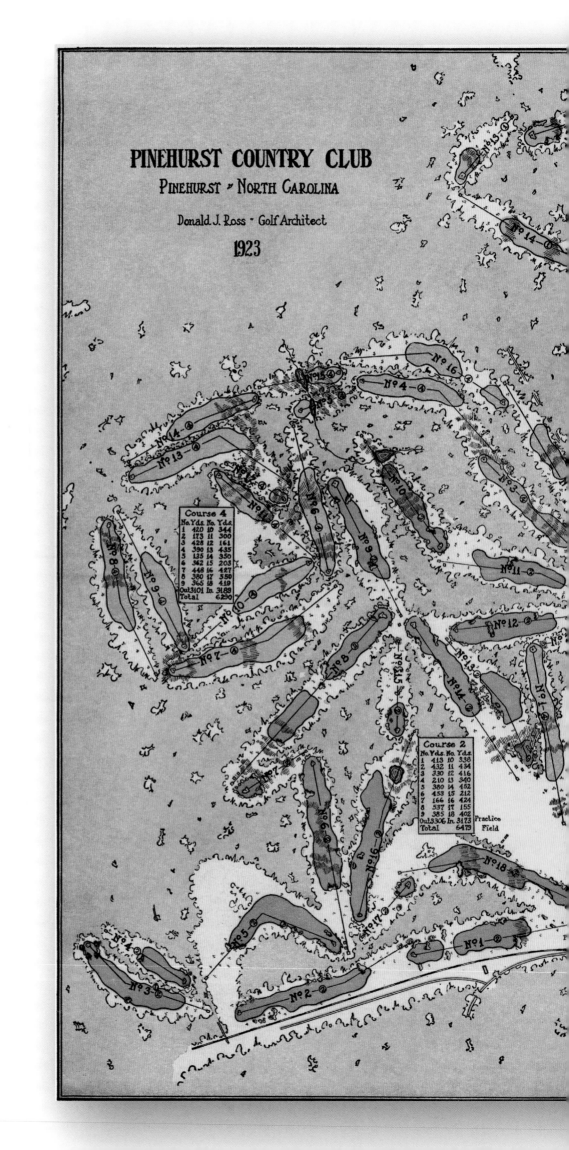

PINEHURST COUNTRY CLUB

PINEHURST · NORTH CAROLINA

Donald J. Ross · Golf Architect

1923

Course 4		
No.	Yds.	No.	Yds.
1	420	10	344
2	173	11	300
3	428	12	161
4	390	13	435
5	135	14	350
6	362	15	203
7	448	16	427
8	380	17	550
9	365	18	419
Out 3101	In 3189
Total		6290

Course 2		
No.	Yds.	No.	Yds.
1	413	10	338
2	432	11	434
3	330	12	416
4	210	13	340
5	380	14	452
6	453	15	212
7	166	16	424
8	537	17	155
9	385	18	402
Out 3306	In 3173
Total		6479

Practice Field

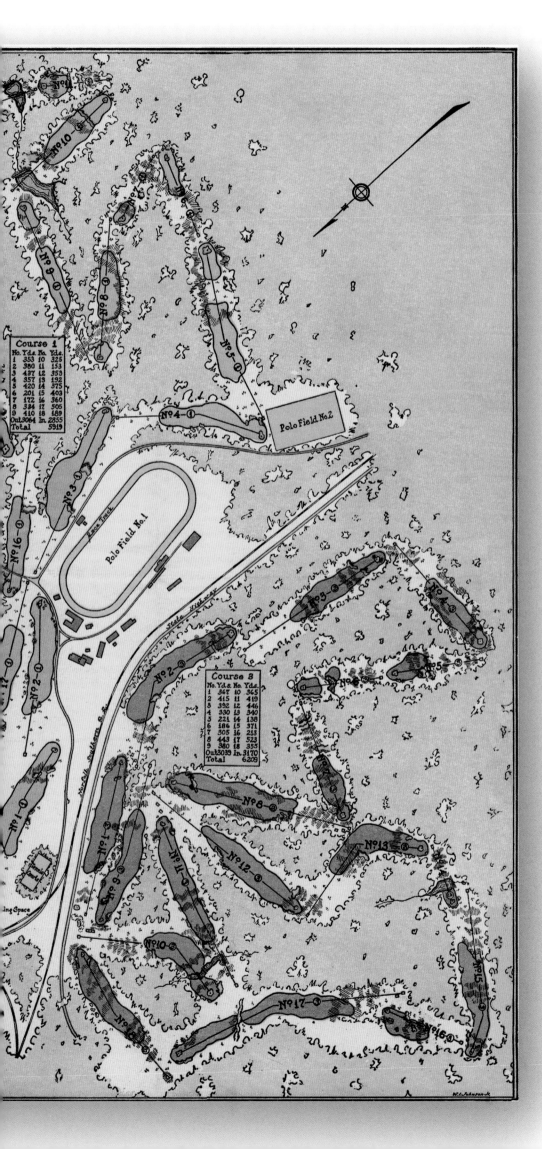

(Courtesy: Tufts Archives)

Pinehurst Number Two Course in 1923
[Overlaid on Present Resort]

Here Bobby Jones putts on the fifth green of Course Number Two (today's seventh) on March 26, 1935.
Note the severe back to front slope of the postage stamp putting surface.
(Courtesy: Tufts Archives)

But the most experimental task Ross undertook that season was the ultimate player satisfaction survey on Number Two. He built a new grass green on the site of the existing third green and a new sand green just over some mounds to the left of it. He simply wanted to see which putting surfaces would be preferred by the players.

But although Ross gave players a choice, he knew the future of Pinehurst was in grass putting surfaces. To him, survival was vitally dependent upon the ability to provide visiting golfers with grass greens comparable

In 1927, Ross raised many bunker faces to ensure his hazards were clearly visible.
(Courtesy: Tufts Archives)

to their home courses in the Northeast and Midwest. Without them, the resort would inevitably fall behind other courses and possibly fade into history. Ross planted two-thirds of the green with bent seed and the other third with bent stolons. Unfortunately, the turf was still not sufficient enough for widespread use despite its acceptance by golfers. Studies continued.

THE FIRST TWENTY YEARS AT PINEHURST WERE GOLDEN ENOUGH FOR TEAM TUFTS TO CONSIDER ADDITIONAL DEVELOPMENT NOT ONLY WITHIN THE CONFINES OF THE VILLAGE BUT BEYOND THEIR SEVEN-FOOT-HIGH FENCE AS WELL. As the remnants of the rusted fence came down in 1915, Team Tufts marched east toward Southern Pines with an eye on expansion. The family decided the timing was right to develop elsewhere in the Sandhills and began plans for a new residential community called Knollwood. A wide boulevard named Midland Road was built that connected Pinehurst and Southern Pines along roughly the same pathway of the ancient Yadkin Trail. Knollwood was planned along the road equidistant from both towns.

In 1920, a stock offering was sponsored by Knollwood, Inc., a company put in place by the Tufts to buy and develop the land. Capital stock of $750,000 was authorized and divided into three hundred shares of $2,500 to support the project. James Barber (the founder of Barber Steamship Lines of New York), Leonard Tufts, and descendants of Allison Francis Page were some of the leaders pushing this new project. Leonard stated,

Midland Road was the first divided highway in North Carolina.
(Courtesy: Moore County Historical Association)

Warren Manning
(Courtesy: Tufts Archives)

"It is a Sandhills business scheme handled and controlled by Sandhills businessmen and men who are known by everyone in the Sandhills. When we come to you with a business proposition, it is a guarantee that the proposition is a good one,"

Turning to the legacy of Frederick Law Olmsted, Leonard hired Warren Manning to plan a 5,000 acre residential community that would include 36 holes to be designed by Ross. Ross had his pick of the property in which to route his golf courses, yet he knew very well that residential development would govern his design. The first golf course, to be called Mid Pines Country Club, was planned for the south side of Midland Road. In January 1921, Barber was elected President of Knollwood, Inc. and Leonard Tufts was Vice President and General Manager. The Mid Pines board then voted to buy 180 acres from the parent company (Knollwood, Inc.) for $22,500. At $125 per acre, the investment was a dramatic increase from what James Tufts paid for Pinehurst twenty-six years earlier.

Mid Pines Country Club opened in November of 1924 as the first private club in Moore County. Four clay tennis courts, a 118 room Georgian style hotel designed by architect Aymer Embury II of New York, and additional outbuildings cost $263,000. Golf course construction came in at $40,152.96, 60 percent over the intended budget of $25,000.00.

Ross chose the site because of its rolling hills and valleys but also because it was mostly protected from prevailing winds by a ridge. Ross indicated, *"It is less exposed to cold winds than any other course hereabouts, due to its sheltered location just behind a hill. The hill, acting as a chute, deflects all wind upward, over the course, which is really a fine thing."*

Mid Pines Hotel
(Courtesy: Tufts Archives)

The design challenges for Ross included considerations for building lots fronting the golf course. Swampland dominated the site as well. To combat the swamp issue, Ross built ponds in these natural lows and routed the golf holes around the water. In a letter to Leonard in April of 1924, Ross stated his intention to eliminate even more swamp land: *"Before next year, we should widen the fairways through the swamps and other items."*

The course began with a prototype Ross starting hole that provides the golfer a relatively easy beginning. The concluding hole was a standard Ross finishing hole that plays downhill through a valley to a green on a natural rise 420 yards away. In between, many of Ross's tees and greens were perched on high points. Each hole followed the predominant slope of the land, almost always feeling as if the course played downhill, either directly or along broad, sweeping ridges.

Although Ross's design philosophies evolved toward the strategic in Pinehurst, at Mid Pines he demanded accurate play by undulating the fairways and requiring that a golfer both slice and hook a tee shot. It was intended to play long and narrow. He also ventured into tree placement for practical and strategic purposes. Instead of cutting down numerous groups of dogwoods and other trees, Ross chose to move them to more strategic positions. He also left trees near the clubhouse to provide a cool and shady place for guests.

The swampy bottom of Mid Pines' fifth hole was dug into a
pond to allow for continuous fairway from tee to green.
(Courtesy: Moore County Historical Association)

IMMEDIATELY UPON MID PINES' OPENING, LEONARD TUFTS BEGAN PLANNING THE CONSTRUCTION OF THE SECOND GOLF COURSE IN HIS KNOLLWOOD DEVELOPMENT

Original Mid Pines Golf Shop
(Courtesy: Tufts Archives)

ON 431 ACRES DIRECTLY ACROSS FROM MIDLAND ROAD. Stockholders in the new venture were given a home site for every three thousand dollars they invested in the project. The two primary investors were Eldridge Johnson, inventor of the Victor Talking Machine ($124,000) and Pinehurst, Inc. ($150,000). Through purchase of common stock as well as a mortgage from Virginia Trust Company ($250,000), funding was in place to begin construction on both the golf course and a hotel. Ross was to oversee construction of the golf course and the Tufts were to run day-to-day operations.

Unlike Mid Pines, the second layout wasn't planned as a stand-alone golf course but routed with three hundred home sites lining the fairways. Tufts and Ross planned for lots from 175- to 225-feet deep separated by a road with the golf course backing up to homes on both sides. Nine holes at a time were to be built with the first tee and final green of each 18 hole layout surrounding a grand hotel. Architect Lyman Sise of Boston, an in-law of Leonard Tufts, designed an English Tudor style hotel located on one of the higher points of the property.

The project was called *"Pine Needle Inn"* early in planning, but was simply nicknamed *"Pine Needles"* by the media. In addition to serving the residents of Knollwood, Pine Needles was to alleviate overflow golfers from the Carolina Hotel and inns of Pinehurst.

By November 1925, Ross's assistant, Irving Johnson, soon began copying the topography of the site based upon Warren Manning's land plan in preparation for his boss's routing. Ross's intention was to utilize the low areas for golf and leave the ridges for home sites:

> *"There are certain valleys on the property which will be useless for building purposes but wide enough for two holes parallel. It is well to be economical in using the land where such a condition exists. I think it would be good judgement to use it up for golf, leaving lot lines on the higher land."*

Construction began in early 1927 and a mild winter helped expedite the process. A local reporter commented on the easy going attitude of the work force:

> *"Generally the weather throughout the winter has accelerated progress of the work to a marked degree, although during rain and shine the mules continue to plod their way with*

scoops loaded with earth to the accompaniment of 'gee' and 'haw'. Apparently the mule does not know what all this activity is all about. Occasionally he bites off a sprig of young pine, though, and enjoys the kick resulting from the turpentine hooch."

Proof that some of today's stubborn golf course shapers
descended from the real thing.
(Courtesy: Tufts Archives)

The original layout began with today's eighteenth hole and the green sat in an old streambed. The ninth hole (today's eighth) ended just across the street from the hotel. The fourth hole (today's third) required over two-thousand feet of drain tile to dry up what was originally a swamp. Early in construction the *Outlook* newspaper declared the sixteenth hole (today's fifteenth) as Ross's favorite:

"Mr. Ross made his suggestions to Frank Maples for widening the fairway here and narrowing there, and throwing up sand bunkers at strategic points to make the game more adventurous for stars and dubs who will follow in his wake."

The final construction bill (including land, hotel, and other buildings) was $750,000. In the process, ground was reserved for a second eighteen. Home sites were surveyed to leave future fairways free, allowing for new home construction to begin anywhere within the property. The debut of Pine Needles was a success and quickly dubbed the best of the south (see Robert Hunter's narrative on page 124).

THE MYSTERY OF SOUTHERN PINES COUNTRY CLUB CONTINUED INTO THE 1920'S. Local lore always credited the Town of Southern Pines for building a new Southern Pines Country Club in 1923 with Donald Ross as the architect of record and a new clubhouse built the following year, but no evidence

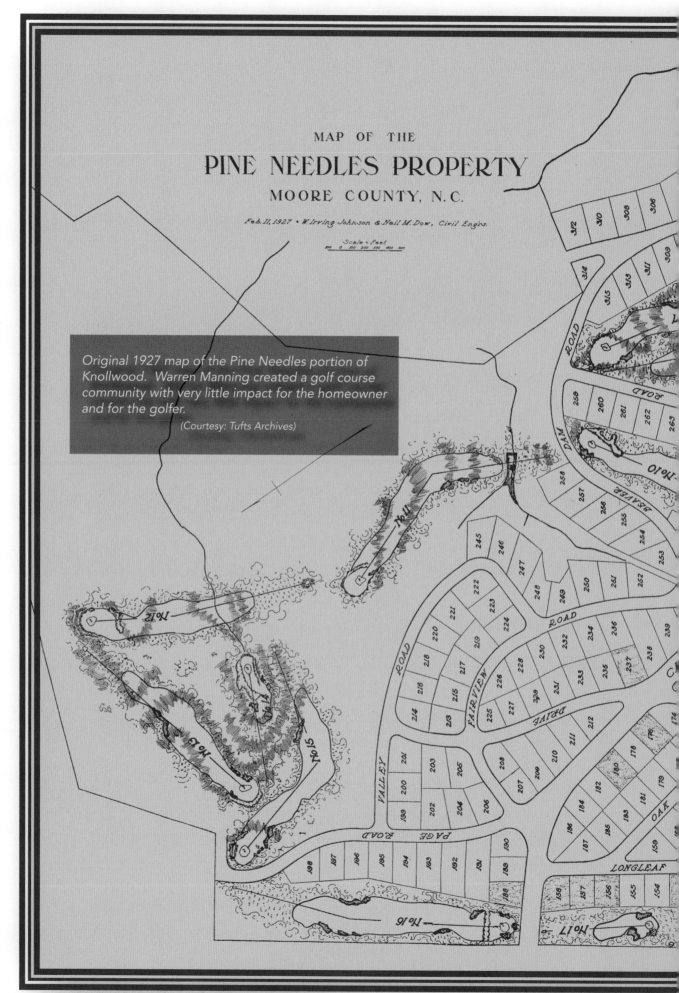

MAP OF THE

PINE NEEDLES PROPERTY

MOORE COUNTY, N.C.

Feb. 11, 1927 • W. Irving Johnson & Neil M. Dow, Civil Engrs.

Original 1927 map of the Pine Needles portion of Knollwood. Warren Manning created a golf course community with very little impact for the homeowner and for the golfer.

(Courtesy: Tufts Archives)

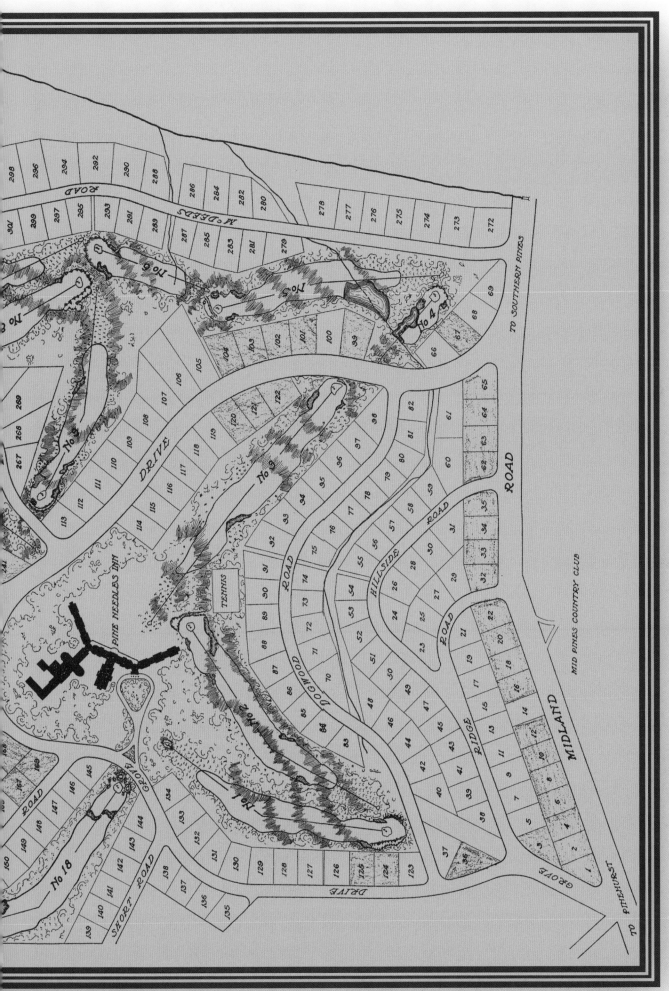

Pine Needles Golf Course
by Robert Hunter
(from *Pinehurst Outlook*, January 17, 1928)

Having pursued for a number of years the delightful occupation of visiting the best golf courses in this country and Europe, it is a real pleasure to find here in my old hunting grounds an ideal golf course. The design of the holes, the construction of work and the natural contours combine to produce at Pine Needles - I do not hesitate to say it - one of the finest golf courses, but I doubt if he has done anything better than this. He is fortunate in having with him an artist like Frank Maples who is doing some impressive construction work. His artificial contouring and the lines of his bunkering are as beautiful as one will find anywhere.

As I see it, the ideal golf course, is one which will be a test for champions and yet delightful to play for even the most indifferent golfer. It cannot, of course, be expected that the latter will get pars and birdies; but he will not face, hole after hole, serious penalties for every mistake made. On every hole at Pine Needles, one who can hit a straight ball will have his reward and lots of pleasure. He need not be long. But with a few additional back tees the champion seeking birdies will have a man's work to do.

Last year I visited many courses in Florida. This year I have seen many courses in this section of the Middle South but in neither place have I seen anything which will give so much pleasure to all classes of golfers as the new course at Pine Needles.

It used to be said by golf course architects that even the best courses have a few weak holes. There is not one weak or unfair hole at Pine Needles. Five of the holes are as fine as anything I have ever seen. The three starting holes are excellent and the finish, the 16th, 17th, and 18th - are really superb.

An impressive thing about Pine Needles - besides the high quality of golf offered - is the beautiful construction work and fine turf. The contours are beyond criticism. Such soft, beautiful, flowing lines are in my opinion essential to the best golf. Many golfers and casual observers do not see contours or care about them. Certainly they are not always easy to see where the grass is brown. Various shades of green throw contours into relief while brown fairways and sand "greens" seem to obscure the beauty of such lines. I have never seen finer contours than those at Pine Needles and the architect and constructor may well be proud of this work there.

The progress Pinehurst has made in the ten years I have been away is extraordinary. Good golf courses have done wonders here - and it is an especial joy to me to see this new course - the finest fruition, I venture to say, of the genius of Donald Ross and his capable aids.

Planting wire grass in the bunker face of Pine Needles' original thirteenth hole (today's twelfth).
(Courtesy: Tufts Archives)

Original eighteenth green at Pine Needles (today's seventeeth).
(Courtesy: Tufts Archives)

Construction (above) of original twelfth hole at Pine Needles and immediately after shaping (below). This is the eleventh hole today.
(Courtesy: Tufts Archives [top]; Pine Needles/Mid Pines [bottom])

substantiates this claim. In fact, on September 26, 1923, the Town Board of Commissioners voted to authorize the laying of a four inch water main from the corporation limits to the new clubhouse of the Country Club, with the entire cost to be paid by the Club. If the Town owned it, there would be no demands for payment. Land records show the property was owned by individual property owners since at least 1906.

Nonetheless, Southern Pines Country Club began developing grand plans during the roaring twenties. The February 18th, 1926 issue of the *Pinehurst Outlook* revealed plans for a new full-length course, eighteen "mini" holes and a new clubhouse. Additional property was to include roads and lots on *"all of that fine ridge and rugged land east of the present links"*, according to the *Outlook*. Interestingly enough, Donald Ross is not credited by the newspaper as the architect of choice for the expansion. The reason is because the expansion was drawn by Irving Johnson. It is unclear whether he was actually going to be the architect for the expansion or if the locals were simply so familiar with Ross's organization that it was understood that Johnson was simply carrying out his boss's charge. Strangely, there was never any mention of the ambitious plans beyond the newspaper article.

IN 1927, SANDHILLS GOLF DEVELOPMENT CONTINUED WITH TWO MORE PROJECTS ON THE DRAWING BOARD, EACH WITH A CONNECTION TO THE TUFTS FAMILY. Montevideo Park was a proposed development of 530 rolling acres from Highway Five to the valley of Aberdeen Creek south

Southern Pines Country Club   Southern Pines, N. C.

The Eleventh Hole of Southern Pines Country Club
(Courtesy: Moore County Historical Association)

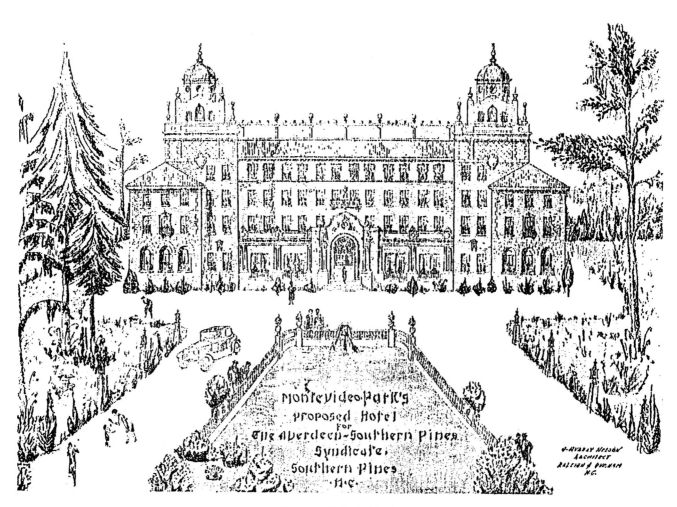

(Courtesy: Tufts Archives)

of Pinehurst. An ambitious project was proposed with 12 miles of road and residential lots (starting at $500 each) surrounding an 18-hole golf course laid out by Frank Maples. The project was to flank both sides of the Seaboard Airline Railroad with Aberdeen Lake forming the northeast corner of the property. Montevideo Park was the only golf course Maples ever designed, but unfortunately it was never built. Beyond an article in the *Sandhill Citizen* introducing the project, no more written mention of Montevideo Park was ever made.

Frank Maples
(Courtesy: Tufts Archives)

ANOTHER MYSTERY WAS A GOLF COURSE REPORTED AS DESIGNED AND UNDER CONSTRUCTION IN 1927, YET THERE IS NO EVIDENCE OF IT ON THE GROUND AND NO ONE TODAY CAN VOUCH FOR ITS EXISTENCE.

One of the original Knollwood developers, James Barber, commissioned Ross to develop a golf course on property bisected by Seals Road (now Airport Road). Midland Road was the southern boundary of much of the area and the Southern Pines/Carthage Road (Route 22) was the Northeast boundary. Conflicting reports describe a residential golf development and a stand-alone private golf course.

Through Ross's eyes, the golf course was to be built in a valley beneath a ridge proposed for excellent building sites for homes (very much like Mid Pines). From the hills above the clubhouse site, three dams along Mill Creek were to cover nearly a mile, making one of the most picturesque valleys in the Sandhills the dominant feature of the golf course.

The first aspect of this mystery is that in early 1926 Barber passed away and left the land to his son Edward. Ross completed a routing for the elder Barber that was dated the following year. The son had no idea of his father's plans so he looked to Ross and Leonard for answers. It was Ross who revealed the father's intention to create a private 18-hole layout where he could take his friends to play. Barber had also kicked around the idea of selling the property to a club that would have rooms similar to Mid Pines.

Ross suggested to Edward that the project should be connected to the Knollwood development. If the roads were laid out properly, Ross reasoned, people would travel from Pinehurst to Knollwood through Barber's development and the property would gain value. In a letter from Leonard to Edward dated March 12, 1928, he advised Edward to sit on the land for a year, sell some lots, and then go ahead with the development.

But according to an issue of the *Pinehurst Outlook* in November of 1927, the course was already under construction. The newspaper reported that a stone clubhouse was built on a hill overlooking two lakes (above the future fourteenth hole of Longleaf Country Club). The only logical explanation is that construction was started and halted upon James Barber's death. The questions that remain are: Why is Ross's drawing dated 1927 (a simple typographical error?) and why Edward had no clue as to his father's intentions. Nonetheless, there was no other mention of Barber's course.

Supposed Barber Course Clubhouse. This photo was taken in 1933.
(Courtesy: Tufts Archives)

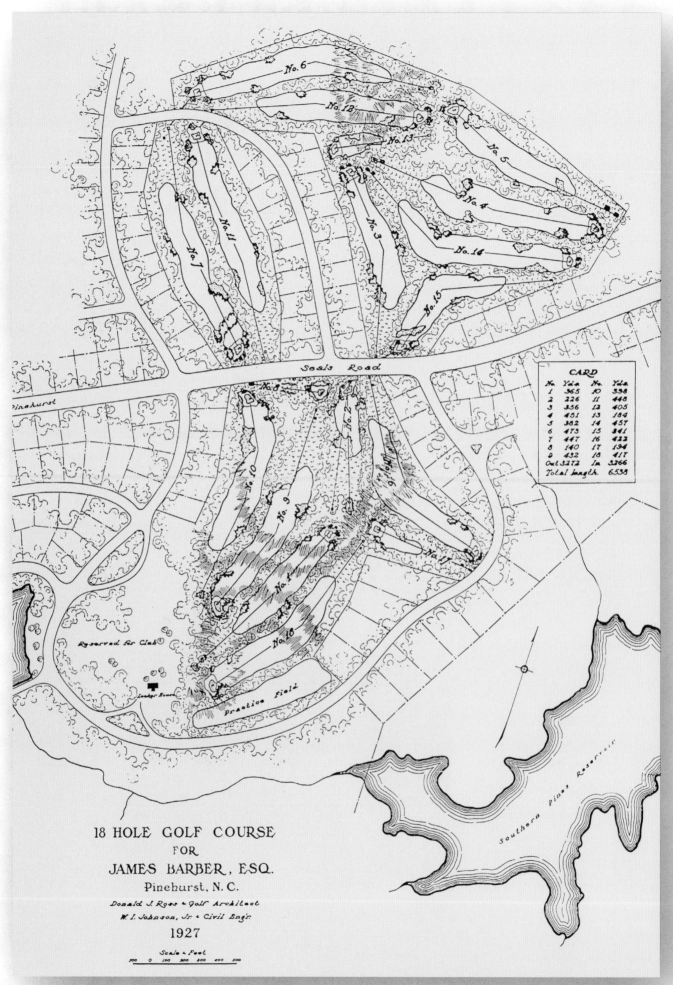

CARD

No.	Yds	No.	Yds
1	365	10	398
2	226	11	448
3	356	12	405
4	451	13	184
5	382	14	457
6	473	15	341
7	447	16	422
8	140	17	194
9	432	18	417
Out 3272		In 3266	
Total Length		6538	

18 HOLE GOLF COURSE
FOR
JAMES BARBER, ESQ.
Pinehurst, N. C.

Donald J. Ross • Golf Architect
W. I. Johnson, Jr • Civil Eng'r.

1927

Scale • Feet

ONE BARBER COURSE THAT DID SURVIVE WAS ACTUALLY AMERICA'S FIRST MINIATURE GOLF COURSE. In 1916, James Barber built an 18-hole "*lilliputian*" golf course on the grounds of his home behind the Carolina Hotel. It was designed by Edward H. Wisell and named the "*Thistle-Dhu*". Wisell's charge was to design a postage stamp course incorporating all the elements that made "*real*" golf such a pleasurable challenge.

Thistle-Dhu "Lilliputian Golf Course"
(Courtesy: Tufts Archives)

Rumblings of economic disaster throughout the country did not go unnoticed in the Sandhills. Both the Montevideo Park project and James Barber's course were probably halted due to the coming depression. Expansion plans at Southern Pines Country Club were also likely affected by black clouds on the horizon as investors across the nation pulled financing close to the vest. Tourism and golf suffered as people focused more on their personal economic stability. The Tufts family was well aware of the financial challenges to be faced on Wall Street and in North Carolina. They were at a crossroads: Continue what they had planned and maintain their philosophy of developing ahead of the curve? Or pull back and wait out a pending storm of uncertainty?

CHAPTER SEVEN
TARNISHED PINECONE

"I am asking you therefore to do not one penny's worth of work over there more than is necessary. Let's not be too artistic. And don't put in any more traps or change around any more holes."

- Leonard Tufts to Donald Ross (May 17, 1929)

SO WHAT ENDED THE GOLDEN AGE OF GOLF ARCHITECTURE? Was it a waning popularity of the game in the thirties and early forties? Or was it the Great Depression and World War II? If the game of golf slipped in popularity it was because current events moved the game out of the forefront of many American's minds. Golf's growth slowed because many of the leading developers of the game found themselves in ever-stretching bread lines. A decade later, World War II deflected attention away from personal gratification and more toward a national effort.

The end of the golden age in the Sandhills came about as a result of all these factors. Gone were the days of long annual visits to Pinehurst, replaced by a cautious conservatism by the end user as well as the fat cats previously willing to invest in the game. For the first time in the history of Pinehurst, timing was not on the Tufts's side. By the time Black Tuesday hit, Team Tufts had just expanded and were juggling 108 golf holes along Midland Road and a glut of hotel space.

The Tufts found themselves in a different boat this time and it meant they could no longer dictate development in Pinehurst. The *"build it and they will come"* attitude shifted to a *"batten down the hatches and prepare for a storm"* philosophy. While James Barber's project died on the vine and both Montevideo Park and expansion plans at Southern Pines Country Club never got off the pages of the *Sandhill Citizen*, the Tufts wondered if they hadn't bitten off more than they could chew with their infant Knollwood development and

Donald Ross analyzing new practice green adjacent to first
tee of Course Number Two as Richard Tufts (left) looks on.
(Courtesy: Tufts Archives)

the infrastructure of 36 more golf holes. The golden pinecone began to tarnish.

Nonetheless, despite pending fears that they grew too quickly with Mid Pines and Pine Needles, the Tufts moved ahead with a foreboding that wouldn't reveal itself for years to come. Discussions about a fifth golf course began in 1928. This time golf wasn't the primary motivation; potential residential development was the driving force.

The plan was to build a new course south of Midland Road and east of Number Two with the sole motivation of selling home sites. Leonard Tufts was so enamored by the potential of a new nine he was even willing to break up Number Two and insert these new holes. However, there was also a practical quality to what he was contemplating: converting the banished nine holes of Number Two into a separate employees' course isolated from the rest of the resort:

> *Dear Donald:*
> *"In further regard to the course for the employees it seems to me that we could rearrange the*
> *course so as to make the #2 course 1 - 2 - 3; then put in nine new holes; then come back*
> *on 4- 5 - 6 - 16 - 17 - 18. Then we could put our employees on the nine hole course on #2*
> *course, consisting of 14 - 15 - 7 - 8 - 9 - 10 - 11 - 12 - 13. No one would object to this*
> *because these nine holes are separated from the rest of the golf course."*
>
> - Leonard Tufts, March 21, 1928

1939 Aerial Photograph of Employee's Course. Note how some holes cross the future 15-501 corridor.
(Courtesy: Tufts Archives)

Luckily, cooler heads prevailed and the decision to keep Number Two intact was made. From a real estate perspective, these holes would lead to additional development along Midland Road in the direction of Knollwood. That project was called Midland Farms and included plans for another 36 holes. Pinehurst Number Five would become the starting point:

March 29, 1928

Dear Donald and Richard,

After thinking over the sketch that Donald showed me yesterday for the extension of the golf course I am wondering if this would be a mistake or not. Looking at it from the standpoint of immediate financial return it seems to me that we ought to have holes on that golf course practically parallel with the double road to Southern Pines, just as far down as our property runs, and at no point over 300 feet away. This arrangement as suggested is probably all together too compact as it wouldn't give space enough for lots between the holes but it illustrates my idea of getting the holes parallel with the double road. It would probably be possible to sell enough lots on the double road next year to pay for the entire cost of this course and these lots should be sold to individuals with restrictions that they build within a reasonable time - as we must remember that we want to get the two towns growing together.

As I remember it, Donald proposes to put in five holes east of the present #3; to put in six holes at other points and to abandon two holes. From the standpoint of immediate financial return we would get one half as much out of this layout as we would if we put the whole nine out on the double road.

Looking at it from another standpoint we should have 1,000 acres of land between here and Southern Pines for our next development after we are through at Pinehurst and Knollwood. This should be mostly on the southern side of the double road and in my opinion should include a large hotel of 300 rooms, two 18-hole golf courses, and about 400 lots and a village center with stores. This shouldn't go far enough north of the double road to interfere in any way with the future water supply. The nine holes suggested can later be used as part of the new development.

I believe we are strong enough now and firmly enough established so that we can move quite a way out from this section in the establishment of a resort. I believe with our present organization we could build, for example, down below Pine Bluff or even up towards Eagle Springs and by putting the developments around in different places in the section we will have the advantage of the open spaces necessary for attractive rides and drives, golf courses, estates, etc.

However, to get back to our next development - it might pay better to adopt Donald's plan as outlined to me yesterday as this would give us enough extra golf and would not put a whole lot of holes that might interfere with the development of our scheme of 1,000 acres between here and Southern Pines (Future Midland Farms). It looks to me as if the best thing for us to do is to put nine holes of golf out between here and Southern Pines, East of #3 hole and South of Midland Road. Whatever is to be done will have to be done in a hurry but if all nine holes are put out beyond #3 we won't have to interrupt the present golf courses any and we can do the work a little more gradually than we could if we adopted Donald's scheme.

Regards,

Leonard

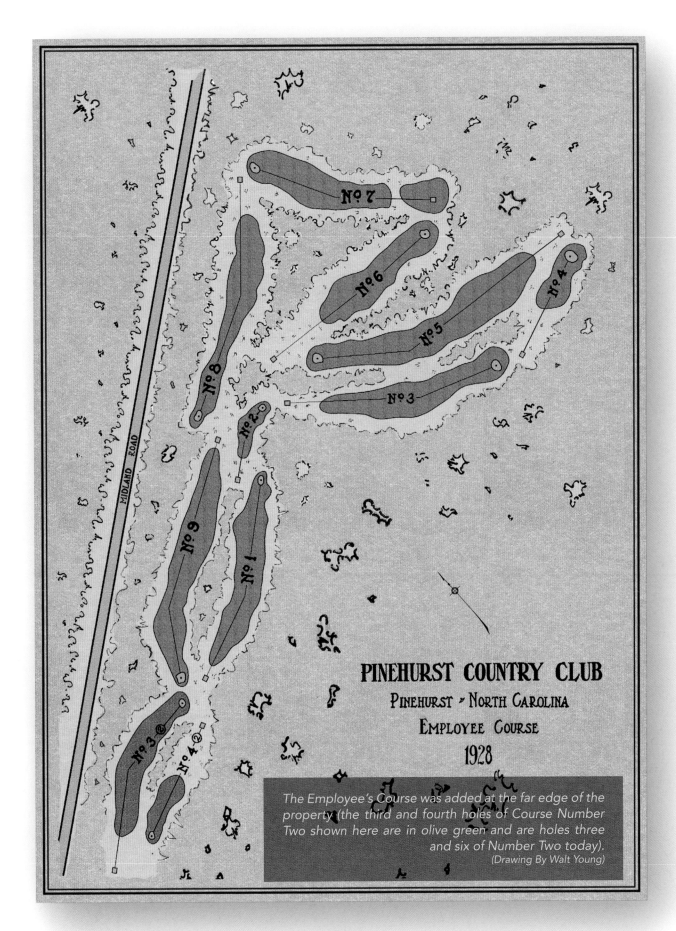

PINEHURST COUNTRY CLUB
PINEHURST ~ NORTH CAROLINA
EMPLOYEE COURSE
1928

The Employee's Course was added at the far edge of the property (the third and fourth holes of Course Number Two shown here are in olive green and are holes three and six of Number Two today).
(Drawing By Walt Young)

Ross followed Leonard's suggestion and laid out the initial holes in the field beyond the present third and fourth holes of Number Two that he had added five years earlier. In a late December letter to Ross, Leonard discussed the opportunity of revising the routing to squeeze more home sites between the golf holes:

> *"This morning I walked over #5 golf course to see if it would not be possible to throw #3 course [hole] farther south, leaving a wider space between #3 and #5 [holes]. There is approximately 200 feet between the actual fairways of these two courses [holes] at about the widest place and it seems to me as if it might be practical to throw #3 fairway over farther and leave perhaps 250 feet or more between the courses and in this way get a line of building lots between the two. This particular ridge along there seems to be very attractive."*

Today, Tufts's suggestion is Muster Bridge Road as well as home sites along Pinehurst Number Seven but Midland Farms never got off the ground.

THE IDEA OF A GOLF COURSE STRICTLY FOR EMPLOYEES HAD ITS NAYSAYERS. Many homeowners resisted the idea of the workers playing behind their homes. In an effort to appease the locals, Leonard softened the focus and didn't refer to it as an *"employees' course."* Instead,

> *"it will be just an added nine holes on which the people of Pinehurst can play as much or as little as they like. We will, however, make an arrangement, and charge $5.00 a year to all employees and restrict their play to this nine hole course."*

The nine opened in October and was nicknamed the employees' course anyway, despite Leonard's attempt at marketing the layout as something else. Ross was very high on his newest design. *"The new nine holes are about the best in Pinehurst. They have excellent golfing quality and from a scenic standpoint, they are very beautiful."*

The most scenic hole was the first, a long downhill par five. The hole started at the end of a high ridge where the third and fourth holes of Number Two stopped and then played down into a valley. From there, the golfer played along the valley floor to a green placed on a saddle point surrounded by a natural amphitheater.

The most difficult was the parallel ninth hole, which started over a small rise and moved back down into a valley. The hole then traveled along the northernmost ridge to a putting surface on a peninsula below the third green. The challenge of the ninth hole was on the tee shot. One could play down the left side and use the downhill slope to gain a shorter approach to the green. However, Ross's sprinkling of bunkers along this line of flight demanded a very precise shot. The less daring could play along the high right side with a more friendly opening to the green, but this route would cost a half stroke to a full stroke more to get home. The other holes crossed over the future route 15-501 and returned through the future World Golf Hall of Fame property.

**Employee's Course
in 1928**
[Overlaid on Present Resort]

LATER THAT YEAR, A MINOR AGRONOMIC BREAKTHROUGH ENABLED ROSS TO CONVERT THE CLAY TEES ON ALL THE COURSES TO RYE GRASS WITH THE MODEST GOAL OF TURF SURVIVAL FOR THE SPRING SEASON. He knew year-round playing conditions were out of the question, but grass during the months of March and April would be a great success. At the same time, planted Italian rye grass began establishing itself in the approaches to every green. It wouldn't survive on the putting surfaces yet, but Ross was getting closer and on track to a full grass conversion.

Although small changes were constant at Pinehurst throughout the twenties, a large-scale conversion of the tees and greens of all five courses was an incredible undertaking, especially with economic strife on the horizon. Some employees were less than thrilled about the prospect of major renovations. They weren't sold on much of Ross's past tweaking, either. A letter from Isham Sledge (the Tufts's long-time hotel manager and secretary/treasurer from 1911 until his death in 1958) to Richard makes a relevant point:

> *"We seem to get in some work on each course each year and I am wondering if we are correct in this. For instance, new work on #1 so far this year amounts to $211.73. I wonder if this is not just for changing around a little and the course is not $200 better than it was last year."*

Pinehurst Number One Scene
(Courtesy: Tufts Archives)

Nonetheless, certain tasks were vital to the health, safety and welfare of the resort guests and locals. Richard fully recognized this and urged Donald to act but with caution in a letter dated May 8, 1929:

May 8, 1929

Dear Mr. Ross:

I think that the changes which you have suggested for the sixteenth of No.1 course, would be a great improvement as I have often noticed how inconvenient it is to have this road across the hole. Since this work would apparently not be very expensive, I think it would be alright to undertake it this summer.

I have also often thought that sometime it might be a good idea to consider making the 17th hole shorter in order to get that green off the top of the hole. During winter weather it always is bad and it might in some way be possible to make these two holes into two two shotters.

I would not undertake anything else this summer however, as we have got to reduce the new work to a minimum in order to build up a reserve for the construction of the addition to the Holly Inn next summer. I wish that sometime before the first of June you could get Frank to make out an estimate of the cost of all new work, changes, etc. to be done this summer and divide the cost so that we would know how much it would amount to before that date and how much after. This would be necessary in order to know what other work we should be able to undertake.

Yours very truly,

Richard S. Tufts

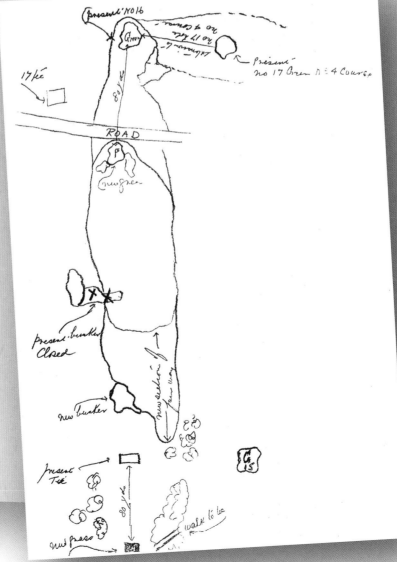

(Courtesy: Tufts Archives)

The Tufts were still wary of continued spending, regardless of the benefits that grass would provide the resort. In a letter to Ross dated May 17, 1929, Leonard ordered him not to spend much money on the golf courses due to tough economic times:

May 17, 1929

Dear Donald,

We have rather a serious situation to face this summer. As you know, this spring we intended to put an addition on to the Holly Inn but unfortunately the money rates were so high, due to the New York speculation, that we gave this up. Since then our business has been very poor as you know and instead of coming out with about our usual profit, we will probably end up the year with a profit of only about 2/3 of what we have been making. In fact I shall be surprised if we do as well as that.

This makes it very, very important for us to keep down our new work this year to the very minimum. We have got to do something to talk about so we are putting on a small addition to the dining room at the Carolina, fixing up the help's dormitory and rest room at the Holly Inn and moving the Gun Club. Not one of these will increase the income of Pinehurst, Incorporated a cent and changing of the tees at the Country Club will not add anything to our income over there.

I am asking you therefore to do not one penny's worth of work over there more than is necessary. We will, of course, have to build 18 new tees at the least account of the talk that was made and what we told the Board of Governors. And Richard thinks it necessary to put in grass tees at all of the four 18 hole courses, but as soon as this is done I hope you will tell Frank to cut down to the smallest possible maintenance force and not do any more work. And if you think it feasible I certainly wouldn't put them all in but this I will leave to yours and Richard's judgement, but if you can put one in for $4.95 and put in a good deal better one for $5.00, only use the $4.95 variety. Let's not be too artistic. And don't put in any more traps or change around any more holes.

The difficulty with this business is, we never know for sure what we can do until the hotels are closed for, as you know, we spend all of our profits each year in improvements.

Regards,

Leonard

Twelfth Tee of Number One Course circa 1935
(Courtesy: Tufts Archives)

Despite Tufts's concern, Ross converted all the tees to grass and pushed forward with efforts to convert the greens. In 1931 (after twelve years of searching for the right mix of sand, soil, and fertilizer), Ross and Maples developed a strain of Bermuda grass that could survive the Carolina winter and handle traffic on the greens.

But before full implementation of the putting surfaces could become a reality, an upgrade to the primitive irrigation system on Number Two (installed back in 1911) would be vital. Team Tufts's first attempt incorporated a quarter of a mile of old two inch pipe in hundred-foot sections. They were coupled with short pieces of fire hose and placed along the center of each golf hole. Couplings were placed every 80 to 100 feet to let the water flow out on a modified dust pan at the end of the hose. The best that could be soaked was about two holes a day.

This system drained the entire village's supply of water in one week and only covered 15 holes. So they decided a more permanent and efficient method was necessary and spent $20,000 on a Buckner irrigation system in the fall of 1932. Five miles of 6- and 8-inch pipe was buried and connected to the village water system, a booster pump was installed to increase the pressure, and outlets were placed flush with the grass at appropriate points. The new system took only fourteen hours to cover all 18 fairways and opened up major possibilities. Now that the ability to irrigate was feasible, Ross and Maples were more than eager to implement their research immediately. They added experimental grass greens to the first and second holes of Number Two in 1934.

Enough positive response was garnered from the three grass greens that the decision was made to convert the remaining greens of Number Two with the homegrown Bermuda variety that Maples and Ross had been developing since the late 1910's. The final ingredient necessary for successfully converting from sand to grass was much larger putting surfaces (to help spread out wear).

Converting from sand to grass let Ross create much more interesting putting surfaces than the relatively round, flat greens of the Sandhills. Without erosion concerns and because the old practice of smoothing out the sand surfaces was no longer necessary, Ross freely developed interesting highs, lows, swales, and ridges on his putting surfaces to provide more challenge to the golfers. In addition, the new greens were more manageable for the ever-developing aerial game required by modern golf equipment.

Sand greens had limited the ability of the golfer to land a ball directly onto the putting surface. At the 1931 North and South Women's Tournament, Maureen Orcutt explained the challenge the hard sand greens presented: *"We used what was called the 'Texas wedge'* [putter] *from fifty yards in. You couldn't hit the ball to the green because it would bounce over those hard greens."*

*Second Green of Number Two Course in 1936 North and South Men's Open.
Note the severe slopes of the putting surface, especially the 2 - 3 foot high
point over the caddy's shoulder to the left.*
(Courtesy: Tufts Archives)

The primary intention for introducing rolls around the greens was to promote the art of chipping at Number Two. Ross never intended for each green complex to be shaved at fairway height as they are today. He wanted golfers to chip around the greens with irons more so than using the putter. Peter Tufts (Richard's son and Donald's godson) explained Ross's grassing patterns at that time:

> *"He stopped the fairway mowing at the edge of the green. If you missed a green it might roll a little ways down on the green surface but the different heights in the fairway cut and the green cut would stop it so it wouldn't roll twenty or thirty feet. Chipping was really tough. And that's what Donald Ross had in mind in building the greens. He wanted to bring chipping into the green in a strong manner. He did a wonderful job there."*

Legend tells us there were no construction drawings for the new greens. *"I remember when DJ [Ross] and my dad [Frank] changed the greens at Number Two from sand to grass. They didn't have a single blueprint. They did it all from their heads,"* Ellis Maples said. Ross paid as much attention to the approach to each green as he did the putting surfaces themselves. Always promoting the ground game, he created rolls or humps in front to demand the perfect approach from the golfer. An example of this is a hump about 20 or 30 yards in front of the new number eight green. If the golfer didn't place his approach dead perfect the ball would roll off to a side.

Construction of New Eighth Green Complex of Pinehurst Number Two in May 1935
(Courtesy: Tufts Archives)

Construction of New Seventh Green Complex of Pinehurst Number Two in May 1935
(Courtesy: Tufts Archives)

Where green complexes were flat, Ross scooped out areas surrounding the intended putting surface and used the material to create greens with swales, hollows and mounds. Each green's construction crew consisted of about fifteen workers and a mule and a drag pan. Ross would direct the man tending the mule to dig the pan into the earth until it was full. He would then tell the man to dump it at another spot a few yards away. The

Fifth Green of Pinehurst Number Two During 1936 North and South Men's Open
Note the dramatic rolls off the putting surface edges into Ross's dips and swales
are as severe in 1936 as they are today.
(Courtesy: Tufts Archives)

Gene Sarazen Putts Downhill on a Newly Converted Grass Green on Pinehurst Number Two
Note the severe back to front slope.
(Courtesy: Tufts Archives)

Seventh Green of Pinehurst Number Two in 1936
(Courtesy: Tufts Archives)

other workers shaped the material with shovels where Ross told them to build up or cut down an area. The men reworked the surface until it was exactly the way Donald wanted it. The entire process took a week to ten days to complete each green complex.

As part of the greens renovation, it was necessary for Ross to rebuild the sand bunkers. He also eliminated about thirty bunkers, reducing the total to 125. Just as his greens evolved into more complex land forms, the bunkers followed suit. Ross developed a philosophy of "*form follows function*," requiring different construction techniques based on site conditions.

Two general principles were the basis for his decision making. Number one, Ross always fit bunkers into a space in a most naturally-appearing way as possible. Each of his bunker complexes were built with material that was immediately available in that location. If site conditions necessitated flat-bottomed sand bunkers it was achieved by simply cutting along the slope. Yet, most of Ross's bunkers were of the concave bottom variety to ensure balls rolled to the middle. Little extraneous earthwork was undertaken, unless it was absolutely necessary.

Note the concave-bottomed bunkers surrounding the tenth green of Pinehurst Number Two in 1936.
(Courtesy: Tufts Archives)

The second principle he followed, which had a profound effect on construction technique, was flashing enough sand up slopes to ensure visibility from the spot where each shot would be taken. In fact, many of the bunkers in 1935 had much more dramatic sand flashing than what is commonly attributed to those same bunkers today.

Hole 1, #2 Course.

Along right side of fairway plant a series of clumps of trees dividing the fairway from instructor's field. Also on the left short of first mound plant a clump of trees.

Close first bunker on the left and open a new bunker leading from rear end of first mound on the left out 20 yds. into the fairway. Leave a space of 75 yds. on the right of new pit as open fairway.

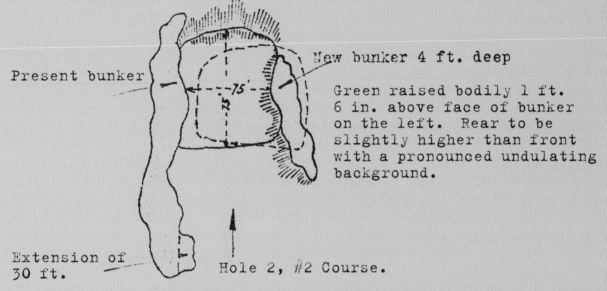

Present bunker

New bunker 4 ft. deep

Green raised bodily 1 ft. 6 in. above face of bunker on the left. Rear to be slightly higher than front with a pronounced undulating background.

Extension of 30 ft.

Hole 2, #2 Course.

Deepen the bunker on the right short of green.

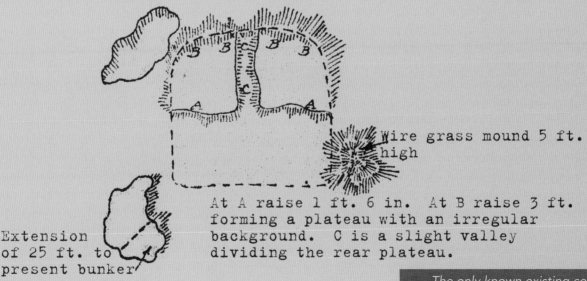

Wire grass mound 5 ft. high

Extension of 25 ft. to present bunker

At A raise 1 ft. 6 in. At B raise 3 ft. forming a plateau with an irregular background. C is a slight valley dividing the rear plateau.

Hole 3, #2 Course.

O. K.

The only known existing construction drawings of Pinehurst Number Two by Donald Ross. It is not known if these were ever utilized.
(Courtesy: Tufts Archives)

*Ross built dramatic flashed-sand bunkers in scale with the open spaces of the new
fifth hole of Pinehurst Number Two.*
(Courtesy: Tufts Archives)

While the greens on Number Two were being renovated, the employees' course was shut forever in a cost-cutting effort by Pinehurst, Incorporated, and the first and ninth holes became the new fourth and fifth holes of Number Two. Once the new holes were in place, the old ninth and tenth holes were the logical choices to be eliminated. These were the last of the three holes that played to the south and their elimination kept the

*Ross mixed elaborately edged bunker faces with simple shapes, yet strove not to sacrifice
the need for visibility in his efforts. This is the seventh green of Course Number Two.*
(Courtesy: Tufts Archives)

A dramatic contrast to today's bunkers, Ross's original flashed-sand bunkers were roughly carved into the fill pad of the eleventh green circa 1936.
(Courtesy: Tufts Archives)

Even on downhill holes such as seventeen of Number Two, Ross made a conscious effort to flash his sand for maximum visibility.
(Courtesy: Tufts Archives)

DONALD J. ROSS — GOLF ARCHITECT

Various Types of Mounds & Bunkers.

Fig.1 Typical face for bunker under 3' deep; steep from A to B; sloping from B to C

Fig.2 Typical face for bunker over 3' deep; sloping gradually from A to B.

Fig.3 Bunker depressed and the face raised above the surface.

Fig.4 Type of bunker dished out of the face of a mound with a sanded face.

Fig.5 Type of bunker with the face cut out of slope.

Fig.6 Series of mounds & hollows all above the surface.

Fig.7 Series of mounds & hollows which should be built only on land which drains readily.

Perspective of Fig. 6.

Perspective of Fig. 7.

(Courtesy: Tufts Archives)

layout more compact and on the higher elevations of the property. The old eighth hole became the new tenth. Play then moved north to the eleventh tee.

Number Two was also lengthened to 6,952 yards by adding back tees to the fourth, fifth, sixth, and eighth, and every hole on the back nine except number fifteen. Ross moved the tenth green back 80 yards and narrowed the fairway in spots with new bunkers. This remodeling primarily was done to challenge the long hitters, yet it still provided areas where shorter hitters had ample room to spray their tee shots.

Although length was added to the course, it was not Ross's intention to present a much tougher challenge to the player. In fact, he felt the changes made the course more fair for each golfer.

> *"Bearing in mind that golf should be a pleasure and not a penance, it has always been my thought to present a test of the player's game; the severity of the test to be in direct ratio with his ability as a player. I carried out this thought in the changes made on Number Two. I am firmly of the opinion that the leading professionals and golfers of every caliber, for many years to come, will find in the Number Two Course the fairest yet most exacting test of their*

A golfer tees off on number sixteen (Course Number Two) during the 1936 North and South Men's Open.
(Courtesy: Tufts Archives)

game, and yet a test from which they will always derive the maximum amount of pleasure. This, to my mind, should be the ideal of all golf courses."

Upon the opening of the newly-renovated course, Ross's grass greens were considered a smashing success by architects, professionals, and locals alike. A. W. Tillinghast was quoted as saying,

"These new greens are quite as fine as anyone could wish to play to or putt over. They are undeniably fine, of lovely uniform color and true as steel. Nothing was lost on me, and after our round together, I told him [Ross] with all honesty that his course was magnificent, without a single weakness, and one which must rank with the truly great courses in the world today."

The *Pinehurst Outlook* also heaped praise on Ross's work:

"The grass greens and the elimination of that old #10 hole, with its stiff climb up to the green, have been attractive to the rank and file of players. Few complaints on the part of the visitors as to the way the surfaces putted and the only criticism later, was that the undulations of the greens were too severe in relation to the length and hazards of the course. In the 1936 North and South Amateur, winner George T. Dunlap averaged under two

The old tenth hole was eliminated as part of the 1935 renovations to Pinehurst Number Two. Along with the ninth hole, it was replaced by the new fourth and fifth holes.
(Courtesy: Tufts Archives)

The Fifth Green of Course Number One, circa 1943
(Courtesy: Tufts Archives)

putts per green proving that there was no real foundation for any criticism on the part of the professionals for those dips and hollows which Donald Ross so masterfully conceived to make approaches and putts as much a problem for the experts to solve as the ability to keep their drives away from the natural hazards of the woods and the artificial hazards of the sand bunkers."

- April 18, 1936

Archery on the Closed Number Four Course
(Courtesy: Tufts Archives)

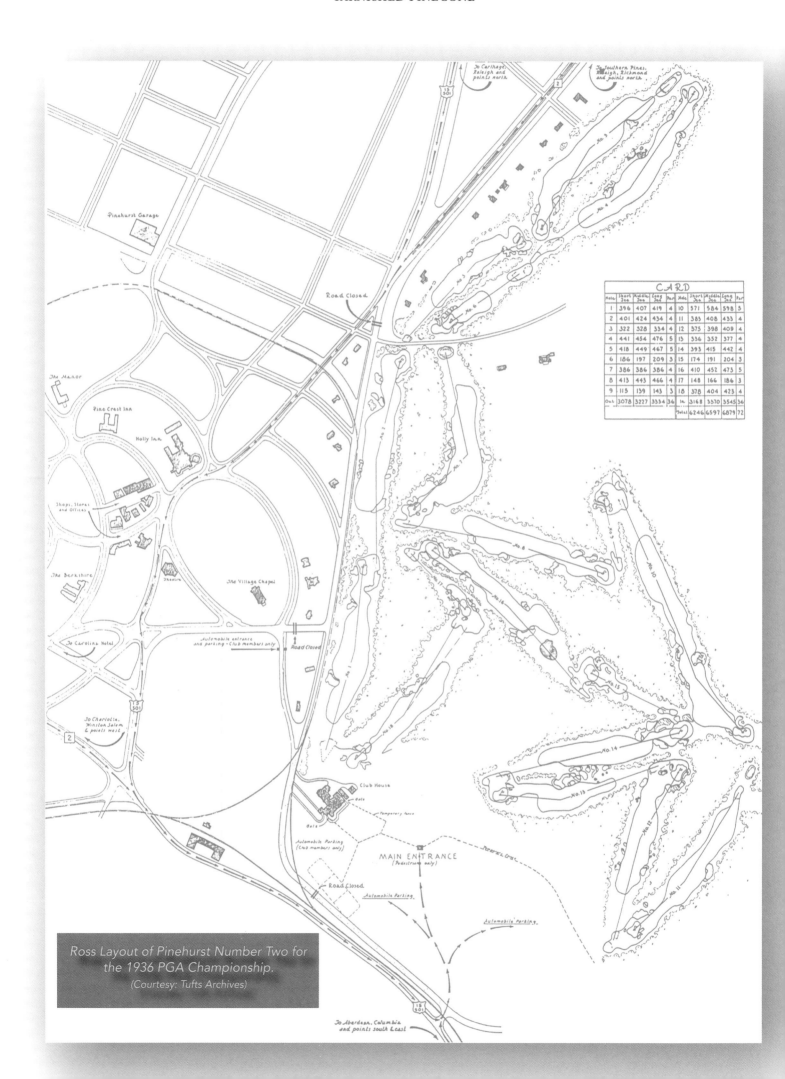

					C A R D						
Hole	Short Tee	Middle Tee	Long Tee	Par	Hole	Short Tee	Middle Tee	Long Tee	Par		
1	396	407	419	4	10	571	584	598	5		
2	401	424	434	4	11	383	408	433	4		
3	322	328	334	4	12	375	398	409	4		
4	441	454	476	5	13	336	352	377	4		
5	418	449	467	5	14	393	415	442	4		
6	186	197	209	3	15	174	191	204	3		
7	386	386	386	4	16	410	452	473	5		
8	413	443	466	4	17	148	166	186	3		
9	115	139	143	3	18	378	404	423	4		
Out	3078	3227	3334	36	In	3168	3370	3545	36		
						Total	6246	6597	6879	72	

Ross Layout of Pinehurst Number Two for the 1936 PGA Championship.
(Courtesy: Tufts Archives)

Number Fourteen of Course Number
Three in 1932
(Courtesy: Tufts Archives)

The Same Hole After Grassing in 1942
(Today this is the seventh hole.)
(Courtesy: Tufts Archives)

Immediately after the successful transformation of Pinehurst Number Two from sand greens to the now-legendary plateau greens, the 1936 PGA Championship thrust Pinehurst into the national spotlight and as the future Home of American Golf. The aggressive grassing schedule continued as Number Three's greens were grassed in 1936 and Number One's were grassed the following year.

IN THE NAME OF PROGRESS, THERE WERE ALSO CASUALTIES. As the PGA Championship exited stage right, the decision to abandon nine holes of Pinehurst Number Four was made. Two years later, the other nine was also set to pasture. Literally. For a prized herd of cattle. It was also used as the new '*helps*' course for a brief period before someone converted it to a novel archery course, with targets appropriately placed to determine "*strokes*" taken. Eventually, Number Four served a prize herd of cattle owned by Pinehurst.

Rod Innes, a professional under Ross at Pinehurst, recalls the challenge the resort faced and the decision to close the Number Four course:

> *"It was closed and it stayed closed for a long time. It had beautiful water holes. We didn't need four courses. The people down here that lived in those houses, they played maybe once or twice a week. They* [the Tufts] *started bringing these groups in, Plumbers Union, or*

whatever it was, and these guys would come in and get a special rate at the Carolina Hotel. Instead of getting the fancy fare they were getting convention chow. These guys would get up in the morning, have breakfast, have their lunch over at the clubhouse, and they would come home at night and eat in the dining room but it was not that famous menu that they had back in the old days."

Golf had ceased to be the cash cow it was previously, forcing the Tufts family to make radical changes to their business model. There were no discussions to sell the resort at this time nor close any more golf holes. Instead, an effort to reign in Ross and his numerous changes (as well as efforts to make the courses more maintenance friendly) was the focus. The grassing advances required a shift in maintenance strategy to establish the conditions Ross and the Tufts envisioned. Where to cut costs was on everyone's mind:

"Frank brought in today his figures on the golf courses but I have not yet seen the figures for the country club. There does not seem to be much that we can cut out of the golf course figures unless it be the work on the tenth hole of No. 2 course, building an approach green near the clubhouse and putting down the wooden blocks in front of the workshop. The work on the fairways of #4 and #5 holes on No. 2 course, I think is very important as I have heard some criticism of the condition of these two holes. Apparently Frank has to have a

The Fifth Hole of Course Number One After 1939 Renovations
(Courtesy: Tufts Archives)

Prior to the 1939 renovations, the tenth hole of Course
Number One played straight uphill as shown.
(Courtesy: Tufts Archives)

Ross's renovations included moving the new tenth hole down
the hill to the left, eliminating the blind uphill approach.
(Courtesy: Tufts Archives)

new tractor and nearly everything else he has listed is small. I would like to get your ideas on dropping out the three items I have mentioned above, if we find we are going to have difficulty sticking to the figures."

-Richard Tufts to Donald Ross, May 16, 1938

Ross again ignored Tufts's suggestions and rebuilt all eighteen holes of Number One the very next year, completely changing seven of them. Irrigation was installed on the course and all the greens were built from the ground up with a layer of topsoil added to the surface to establish a proper growing medium for the new grass. This was done despite the conversion from sand two years before. All the fairways were re-planted and many new tees were rebuilt, also with a layer of topsoil added to the surface. Among the changes included rebuilding the par-three fifth hole as well as new sixth, seventh, eighth, tenth and eleventh holes. Most likely the changes were precipitated in an effort to eliminate two of the more *"mountainous"* holes and make the course more playable. The holes that were replaced, the old ten and eleven, played forty feet straight up a ridge (roughly where today's eight tee sits) and then back down. The final changes were the re-orientation of the eighteenth hole to the west and installation of new irrigation.

RICHARD TUFTS FELT HIS FAMILY FIRST FACED FINANCIAL STRAIN FIFTEEN YEARS BEFORE NUMBER FOUR CLOSED WHEN THEY FIRST INVESTED IN KNOLLWOOD: *"IT WAS OF COURSE THE EFFORT TO SALVAGE KNOLLWOOD WHICH GOT US INTO TROUBLE."* Despite all the

Original Fourth Hole at Pine Needles in 1938
(Courtesy: Tufts Archives)

Seventh Green at Southern Pines Country Club
(Courtesy: Andy Page)

expansion efforts and conversion to grass, the stock market crash and resultant depression made it impossible for the Tufts to maintain so many holes in Pinehurst and Southern Pines. In order to keep the resort afloat, further closures were necessary. Once the remaining holes of the employees' course were shut, they continued the bleeding down Midland Road.

The Tufts closed Pine Needles in 1931 and on November 8, 1934, the Homeland Investment Corporation acquired Mid Pines by auction for $90,000. On June 5, 1935, the Patuxent Development Company bought Pine Needles and 531 adjoining acres for $75,000. Patuxent was led by longtime Pinehurst resident George Dunlap. The new ownership followed the resort's grassing plans with their own greens conversion in 1937 (Mid Pines followed suit the next year). Maples and Ross did the work themselves in less than a month. Upon completion, Ross described them as *"the most perfect in the sandhills for the average player"*.

THE HISTORY OF SOUTHERN PINES COUNTRY CLUB DURING THE DEPRESSION ERA WAS ALSO OF FINANCIAL STRUGGLE AS IT REGULARLY BATTLED THE TOWN REGARDING WATER, SEWER, AND OPERATIONS. In the wake of the depression, the Town bailed the Club out of murky water. In April of 1932, M. G. Nicholls approached the town Board of Commissioners as a Director of the club (he also was the deed-holder of the land at the time) stating that it would be forced to shut down all 18 holes if sufficient arrangements could not be made for the purchase of fertilizer. In response to this cry, a representative from the town Chamber of Commerce, a Mr. Richardson, recommended the Town donate $2,500 to the cause. The recommendation was not accepted, yet the Commissioners did declare their intentions as individuals to help in any way possible to re-finance the Club.

Less than three months later, Nicholls returned with another request for fertilizer. Once again, the Club's plea was turned down, mostly because of a perceived conflict of interest. The Town recognized the Country Club as a private corporation and *"nothing other than a real estate development for the purpose of making a profit from the sale of lots for the benefit of the stock holders,"* according to Town Board minutes.

Nicholls returned in subsequent years with similar requests. In May of 1934, it was for relief of hydrant costs owed to the tune of $266 on the grounds that the Club was in very bad shape financially and had been unable to meet the bills and payroll. By 1936, Town water bills were mounting as well. The Town Clerk had noted that the Town carried the Country Club account for about three years due to financial problems and declined to discontinue service on the grounds that it would have possibly meant the closing of the club. The commissioners then relieved the club of the account in the amount of $593.13.

By spring of 1937, the club's Directors had enough of the eternal struggle. At a Board of Commissioners meeting, J. C. Barron (representing the club) approached the Town about taking over operation of the facilities and golf course. Several years earlier, the Town made a proposition to assist the club provided the Town was given some voice in the club's management. That proposal was not accepted, but now the Executive Committee returned with their hats in their hands.

It recommended a lease be drawn between the Club and the Town in which the Town would pay $2,500 for the club and its golf course. The mayor opposed the request, saying Southern Pines shouldn't have to pay the club any definite sum. Instead, the club should simply allow the Town to assume operation and pay

Southern Pines Country Club Clubhouse
(Courtesy: Andy Page)

1939 Aerial of Southern Pines Country Club
The original eighteen greens are grass but the third nine still has sand greens.
Note nine additional holes already cleared in the southeast corner of the site.
(Courtesy: Moore County GIS)

(Left to Right) The First, Eighteenth, and Seventeenth Holes of Southern Pines Country Club After Grassing
(Courtesy: Tufts Archives)

all expenses. On July 21, the Town and Southern Pines Country Club agreed to a one year lease, subject to an annual renewal of the lease for a period of five years. In addition, the Town directed $5,000 to meet the club's operating expenses from July 1, 1937 to April 1, 1938.

In April of 1938, Frank Maples walked the golf course to consider re-building the greens and installing a partial sprinkler system. He pointed out that because of the successful installation of grass greens at Mid Pines and Pine Needles, it was necessary that the same be done at Southern Pines Country Club if the Town expected to draw a large percentage of visiting golfers. He also stated his willingness to take full charge of the job at a fee of 15% of the cost of construction, provided the Town furnish the necessary equipment. His total cost estimate for the project was $10,000. No action was taken by the Town.

The following week, the Town Clerk inspected the grass greens at Pine Needles with a few Commissioners and discussed the cost of replacing the sand greens with Angus Maples (superintendent at Pine Needles and Frank's brother). The new owners of Pine Needles offered Maples' services in building the greens at fifty cents an hour. It was estimated that the capital outlay, including fertilizer, proposed pipe lines, lawn mowers and sprinklers (including tank wagon), would cost $1,500 or less. It was decided to quickly go ahead with the installation of the greens to take advantage of the summer growing season. The town also decided to install permanent irrigation lines to a few tees and greens.

During all these challenges, Southern Pines Country Club somehow managed to open a third nine holes sometime between 1932 and 1939 and also clear land for a fourth nine that was never completed. There is no evidence in the Town of Southern Pines Board of Commissioners meeting minutes (or anywhere else) of who initiated the project or when it was completed.

The new grass greens were an immediate success. On April 28, 1939, Mayor Stutz advised the townspeople that since the installation of the greens, the club had showed a remarkable increase in business over the previous year. Hotel and cottage rentals around town had spiked and the plan was to continue with even more improvements to the golf course. The following week, the Town Clerk advised that due to the tremendous amount of play during March and April, there was danger of losing this business due to a lack of manpower. The Town eagerly permitted the use of its equipment and employees for three weeks to install grass greens on the third nine (referred to as the '*little course*'). The tees on the first eighteen were slated for enlargement as well.

The end of the golden age began with the onset of the great stock market crash of 1929 and slowly deteriorated over the next few decades. The Tufts sacrificed their Knollwood development to ensure survival of Pinehurst Country Club. Many courses weren't as lucky, though, as more than six hundred other golf clubs shuttered their doors forever. New projects like the Tufts's Midland Farms vision (between Pinehurst and Knollwood) would have to wait. But the truth was the family never regained the momentum they enjoyed earlier that century. Team Tufts would never make it to Eagle Springs or Pine Bluff either.

> *"We very, very foolishly were induced to take the management of Mid Pines Club and failed to get the financial backing we were promised so we put up more money. We did the same at Knollwood and Pine Needles and made a financial success of each til it was taken over by the stockholders, except in the case of Pine Needles, where we made a mistake of thinking that we could send our overflow from here* [Pinehurst] *but to our surprise our patrons didn't like it. We were building up a fine clientele of older, quieter people of large means when we were forced to close it by the depression. In these three ventures we very foolishly lost $510,000."*
>
> - Undated letter from Richard to Leonard Tufts and assorted banks

Mid Pines Thirteenth Tee
(Courtesy: Tufts Archives)

THE STRUGGLES FOR SOUTHERN PINES COUNTRY CLUB CONTINUED AS WELL, DESPITE THE FIRST REAL SUCCESS THE CLUB EXPERIENCED (WHICH INCLUDED PLANS FOR A NEW CLUBHOUSE). By June 1940, M. G. Nicholls had passed away, sending the club back into a state of uncertainty and confusion. Ownership of the property was entirely in the former club president's name because of a loan through Citizens Bank and Trust he provided to cover expenses back in 1937. Upon his passing, the club assets were transferred to his wife, Harriet. She immediately began in-depth discussions with the Town about the purchase of the club, despite some members' resistance. On August 18, 1941, the Board authorized the mayor to purchase Southern Pines Country Club from Mrs. Nicholls. The purchase price was $20,000 and included the golf course, clubhouse, and remaining unsold lots. It was pointed out that the building lots could be sold over a period of years to pay off the principal or at least a large part of it.

Mid Pines Eighteenth Fairway
(Courtesy: Tufts Archives)

During the next few years, the Town lost money on an annual basis. In 1944, the Town converted the facility to a true public course, buying out the membership and converting the clubhouse into a town community center. Losses continued that year to the tune of $3,500. Numerous offers to purchase the club were floated to the Town, but they were all turned down until a man from West Hartford, Connecticut named Wilton W. Sherman offered to purchase it in 1946. Based on his experience running a club in Connecticut, Sherman planned to operate the course at a higher standard and keep it open during the summer months, something the Town eliminated a few years before to save expenses.

Sherman was also prepared to enlarge the greens on the back nine of the original 18, start work on the fourth nine, and install a new sprinkler system for the two golf courses at the very earliest date possible. With his investment of approximately $65,000, the Town would have thirty-six holes. A motion was approved to sell the property to Sherman for $31,000 (considerably less than its value). The Town also had first right of refusal in any future purchase and would put some restrictions on the sale or cutting of timber. Sherman brought a young accountant down with him named Julius Boros who just so happened to be a fine amateur golfer.

Southern Pines Country Club's Accountant:
Julius Boros
(Courtesy: Tufts Archives)

After three years, none of Sherman's goals were achieved. He asked the Town Board of Commissioners that he be given permission to abandon the nine hole course and shut operations for the summer months. Word of a golf course for sale quickly spread. John Sullivan, a longtime Elk and former Exalted Ruler, remembered how talk of the local Elks purchasing the club came about:

"At that time, the Elks were in a little building downtown here and John Cline, who was president of the telephone company and also our first exalted ruler, Jack Carter, and another man were going to buy a golf course for investment. So they were down there in the club one night and John said, 'What the heck. All of us play golf, why don't we buy it?' John and Jack pulled their money in with the Elks. At that time, Mid Pines, Pine Needles, and this course were up for sale. They looked at Pine Needles and they didn't want to get into renting rooms and stuff like that. Then, they went over to Mid Pines and, of course, that didn't have much ground, so they came over to Southern Pines. Five hundred acres of ground and 27 holes of golf."

On February 14, 1951, Cline notified the Town that the Elks Home Incorporated of Southern Pines purchased the club from Sherman for $58,500. It was the aim and desire of the Elks Club to again make

Southern Pines Country Club a place of recreation for the people of Southern Pines and adjoining towns. The Town of Southern Pines and Wilton Sherman were officially out of the golf business.

PATUXENT DEVELOPMENT CORPORATION GOT OUT OF THE GOLF BUSINESS. Tired of running Pine Needles, the corporation sold the hotel and golf course on June 4, 1948 to the Most Reverend Vincent S. Waters, Bishop of the Roman Catholic Diocese of Raleigh. Patuxent took an even bigger loss than Homeland Investment's at Mid Pines. Although the property was appraised at $750,000 ($390,000 for the hotel), the Diocese bought the resort for just $406,000. They converted the hotel to a hospital and sanitarium called St. Joseph's of the Pines and ran the golf course for five years.

Peggy and Bullet Bell
(Courtesy: Pine Needles)

They then sold the course to Peggy Kirk and Warren "Bullet" Bell, Pop and Maisie Cosgrove, and Julius Boros for $50,000, keeping the hospital and surrounding land. In 1955, the Bells bought out the Cosgroves for $60,000. Peggy Kirk Bell owns Pine Needles today and remembered how their initial foray into the golf business clashed at times with the Catholic Diocese. *"The eighteenth hole used to be the first hole back then and we had to plant shrubbery along the tee to block out the nuns,"* she recalled. *"They would hang their clothes out to dry and it got to be a distraction."*

Original Pine Needles Clubhouse
(Courtesy: Tufts Archives)

In 1957, the Bells decided to buy 20 acres along Midland Road for a new clubhouse and a series of lodges, which required re-numbering the golf holes. Now that the clubhouse was down the hill from its original location, the original second hole became the first hole and the old first hole became the new finishing hole. At least with this configuration, golfers may not notice the Nun's excesses as much. Among other innovations, the Bells were the first to stay open all year. Mrs. Bell recalled:

Leonard Tufts
(Courtesy: Tufts Archives)

"They [the Tufts] *just closed up Pinehurst, went up to Maine; the Mid Pines' Cosgroves went up to the Boston area. We closed up the first two years and were having trouble getting employees to come back. So I decided to stay open year-round and see what happens. Then about four years later, Pinehurst stayed open year-round and then Mid Pines."*

THE YEARS FOLLOWING THE END OF WORLD WAR II BROUGHT ABOUT ENORMOUS CHANGE FOR THE PINEHURST RESORT. From an operations standpoint, there were fewer golf holes to maintain. From a personnel standpoint, the main players of Team Tufts underwent a dramatic turnover, starting with Leonard Tufts's passing from pneumonia on February 19, 1945.

Donald Ross died of a myocardial infarction on April 26th, 1948. It was very unexpected because he had fallen ill only a few days earlier. Ross had many projects on the drawing board, including ambitious plans to remodel six greens per year on all three courses. According to his 1946 diary, the impetus for reconstruction was primarily because weather and maintenance practices had shrunk the putting surfaces, thereby altering his original design.

A somber funeral took place just yards from his beloved Number Two course in the Pinehurst Chapel, where Ross was a founding member. While most are familiar with Ross the architect, few people today can recall Ross the person as well as Rod Innes, who grew up in Dornoch and worked under Ross as a professional in Pinehurst. Innes recalled that he was not only a great golf course architect, he was also a great manager of people and did very well for himself as a professional.

Donald Ross
(Courtesy: Tufts Archives)

At Pinehurst, Ross managed three teachers who taught on a commission basis and sold balls and clubs. He was also in charge of three club repair professionals. Innes was one of those three and fondly remembered a witty character who was very focused and strict when it came to his businesses, whether it was golf course design or club repair:

"He came in one day and he was looking over the bench and it so happened that there was a wood chisel that had a blade about like this up front. We used it to flick [pry] the tacks off the shaft to release the grip because the grips were tied down with these little tacks. Everybody at the bench used it but it so happened on that day to be in front of my table and he picked it up and looked at it [in very dull condition] and said 'This should never happen, this should never happen'."

Donald Ross's Pro Shop at the Pinehurst Country Club, circa 1919
(Courtesy: Tufts Archives)

"There was a grinding wheel in the back room, one of those that you turn by hand and so he got John Womble, another pro, to turn the wheel and he sat there and ground that thing to get those nicks out of that blade and put a hollow ground edge to it and took it out and put it on the shelf. It was like a razor when he got through with it. He said, 'Now this is the way a tool should be'. He said he didn't ever want to come in and see that again. I took that chisel and I wrapped a piece of cloth around it and stuck it up in the thing [cabinet]

so nobody could get it. I didn't want him to come back in and blame me for that again."

FRANK MAPLES WAS NEVER ABLE TO IMPLEMENT ROSS'S GREENS RENOVATION PLANS BECAUSE HE PASSED AWAY FROM AN EMBOLISM ON NOVEMBER 2ND, 1949. Ross, Maples, and Leonard Tufts had spent over forty years together at Pinehurst, transforming a raw, stark series of fields into the prototype of American golf resorts. The end of the forties brought the end of an unparalleled era of golf history with their passing.

Frank Maples and Donald Ross
(Courtesy: Tufts Archives)

Ellis Maples
(Courtesy: Tufts Archives)

Yet ironically, despite Ross's efforts and the national acclaim Pinehurst Number Two was afforded, the locals had a lesser view of the course at the time of his death. In fact, Number Two was the least popular of the three courses in use, according to the Pinehurst Executive Committee meeting minutes of April 6, 1950. Even when the other courses were too crowded, Number Two was not being used anywhere near its capacity.

THE FIFTIES BROUGHT NEW (YET FAMILIAR) FACES TO PINEHURST WITH PLANS TO CLEAN UP NUMBER TWO'S REPUTATION. Upon Leonard's death, transfer of power went to his son Richard. The transition was a smooth one because Richard had taken over most day - to - day operations in 1925. Upon Frank's death, his son Henson took over maintenance of the courses.

*Not even a dummy could ignore the drama of the original Ross
flashed-sand bunker faces at Pinehurst Number Two circa 1937.*
(Courtesy: Tufts Archives)

Unfortunately, there was no son to step in for Ross. He had only one daughter, Lilian, and she had no desire to continue her father's work. Luckily, another Maples was waiting in the wings. Henson's brother Ellis was a project manager for Ross prior to his death and stepped right in to complete Ross's last project: Raleigh Country Club.

The new faces in Pinehurst continued down the path that Ross and Maples paved many years before. But instead of a golf architect leading the charge, it was superintendent Henson. Although course improvements were made to improve playing conditions, some changes were made to cut down handwork and other time-consuming efforts such as sand bunker maintenance.

Prior to the depression and for a period thereafter, all of the sand bunkers at Pinehurst had been hand raked. In an effort to minimize the time it took to rake the dramatic faces Ross implemented, Henson's crew re-built many bunkers on the courses with grass faces, creating a flatter bottom along the way. In other words, the dramatic flashed-sand Ross bunkers were no longer a feature at Pinehurst. Recalls Pinehurst golf architect Dan Maples:

The New Nine Holes of Pinehurst Number Four (in Red) in 1951 Overlaid on Present Resort (Original Ross Number Four Course Shown in Blue)

"Most of the Pinehurst courses were flashed by Ross. The reason I know that is because my dad [Ellis] *told me that my uncle Henson took them off the faces and put them on the bottoms to save money. So that's how I know that what you see in the bottom is not original. My uncle took them off the banks because you could maintain less sand in the bottom. Less sand is flatter and cheaper."*

Henson Maples was the one responsible for lowering the sand lines on Number Two, *not* Donald Ross.

THE DAWNING OF THE NEW DECADE BROUGHT RENEWED ENTHUSIASM FOR THE GAME OF GOLF IN AMERICA. With World War II over, Americans moved forward and turned their attention to a happier life. Government programs focusing on education and other opportunities provided a new era of prosperity. Leisure activities were once again on the minds of Americans and it translated into a period of golf expansion that rivaled the golden age.

It meant Pinehurst was once again in demand and on April 13, 1950 the Membership of Pinehurst Country Club agreed to restore nine holes of the Number Four course. Team Tufts brought in Robert Trent Jones to assist them.

Jones was the exact opposite of Ross in design philosophy and technique. Starting out as an apprentice of Canadian golf architect Stanley Thompson in 1930, Jones eventually became a partner in charge of the firm's work in the United States while Thompson covered Canada. He never officially left his mentor but simply eased out on his own after the depression. The game of golf and the art of golf architecture was never the same.

On Friday, March 2, 1951, a nine-hole Number Four course re-opened for play with a minimal amount of features. A common practice for new golf courses of this period was to open in an incomplete state, with the expectation that the final form would evolve when sufficient revenue was raised. This strategy was adopted by Richard Tufts to lessen maintenance as well. In typical Team Tufts fashion, the new Number Four course was not promoted as a *"work in progress."* Instead, it was touted as an innovation of great strategy without the most common of hazards: the sand bunker. The ground provided hazards of its own in the form of contours and rolls and the tightening of the fairways.

The new nine holes were located in the same spot as the original Number Four course. In fact, the new first, second, third, fourth, and ninth holes were the first, second, third, fourth and eighteenth holes of the original layout. The newer version deviated from the old with a makeshift par three of just eighty-five yards. This connector hole played from the green site of the original fifteenth to the south in order to also utilize the golf course corridors of the old sixteenth and seventeenth holes. In this location, Trent Jones opted to utilize three par fours in their place: the new sixth was a dogleg-right of 395 yards followed by two 290 yard holes, another dogleg-right and a straight hole. The new Jones nine finished with Ross's original eighteenth hole.

The New Eighth Tee of Course Number Two
(Courtesy: Tufts Archives)

Amazingly, the new holes were brought on line at the same time the resort was preparing to host a second professional event on Number Two. Fifteen years after Denny Shute won the 1936 PGA Championship, Number Two returned to the national stage as the host site of the Ryder Cup. The challenge to prepare for the matches was simple: test the best golfers on both sides of the Atlantic. That meant a facelift for the course in the form of lengthening and narrowing.

In any renovation of this magnitude geared to a specific professional-level event, certain courses seem to require added length. Pinehurst Number Two was no exception for the Ryder Cup. Holes four, eight, and sixteen were all lengthened by 15 to 20 yards, stretching the course from 6,952 yards to 7,007 yards. Some green shapes were also changed to bring additional cup locations into the mix. In addition, fairways were narrowed by adjusting grass lines on holes two, five, seven, twelve, and fourteen.

A new tee location on eight promoted a shot down the left side more so than before and created a downhill second shot that was much more difficult. Ross's approach area just short of the green on the right was stiffened by the addition of more rolling mounds. On both ten and sixteen, Maples challenged the ever-increasing length of the pros with carefully placed bunkers and mounds.

Led by Jimmy Demaret, Ben Hogan, and Sam Snead, the Americans dominated the 1951 Ryder Cup by a score of 9 ½ to 2 ½. With no doubt, Henson Maples' narrowing of Number Two favored the American style over British golf and had a major influence on the outcome.

Ben Hogan During the 1951 Ryder Cup
(Courtesy: Tufts Archives)

NINETEEN FIFTY-THREE MARKED THE REAPPEARANCE OF NUMBER FOUR AS AN 18 HOLE COURSE. But the first nine (revised in 1951) deviated just enough from Ross's layout that it was impossible for Team Tufts to restore the rest of the course. Instead, Richard Tufts built a new par-three tenth hole for Number Four and then incorporated eight holes from the Number Three course (two through nine) for the rest of the second nine.

Tufts's decision to utilize holes from Number Three meant he had to create new holes for that course. Suddenly, the four tidy, compact layouts originally conceived by Ross, each with their own corner of the Pinehurst Resort, were altered to the point that numerous road crossings were imperative to maintain four 18-hole layouts. The new configuration completely altered the landscape in the most dramatic change to the resort since the old employees course was incorporated into Number Two eighteen years earlier.

Tufts's first challenge was replacing the original first hole of Number One, which he used as the new first hole of Number Three. However, instead of building a new opener for Number One, Tufts re-numbered the remaining holes and made the old second hole the new starting hole. Tufts then changed two holes, making the seventh a par-three seventh hole and the eighth hole a short par four. Unlike the other holes, though, eight

180

*Ross's first hole of the Number One Course was changed to the
first hole of Course Number Three by Richard Tufts in 1953.*
(Courtesy: Tufts Archives)

deviates from the high-point-to-high-point routing Ross painstakingly refined over the years. Instead, Tufts sent the hole over a rise just off the tee into a valley, which made the entire hole blind from start to end.

The next task for Tufts was to replace the holes from Ross's original Number Three course that were

Ross's original tenth hole of Number Three was converted to the third hole in 1953.
(Courtesy: Tufts Archives)

Pinehurst Number Four in 1953
[Overlaid on Present Resort]

Pinehurst Number One in 1953
[Overlaid on Present Resort]

Pinehurst Number Three in 1953
[Overlaid on Present Resort]
(Original Ross Number Three Course
Shown in Blue)

incorporated into Number Four. He considered many alternatives to develop the best possible scenario, including building nine or more brand new holes on virgin land southwest of where today's Number Three course stands. Instead, he settled on building new holes to the west of the existing holes.

The first hole of Number One was converted to Number Three's first hole, but all the holes he had to connect with were to the north and his connector hole (original first of Number Three along Highway Five) was going south. Tufts's solution flipped the hole 180 degrees so the new green was at the start of the remaining holes. The newly numbered third through ninth holes remained unaltered from Ross's routing (original #10 - #15).

With the difficult connection situation ironed out, all Tufts had to do next was add more new holes. But instead of simply adding them in one string at a logical point in the routing, Tufts added two separate loops of holes. He started with four new holes in a clockwise loop to the west. At that point, he was in position to utilize Ross's original three-hole finish, but would have been two holes short of a full eighteen. So, utilizing Ross's original par three sixteenth (new fourteen) as a connector, Tufts severely shortened the next hole (new fifteen) in order to build two new parallel holes at the northwest corner of the site (sixteen and seventeen). The finishing hole remained the same.

Henson Maples and Richard Tufts on the Sixth Green of Course Number Three in 1960
(Courtesy: Tufts Archives)

FOR THE REMAINDER OF THE 1950'S, THERE WERE NO MORE PHYSICAL CHANGES IN THE SANDHILLS. On paper, it was a whole different story. Although the new Pinehurst Number Five was built in 1961, design of the addition began much earlier. A 1956 traverse map by Rassie Wicker shows the five Pinehurst courses laid out as they mostly appear today, yet there is no record of the Number Five course being started until at least 1960.

Just like their previous expansions, Team Tufts pulled this one off with the prospect of another major tournament coming quickly. The addition of Pinehurst Number Five, however, severely altered all the other courses at the resort except Number Two, which was fortunate considering the fact that the U. S. Amateur was scheduled there for 1962.

Construction of Ellis Maples's Nine Hole Loop (5-13) of the New Course Number Five in 1961
(Courtesy: Tufts Archives)

The New Twelfth Hole of Course Number Five
(Courtesy: Tufts Archives)

Pinehurst Number Five in 1961
[Overlaid on Present Resort]
(Original Ross Number Three
Course Shown in Blue)

*Pinehurst Number Four in 1961
[Overlaid on Present Resort]
(Original Ross Number Four
Course Shown in Blue)*

Construction of New Eleventh Hole of Course Number Four in 1961
(Courtesy: Tufts Archives)

Unfortunately, Richard fell under the spell that captures so many architect-owners to this day in his rush to grow. The Number Five expansion overlooked the practical applications of golf course routing as demonstrated in the original four courses. Progress came at the expense of the very characteristics that made Pinehurst so successful in the first place.

This revelation was repudiated by Tufts, who was confident in his ability to weave yet another 18 holes through the resort while securing the existing clubhouse as a base for all five courses. No consideration was given to preserving the original layouts or creating a fifth course at a different location. There was also not enough additional land to do the job properly, especially considering it had severe topographic variation. There are many examples of inadequacy that point to a lack of space, a lack of topography, or a lack of experience on Tufts's part, or a combination of the three, led by the worst problem of all: the newest course at Pinehurst was not part of a contiguous layout. Instead it was designed as separate nine hole additions to both the Number Four course and the *"new"* Number Five course.

The first nine-hole loop was designed by Ellis Maples. These holes became five through thirteen of Number Five. Number Five also included the original second through ninth holes of Ross's Number Three course (which were transferred to Number Four by Team Tufts in 1953), with slight alteration. These holes

194

became two through four and fourteen through eighteen. Maples extended the par-three Tufts had built in 1953 (as the new first hole for Number Four) to a par four and made it Number Five's opener.

Although Maples is credited with designing these new holes, diverging opinions abound as to how much of Number Five Ellis actually designed. Peter Tufts says father [Richard] was clearly the architect and simply engaged the Maples family to construct the new holes.

> *"Dad actually designed Number Five and probably Number Four. Ellis had the means to get equipment in there and a crew. He could build it and that is why dad hired him, not for the design. Dad wound up in the hospital and I had to take his place. I supervised the building of Number Five and that is where I picked up a lot of knowledge on architecture."*

Dan Maples, on the other hand, recalls how fond his father was of the work he did on Number Five, *"I know he enjoyed doing Number Five because he grew up there and his whole history was there. I know he enjoyed contributing and having a golf course there."*

The second new nine-hole loop was designed by Richard (assisted by Peter) for Number Four. It was on the same land which Ross's original Number Four back nine holes were laid out. The front nine of the resurrected Number Four (from 1953) was then renumbered as the new first through third and thirteenth through eighteenth holes.

The 1961 expansion was a stark reminder that Ross had his choice for the best land and subsequent expansions were doomed to second fiddle. By then, there were already a good number of blind shots and severe doglegs. One example was the tenth hole of the Number Three course. It's a severe dogleg that takes the driver out of the player's hands because it's nearly impossible to bend a tee shot at a sharp ninety-degree angle. The reason it was created this way was because someone wanted to leave enough room for residential development at a later date. As for the new Number Five holes, the land given to Maples was difficult to incorporate without blind shots due to the severe elevation changes that were prevalent, especially in the stretch of holes from eight to eleven.

When expansion was complete, only Number Two remained fully intact and sixteen Pinehurst Ross holes were lost forever. Nonetheless, the resort boasted new holes contributed by two of the leading architects of the time: Robert Trent Jones and Ellis Maples. At its own detriment, Pinehurst once again set the bar for the rest of the country to clear as the resort became the first in the United States with ninety holes originating from one clubhouse.

However, the door was now open for new players to take advantage of the platform that Team Tufts dominated over the past seventy years. Others with the development bug would indeed seize on that opportunity, bringing great expansion to the Sandhills. Unfortunately, this same expansion began an unsettling trend that would undermine the Sandhills' prosperity for many years.

CHAPTER NINE
SANDHILLS DISCOVERED

"The first day I was there, walking around that lake and seeing those magnificent pine trees and all, it just occurred to me, what a hell of a spot for a golf course and a country club"

- Dick Urquhart (Founding Member, Country Club of North Carolina)

BY 1953, THERE WERE FEWER GOLF COURSES IN THE UNITED STATES THAN THERE WERE IN 1929. But the fifties and sixties brought renewed interest in the game and ushered in the modern age for the business of golf course architecture. Golf design was no longer just an art form. Reflecting the increasing exposure of professional golf, maintenance and conditioning became bigger factors while shotmaking and strategy became smaller considerations. In addition, real estate golf development became one of the strongest investments in the country. Developers sought to create golf communities everywhere, including the Sandhills. And the Sandhills was ripe with opportunity.

What always had distinguished the United States of America – capitalism – brought many entrepreneurs to Moore County by the late fifties and sixties. Not only did golfers love playing the Pinehurst courses, they soon fell in love with *owning* golf courses there as well. The sixties began with a flurry of golf development as real estate investors attempted to emulate the very simple business model the Tufts's family had developed, but with one exception: When James Walker Tufts arrived by train, there wasn't a golf course for hundreds of miles. When the nouveau-riche golf developer arrived by automobile and airplane, there were seven golf courses in operation and plans for more.

For the first time in Sandhills history, competition was not from within Pinehurst but from the outside. Despite warning signs from as far back as the twenties, the Tufts pressed on into the sixties. Richard even went

Richard Tufts
(Courtesy: Tufts Archives)

on record in the September 1962 issue of *Golf World* Magazine that the resort most likely would top out at seven courses.

When the USGA came calling to stage the 1962 U. S. Amateur Championship on Number Two, recent technological advancements in equipment meant that additional fortification would be needed against the top golfers in the United States. Renovations to Number Two were inevitable, just like they had been for the Ryder Cup a decade earlier.

After the 1961 North and South Amateur, Richard added new bunkers on both sides of the landing area on the seventh hole and to the left of the fourteenth. He repeated this strategy throughout the course in an effort to tighten up landing areas. Tufts's update was a marked divergence from the golden age strategy of staggering bunkers on opposite sides of a fairway but was standard procedure in the era of Robert Trent Jones.

Along with the insertion of mounds, hollows, and more rough, the new bunkers effectively narrowed the fairways. Even though the Amateur was the reason for these changes, the intention was to make Number Two a fair test for all golfers. Richard Tufts explained his thinking in his book, *The Scottish Invasion*:

> *"For the 1962 amateur, restrictive features have been added at the 240-270 yard range from the tee and where possible, the player has been presented with the option of a challenging carry or of playing into a gradually narrowing area. These changes are not intended to affect the play of the average golfer who would not normally reach these new features, even from the shorter tees, and his troubles have been mitigated by providing wider fairways for both his tee and second shots. Thus the ideal is approached of providing a more severe test for the expert player and of requiring less from those who are more prone to create their own trouble."*

Other changes to Number Two included lowering the sixth fairway as well as adjusting the green shapes and adding more contour to the putting surfaces of holes one, two, six, and nine. New tees on four, five, and eighteen lengthened the course to 7,058 yards. Also for the first time, imported sand replaced native sand in all of the bunkers.

Spreading New Sand on Pinehurst Number Two In 1962
(Courtesy: Tufts Archives)

By the 1967 Men's North and South Amateur, Number Two's bunkers were all grass faced. This is the seventeenth green.
(Courtesy: Tufts Archives)

Construction on the Ninth Green of Course Number Two in 1962
(Courtesy: Tufts Archives)

The 1962 renovation pushed Number Two further away from the strategic design that Donald Ross and Frank Maples had introduced. Irrigation improvements also allowed for the Bermuda grass to slowly creep into the pine needle rough. From both a strategic and maintenance standpoint, the rough took on more importance than Ross's framing bunkers.

Due to the introduction of motorized rakes, the bunkers continued their transition from the dramatic Ross flashing to a lower profile. Because the rakes couldn't maintain the high sand slopes, the bunkers became more grass-faced and lost much of their character. Irregular, natural shapes were

Peter Tufts (in Black Pants) and Billy Joe Patton in 1962
(Courtesy: Tufts Archives)

replaced with boring kidney shapes and circles. Most bunkers had clover-shaped sand lines adjusted for the limitations of the mechanical rakes. The increase in higher maintenance standards also transformed the bunker lines to clean, defined edges instead of rough-edged hazards.

D.A. Hogan, James Tufts and Rassie Wicker discuss renovations on Course Number Four.
(Courtesy: Tufts Archives)

The remainder of the decade was the quietest period of the Tufts's time in Pinehurst. But that didn't mean there wasn't any activity. Numerous changes took place on Number Four with a modern irrigation system installed and four holes completely rebuilt (fourteen to seventeen). In the process, the fifteenth hole was straightened from a dogleg right by moving the tee to the left.

In addition to the work on Number Four, the long-range plan was to include reconstruction of all the greens on Numbers Two, Three, and Five in phases over the last five years of the decade. From the 1965-1966 season to the 1967-1968 season, the plan for Number Two was to rebuild five to seven greens a year and at the end, convert the greens from Bermuda to bent. Ten greens on Number Five were projected for renovation in 1969, along with miscellaneous changes. For reasons unknown, the renovation work was never carried out.

EVEN THOUGH THE FOCUS WAS ON GOLF FOR SO MANY YEARS, THE TUFTS FAMILY ALSO EXPANDED THEIR REAL ESTATE HOLDINGS IN MOORE COUNTY, GOBBLING UP MORE AND MORE LAND AS THE YEARS WENT ON. Property stretched north to Carthage, south to Aberdeen along Highway Five, and all the way to Southern Pines along Midland Road and Morganton Road. Much of this property was sold off to the very prospectors who created intense competition with the Pinehurst Resort and eventually helped expedite the Tufts's exit from the Sandhills golf scene. Many of these developers were also resort clientele who witnessed first-hand the success and inspiration of the Tufts and Pinehurst.

The market that James, Leonard, and Richard developed was now a golfing hotbed, but with a limited clientele. Would more golf courses enhance Pinehurst, already considered one of the leading golf resorts in North America and perhaps the world? Or would the market flood and create a glut of courses for only a few golfers to choose from? The Tufts were well aware of the pitfalls additional courses would create and were already considering an exit strategy.

Golf development beyond the Pinehurst Resort was based purely on the same opportunity James Walker Tufts saw sixty-five years earlier. Three ingredients were vital to success in the 1960's: a niche; strong leadership; and financial depth. These were the characteristics that Pinehurst possessed for the first fifty years of its existence. Without these ingredients, many Sandhills golf courses found it rough from the onset.

One development that did possess these elements was The Country Club of North Carolina. CCNC was the vision of one man: Dick Urquhart. Urquhart recalled:

> *"The first day I was there, walking around that lake and seeing those magnificent pine trees and all, it just occurred to me, what a hell of a spot for a golf course and a country club. The idea, like anything like that, just sort of grew."*

The initial idea was to attract a group of statewide members due to the central location of the project. Armed with a group of deep-pocketed friends and lots of high-brow contacts, Urquhart produced a group of investors from the biggest clubs in the state. Golfers from Raleigh Country Club and Carolina Country Club to the north, the Cape Fear Club on the coast as well as Charlotte Country Club and Greensboro Country Club to the west were very interested in a second club within a few hours' drive. Urquhart's friends were among the most influential men of North Carolina: Charles Cliff Cameron, dynamo banker; Greensboro politician Skipper Bowles; and even Governor Terry Sanford.

That CCNC blossomed into a getaway for members from across the United States was a bonus. Urquhart remembers:

"We sort of shifted our plans and thought we could attract a lot of national guys because Bill Jennings had gotten in the act pretty good and was very enthusiastic about what we could do nationally. You know, we were just babes in the woods."

Jennings just happened to be President of Madison Square Garden and the New York Rangers as well as the founder of the Westchester Classic, a PGA Tour event in Rye, New York.

Although the idea came quickly, assembling the land took a little old-fashioned southern charm and a lot of real estate ingenuity. Urquhart recalled that the first tract of land was obtained relatively pain-free. *"To begin with, we had a magnificent site, which a group of us were able to option in early 1962. I believe we started off with nine hundred acres including Big Watson Lake."* John Warren Watson, a Philadelphia industrialist who invented the forerunner to the modern shock absorber, bought the 900 acre tract in the twenties and dammed up three streams to create a 60-acre lake. His sole intention was to build a hotel and golf course. After building a home and a boathouse, Watson named his home *"Sunny Sands"*.

Unfortunately, Watson died in 1961 and upon his passing, his estate's executor contacted Urquhart.

John Warren Watson's Cabin
(Courtesy: Tufts Archives)

"We bought the original acreage, which included the lake and his home, for $450,000," recalled Urquhart. The original land did not include the majority of property the club sits on today. In fact, most of that original land now occupies a prominent shopping center and all four corners of the intersection of Morganton Road and U.S. Route 15-501 adjacent to the club.

The original property was acceptable if the founders were only content with an 18-hole getaway. But their vision was bigger than that. Much like James Tufts, Urquhart and his partners knew that success lay in expansion.

Pinehurst owned a vital slice of 100 acres and it was the keystone to a cohesive development with the possibility of a second 18 holes at CCNC. The property came within 400 yards of the proposed clubhouse location and prohibited expansion. More importantly, it created a land planning challenge. Urquhart worked out a land swap for the acreage that included the intersection of Morganton Road and the shopping center property.

> *"If we had not been able to maneuver that, we [would have] had one golf course and it would be a different club entirely. We would not have three-hundred and fifty members from North Carolina and others from twenty-eight states."*

Once all the land was assembled and the forty-two founding members had committed seed money, the first decisions to be made were who would design the first golf course and who would develop the residential land plan.

THE PLANNING OF THE COUNTRY CLUB OF NORTH CAROLINA WAS A STORY OF THREE VERY DIFFERENT GOLF COURSE DESIGNERS WHO COULDN'T HAVE BEEN AT ANY MORE DIFFERENT POINTS IN THEIR CAREERS THAN WHEN THEIR PATHS CROSSED ON THE SHORES OF WATSON LAKE. Jones – arguably the biggest name in the business throughout the sixties and seventies – was not the first choice by the founding members. In fact, he wasn't even the second choice. The initial architect of record for the first 18 was a little known land planner from Atlanta who saw an opportunity to break into the business of golf course design. His name was Willard Byrd.

Byrd had founded a landscape architecture firm in 1956 and had a wealth of land planning experience. He also dabbled in golf course architecture but mostly as a by-product of his land planning (although there is no record of any course design prior to his involvement with the Country Club of North Carolina). Urquhart recalled that Byrd had taken credit for a course near Ponte Vedra, Florida and another around Atlanta. According to Urquhart,

> *"I went and looked at them and I was completely a novice; forty-three years old and didn't know what the hell I was looking at. But it looked good to me. What we really thought about the guy after talking to him and seeing the work he had done was his land planning expertise."*

He was chosen over Robert Trent Jones and another land planner named Eugene Mahtini.

It took seven different plans before the final layout of the course and surrounding home sites was agreed upon. Part of the problem came from a change in direction when the founding fathers decided to build 36 holes. At the time, they moved away from just a regional getaway and toward a national market. So Urquhart and his partners decided they needed an architect with more experience in course architecture than Byrd could provide at that point in his career. They turned to Ellis Maples, who had just completed Pinehurst Number Five and cemented his place in Sandhills lineage as the heir apparent to Donald Ross.

Thus began a long-running power struggle for design credit of the golf course, one that far outlasted the memories of many of those involved. From the start, Byrd was against being told he needed help and didn't want input from anyone, probably even Ross if he had showed up at Byrd's door.

Urquhart related the rocky start Byrd and Maples had:

Ellis Maples
(Courtesy: Dan Maples Design)

"Well, Willard and Ellis got to arguing, mainly about who was going to get the fee. I got them in a room together one time and said I was going to walk out and if they didn't come out in fifteen minutes with some sort of rational agreement, both of them were fired. We had already established that $22,500 was going to be the total architect's fee. So, they finally came out and Willard was going to get $5,000 and Ellis was going to get $17,500. The land planning was paid separately."

Despite their resistance to work together, the first eighteen holes at CCNC evolved very quickly. The two nines were to be called Dogwood and Longleaf, and the only routing change Ellis made was moving the second fairway on Dogwood to avoid a natural low area better served as a pond for drainage. This routing decision was classic Ross – weaving a hole from high point to high point and playing over or around the natural drainage swales.

Of course, Willard wasn't happy with the decision because he had some magnificent lots that the new fairway encroached on. *"He hated like hell to give up that piece of land,"* Urquhart remembered,

Country Club of North Carolina Dogwood Course Hole Thirteen
(Courtesy: Country Club Of North Carolina)

"but Ellis demonstrated pretty ably that he had to have that property to make the hole playable. Otherwise, everything would go to the left so quickly that the hole would not be playable." Maples also lengthened the sixth hole by moving the tee back.

Country Club of North Carolina Dogwood Course Hole Three
(Courtesy: Country Club Of North Carolina)

Aerial View of Whispering Pines in 1962
(Courtesy: Tufts Archives)

Even with the initial admonitions from Urquhart and the relative ease with which the final routing evolved, Maples and Byrd continued to squabble. *"It was like tying two cats together and hanging them over a wire,"* Urquhart said. *"Hell, they got to scratch each other, but I really think that we got the best out of both of them."* To this day, though, Byrd insists that he alone designed what is now the Dogwood course and that Ellis had nothing to do with the final product in spite of the existence of original construction documents by Maples for the first eighteen holes at CCNC. Ellis designed all the golf course features and produced all the grading plans. *"All that kind of stuff was absolutely Ellis's domain and he did it and did a hell of a job with it,"* remarked Urquhart.

Ellis' bunkering was the primary feature of the Dogwood course. Similar to Ross's, Maples created high-flashed sand faces even more dramatic than his mentor. The sheer faces, however, were very hard to maintain. The bunker style garnered attention from the national media and CCNC became an instant hit. The course (plus all the equipment) came in at a cost of $300,000. This was just a fraction of the $1,250,000 spent on the entire development, originally referred to as Royal Dornoch Village.

206

WHILE THE COUNTRY CLUB OF NORTH CAROLINA ESTABLISHED ITSELF AS THE PREMIER GOLF COMMUNITY OF THE SANDHILLS, TWO OTHER VISIONARIES HAD THE SAME GRAND PLAN FOR 36 HOLES SURROUNDING A RESIDENTIAL COMMUNITY. In 1959, Ardis B. Hardee (from nearby Lexington) began plans for his own enclave a few miles north of Southern Pines: Whispering Pines. In 1967, roughly the same distance west of Pinehurst, a man named Rowland McKenzie began developing a site for a golf resort called Foxfire. Neither of these developments had the financial backing or central location of CCNC.

Whispering Pines East Course Number Sixteen in 1962
(Courtesy: Tufts Archives)

Two hundred years ago, the land that Whispering Pines would sit upon was deeded by The King of England to Nicholas Smith. Smith built a grist mill to grind corn rations for revolutionary war soldiers. To power his mill, he dammed part of Nick's Creek and created a lake. A few years later, Smith sold his land to a speculator named John Black. The land changed hands several times over the next eighty years before William C. Thagard purchased the land from Cornelius Dowd.

Thagard named the lake after himself. Thagard rebuilt Smith's dam and expanded it into a sawmill and turpentine business. Thagard's heirs sold the land to two brothers named McDonald who continued to expand on the business and then broke into textiles. That business never took off, though, and after a few other transactions, the land was abandoned until 1944 when John Watson bought the property and cleaned up the lake.

Manice Estate Orchard Barn, circa 1960
(Courtesy: Tufts Archives)

Ardis Hardee was a young schoolteacher when he came to a Rotary Club convention at the Pinehurst Hotel in the spring of 1959. Even though he had no real estate experience (except some summer sales work in Virginia), Hardee decided the Sandhills was the perfect place to begin a new career. After a Carthage real estate agent named Ed Comer showed him Thagard's Lake, the idea for Whispering Pines was born. Hardee recounts: *"It was our dream and it became our cardinal policy to make Whispering Pines 'a way of life'. My aim and purpose was to create the finest private residential development as was humanly possible."* That May, Hardee bought 475 acres surrounding Thagard's Lake for $52,000 and began plans for the Country Club of Whispering Pines. Initially, he planned just a boating and fishing community. However, he soon decided a golf course community would attract a more affluent clientele of retirees and year-round residents – yet at a more affordable price point than what Pinehurst offered.

Eighteen holes were designed by Ellis Maples and ready for play by 1962. In July of the following year, only sixty-eight families lived in Whispering Pines. So to increase play, Hardee opened a sixty-room inn

Whispering Pines' Original Seventh Hole
(Courtesy: Avestra Group)

called the Whispering Pines Quality Court Motel and a restaurant for golfers traveling on Route U. S. One. Nine more holes were built a few years later and were combined with the original first through fourth and fourteenth through eighteenth holes to become the East course, making its debut on October 21, 1965. The remaining nine holes were re-named the West course.

By 1967, Ellis designed and began supervising the construction of an additional nine. On September 1, 1969, the 36 hole Whispering Pines Country Club opened for play. Five of the new holes on the West course were west of old Pee Dee Road (now Rays Bridge Road) and the other four were dredged up out of the swamp where the Little River joined the upper end of Thagard's Lake.

AT MOORE COUNTY'S HIGHEST ELEVATION SITS ROWLAND MCKENZIE'S ANSWER TO THE COUNTRY CLUB OF NORTH CAROLINA IN VERY MUCH THE SAME VEIN AS A. B. HARDEE'S WHISPERING PINES. Foxfire Country Club was not an ode to the native foxes of Moore County, nor to the unique Fox Squirrel. Instead, it was named for an eerie, phosphorescent light that was often seen in the woods, the result of a luminous fungus that causes decaying wood to glow. The light is known as "*Fox Fire.*" The site's sporting history goes back to when Native Americans hunted the area with white sawtooth-edged arrowheads. The Indians regularly competed on horseback, grabbing rings from a tree long before John Patrick or James Tufts arrived.

The area was originally known as "*Piney Bottom.*" But when the Scots arrived, they gave it the name "*Pine Barren.*" They manufactured turpentine and sold peaches from 26,000 trees on 300 acres of today's Foxfire property. Three natural lakes on the property were bisected by the railroad, allowing the Scots easy access to move their peach freight. Foxfire was also the site of a Revolutionary War skirmish in 1780. Tory forces led a surprise attack on a camp of Whigs, massacring several American patriots.

The property went through many hands before McKenzie started his project. The Pennsylvania Development Company acquired 6,000 acres at one dollar each just eight years after James Tufts bought his land from the Pages. A decade later, George Silkworth and A.G. Wilcox bought 1,820 of those acres of timber for $22,000. By 1920, E. A. Manice owned 2,275 acres of "*superb pines*" and 600 acres of peach trees, cotton, corn, wheat, and grapes. Through another series of land transactions, Rowland McKenzie was ready to start his golf course development. But a year later he sold the land to Roger Elton. It was Elton who broke ground on Foxfire Country Club in 1969 and hired Gene Hamm. Hamm had started his career as an assistant under Ellis Maples in Pinehurst. In the mid-fifties, he left the golf professional ranks to oversee construction of the Duke University Golf Course for Robert Trent Jones. In 1959, he started his own course design firm. By 1970, Foxfire's 18-hole course was up and running.

Unfortunately, Whispering Pines Country Club and Foxfire struggled due to a lack of golfers and home buyers. Only the Country Club of North Carolina had enough capital to survive in a marketplace that was slow to develop. As for the Tufts family, they seemed more than ready to tackle this outside competition at the start of the sixties but they entered the seventies with grand plans for the resort simply left on the table.

CHAPTER TEN
A DIAMOND FINDS IT ROUGH

"We've got this vehicle and we're going to bring in California La Costa-type ideas."

- Diamondhead Director of Golf, Lou Miller

THE TUFTS FAMILY STRUGGLED FINANCIALLY FOR THE MAJORITY OF THEIR REIGN IN THE SANDHILLS. There is no question that three generations of Tufts were brilliant businessmen, marketers and good managers. They were fortunate to surround themselves with great support staff. The struggle, however, was not because of an internal issue. It was simply the fact that the golf resort business was not an easy way to make a living for an extended period.

From the moment Leonard and his partners began their Knollwood project in 1915, they struggled to generate operating capital for the resort. To support Knollwood, Leonard sold ownership increments to certain residents in the Village of Pinehurst. In addition, a consortium of banks was brought together by Isham Sledge in order to borrow money to keep the entire operation running. For twenty-five years, Pinehurst, Inc. was saddled with a $100,000 loan payment to the banks.

Along with rising costs came a shift in the resort business toward more than just golf and passive recreation. The Tufts recognized that survival was dependent on more than just serving a few high rollers. Sledge's son Bill began working at the resort upon graduating from Cornell University in 1954. From 1963 to 1966, he was the manager of the Carolina and the Holly Inn, and the food service manager. He remembered that the financial problems were a result of the Tufts's expanded business plan, coupled with a lack of capital.

"1960 was the first summer we operated on a year-round basis. Two courses were open rather than one, which I am sure didn't pay but you had to start somewhere. We felt we were charging the most we could charge with the condition the facilities were in. They didn't have any money to keep the properties in the shape that they should have been kept in."

From 1958-1970, the cost of maintaining the staff alone quadrupled.

It was clear Pinehurst would have to compete effectively for a much larger market to survive. In order to do that, it was essential to substantially enlarge both the scope and variety of the recreational amenities in addition to wholesale capital improvements. Both hotels (the Carolina and the Holly) needed renovations to attract a younger market needed for sustenance. Many of the other facilities were equally out-dated and needed expansion and modernization. In order for the Tufts to continue, the family would have had to pull together everything they had to finance these improvements. To maintain its position as a world-class resort, Pinehurst required a multi-million dollar investment.

The dedication and commitment that James and Leonard shared for Pinehurst was steadfast with third-generation Richard. In Richard's mind, the resort would stay in family hands forever. Unfortunately, the rest of the family wanted an exit strategy. They knew all too well that the recession of the seventies could lead to hard times much like

Richard Tufts
(Courtesy: Tufts Archives)

they suffered in the thirties. Back then, they lost resort facilities at Linville, Roaring Gap, Morehead City, Pine Needles and Mid Pines. By 1970, the youngest of Leonard's three sons, James, was sixty-seven and Richard was in very poor health. The possibility that estate taxes would come at a time when the family was so extended was something they hoped to avoid.

Each of the three Tufts brothers owned roughly twenty percent of Pinehurst stock. Another fifteen to twenty percent was held by Isham Sledge's family, having acquired their stock through Leonard's fourth child Esther. The remainder was held by various minority partners. At the time, Pinehurst was run by an executive committee of nine individuals. They included the Tufts brothers (James, Albert, and Richard), A.P.

Thompson, who had replaced Isham Sledge as Secretary/Treasurer, and John Frank Taylor, the engineer for the company. The other four committee members were Bill Sledge, Peter Tufts, Jim Harrington (who was married to Richard's daughter at the time), and Albert's son Leonard.

Richard attempted to re-organize Pinehurst, Inc. and redistribute company stock equally among the next generation of Tufts (seven great grandchildren of James Walker Tufts), but was rebuffed by Bill Sledge:

> *"Richard proposed that everybody on the executive board who owned voting shares would*
> *contribute those voting shares to a pool. They would be divided on a prorated basis among*
> *the nine members of the executive committee. When you went off the executive committee*
> *for whatever reason, those shares went back into the pool and were redistributed. I couldn't*
> *quite bring myself to do that with my shares because they represented shares not just for*
> *myself, but for my mother and my sister who were not on the payroll."*

Instead of the proposed re-organization, the majority decided to sell the resort.

For a few years, the owners quietly courted suitors to purchase the property. Large corporations and wealthy individuals alike showed interest. Local real estate magnate A. B. Hardee spent three months performing due diligence on the resort and was able to secure the $8.9 million asking price. But the short-term, high-cost financing seemed too much of a risky combination and Hardee stepped away.

Once Hardee passed on the deal, a group called the Diamondhead Corporation approached the family. The Tufts performed their own due diligence and concluded Diamondhead was an appropriate fit for Pinehurst. So, on December 30, 1971, the Tufts family sold Pinehurst Resort to the Diamondhead Corporation of Mountainside, New Jersey, for $9.2 million, and an additional 2,000 acres for another $2 million. At the time, some Sandhills real estate operators valued Pinehurst's holdings between $14-20 million and felt that Diamondhead had practically stolen the 7,500 acres. In reality, Pinehurst holdings were placed in the tax books at just $5 million. James Tufts said after the sale:

> *"If you consider the profit we were making, then we got a fair price. On the other hand,*
> *if you look at the value of the land, they got a whale of a bargain. Land sales were the*
> *last thing we thought of. If we had gone out for* [real estate] *sales it might have been*
> *different."*

The final payoff ($11.2 million for almost ten thousand acres) was an incredible return on James Walker Tuft's original five thousand dollar purchase seventy-five years earlier.

FOUNDED BY WILLIAM MAURER, A REAL ESTATE DEVELOPER FROM CALIFORNIA, DIAMONDHEAD HAD GRAND PLANS FOR GOLF RESORTS AROUND THE COUNTRY. His goal was to create resorts for the upper-middle classes, and had already begun resorts in Bay St. Louis, Mississippi; Fairhope, Alabama; and Ardmore, Oklahoma. But like most developers with innovative ideas and aggressive expansion plans, Maurer lacked the capital to put his vision in motion.

His meal ticket was punched by a simple trucker named Malcolm McLean. As large a contribution to society that James Walker Tufts's soda machine was, Malcolm McLean forever changed the way freight was shipped around the world. McLean was born in 1914 just a few miles down the road from Pinehurst in a little town called Red Springs. As a twenty year old, Malcolm started the McLean Trucking Company in Winston-Salem, North Carolina and within a few short years, the company was the fifth largest trucking company in the United States.

Spending long days watching the tedious process of loading and unloading a ship's contents led McLean to his breakthrough idea of "*containerization*." The simple concept was a system where a tractor trailer could be lifted off a truck chassis and loaded directly into a ship's cargo hold. The idea worked and led to the founding of the Sea Land Corporation. McLean's containerization system cut the loading and unloading of ships to a fourth of the time it had been previously. In 1969, he sold his company to R. J. Reynolds for $160 million. He then set his sights on a piece of history: Pinehurst.

The resort had sizable infrastructure needs and the financial pressure facing Diamondhead the day they closed the deal was far greater than anything the Tufts would have faced had they continued ownership. The corporation planned to continue operation of the hotels, golf courses and other facilities just like the Tufts family "*as long as financially possible*," according to Maurer.

Pinehurst's reputation for relaxation and leisure for a small segment of society created a major challenge for Diamondhead if it was ever going to gain a return on its sizable investment. Members of the upper class had often come to Pinehurst as guests of the family. Any allusion to spending money on vacation was considered uncivilized at the resort. Unfortunately, it also made for poor financial success. Mutt Frye, one of the town's full-time firemen, said he knew why change had come, "*Some of these folks that used to come here, they'd check in and sit down. They had boocoos of money but they weren't turning any of it over.*" Anything consciously done to turn over a guest's money would have been rejected as out of keeping with good manners and grace in the Tufts era.

One of Malcolm McLean's favorite sayings was, "*I don't have much nostalgia for anything that loses money.*" So it was only a matter of time before Tufts's nostalgia was swept under the rug in favor of a glamorous resort and residential development. The powers at Diamondhead brought a different attitude to Pinehurst, an attitude that flew directly in the face of the down-home atmosphere the Tufts family presented, both in service and in appearance.

The corporation's new focus was to capture more families and convention business, so the Pinehurst market shifted from the elderly rich to younger, more middle-class guests. "*There are a lot of people in this country who have worked hard to earn their money, and they deserve a place to spend it*," declared Maurer. The ideal Diamondhead guest (and future homeowner) wore a hard hat, carried a hammer in his belt and had a lunch box full of money.

Pinehurst Country Club Members Clubhouse
(Courtesy: Tufts Archives)

In order to attract this customer, rustling pines and quiet solitude wouldn't work. Instead, a complete update was in order. First and foremost, the Carolina Hotel was modernized to the tune of $2.5 million. Gone was the wood detailing and cozy feel, replaced by glitz more characteristic of South Florida or Beverly Hills. The village was to be updated with gas lights, curving brick walks, fine restaurants and specialty shops. A modern shopping center was proposed near the Moore Memorial Hospital.

The most visible amenities were a separate members' clubhouse adjacent to the main clubhouse and the construction of the World Golf Hall of Fame behind the fourth green of the Number Two course. In addition, the entrance to the club grounds was relocated from near the first tee of Number Two to Marshall Park (where it sits today). The goal was to create a strong axis that tied together both the hotel and the club. The tennis courts were also moved to Marshall Park, two new traps were added to the skeet fields, the old riding stables were renovated and a major horse show ring was built. Plans also called for a skating rink and bowling alley in Marshall Park, as well as a 200 acre lake (today known as Pinehurst Lake) and two or three more courses.

The transformation of Marshall Park from a sleepy corner of Longleaf Pines and a few benches into a focal point of the resort was the first of many Diamondhead moves that alienated both the locals and the remaining members of the Tufts family. Peter Tufts was in charge of golf operations when Diamondhead began negotiations with his father. He knew that the direction they were going in was not the same one laid out by his family. Peter recalled:

> *"The entrance to the club was drastically changed. The fact is the entrance goes into the club on land that was donated to the people of Pinehurst forever more as a park and they wrecked that."*

The modernization of Pinehurst was only part of what angered the old guard. What created the most dissension between the residents and the new owners was the focus on residential development for resort guests and permanent homeowners. Fifty split-level cottages were built to augment the hotel's capacity. In addition, thirteen thousand building lots were surveyed and ready for sale almost immediately. More than thirty miles of new roads and streets were constructed along with sewer, water and electrical utilities. Locals were aghast at the frequency with which Diamondhead constructed condominiums. They popped up everywhere, but stood out the most along the fairways of the Number Three and Five courses. However, the locals ignored the fact that the condos were actually built at a much lower density than North Carolina permitted at the time.

The Diamondhead sales force was a hard-selling group of twenty people housed in the basement of the hotel. The team was charged with pushing home sites ranging from six to twenty thousand dollars, each accompanied by a club membership. Sales techniques were different than the *"Tufts's way"* and included such promotions as television giveaways. In addition, printed material promoted amenities that were not as certain to be available as the brochures advertised. Residents envisioned clogged streets, crowded restaurants and – worst of all – difficulty getting a tee time. The last straw was the proposal for condominiums and a 250-room hotel to be built on the Number Two course.

Diamondhead's actions led to the formation of a group called the *"Concerned Citizens of Pinehurst."* *"Concerned Citizens"* was motivated by its perceived commercialization of Pinehurst by the Diamondhead Corporation. The group consisted of about two hundred members, but there were at least that many residents who wanted nothing to do with them. Soon a second group was formed called *"Citizens Concerned about Concerned Citizens."* This new group understood that when a company invests millions of dollars, it doesn't expect a small return each year. Both survival and change often come with a price.

Nonetheless, Diamondhead was well aware of what the bad publicity and misinformation could lead to, so it worked to improve relations with the residents. Even Maurer admitted that *"some condominiums were a legitimate mistake, and it won't happen again."* Diamondhead also knew that a happy community would help the resort and it wanted to do what was best. As part of an agreement between Concerned Citizens and Diamondhead, the decision was made *"not to construct any condominiums or multi-family dwellings adjoining, abutting, or within any portion of golf course Number Two, as same is now situated or hereafter redesigned."* The company also agreed not to build any more condominiums adjoining the golf courses within the village boundary at more than eleven units per acre. In addition, a twenty-five-foot buffer between the courses and the condos was established and no further buildings (except for recreational purposes) were to be built in Marshall Park.

Local opposition was not Diamondhead's only problem, however. Another revolt came from many of the long-time employees of the Tufts family. The laissez-faire attitude the Tufts enjoyed with their guests also held true with their employees. Although loyalty was high and the deep love and respect for the Tufts family was a major element to the comfortable success Pinehurst once enjoyed, these attitudes were costly. Diamondhead made a big investment in Pinehurst and tried to maintain existing policies as long as possible. But there was no way a profit (or just a break-even point) could be established and adjustments had to be made. Simply put: Accountability and consistency were policies of the new culture.

Sadly, Henson Maples and one hundred other employees, many of whom had worked for the Tufts their whole lives, left the resort because of new maintenance and operations policies. Diamondhead officials simply could not afford employees who were so married to the old ways. They made sizable settlements with those they dismissed, and most former employees found new jobs.

Henson Maples Discusses the Day With His Maintenance Staff
(Courtesy: Tufts Archives)

Although Diamondhead planned to make their fortune in real estate, they also wanted to provide the best possible playing conditions for a clientele looking for the ultimate vacation resort. So they carried their aggressive building renovation program to the five Pinehurst golf courses, hoping to attract the same golfer who traveled to newer resorts such as Doral and PGA National in Florida. Lou Miller, Director of Golf from 1975 to 1980, explained the Diamondhead concept: *"We've got this vehicle and we're going to bring in California La Costa-type ideas."* Future professional events were planned as well, including a marathon 144-hole event called the World Open.

In essence, Diamondhead planned to erase all the elements that made Pinehurst special and bring in standardized playing conditions found everywhere else - all in the name of progress and creating player-friendly conditions. Initial renovations to the Pinehurst courses were to include an upgrade of grasses for the greens and the addition of Bermuda grass rough from tree line to tree line, replacing the native wire grass that framed the holes and the natural pine straw rough that gave Pinehurst much of its character and identity.

Number Two was the first course to undergo the *"Diamondhead modernization."* A series of renovations from 1970 to 1973 increased the length of the golf course to 7,274 yards in preparation for the inaugural World Open in 1973. In late 1972 and into 1973, the home-grown Bermuda was removed from the putting greens and replaced with the newest of turfgrass varieties, Penncross bentgrass.

Penncross bentgrass differed from Bermuda because it was a cool-season grass that stayed green year-round and required much more water and precise mowing to keep it alive in the heat of summer.

Jack Nicklaus Wins the 1975 World Open
(Courtesy: Tufts Archives)

Diamondhead made no changes below the grass and the additional irrigation needed for the Penncross stressed the subsurface drainage. The consequences were soft and wet playing surfaces.

An even bigger change to Number Two was the removal of the remaining native wire-grass rough and the installation of conventional Bermuda rough to keep balls in play and out of the pines. In some places, particularly between the thirteen and the fourteenth holes, love grass was established. Fairways were widened

Ninth Hole of Pinehurst Number Two in the Early 1970's
(Courtesy: Tufts Archives)

and bunkers were removed. Much of the contouring created by Team Tufts was either softened or entirely removed. The worst example of this conversion was the third hole. The left side mounds and rolls were flattened and the wire-grass rough running down the entire right side was replaced with a couple of pot bunkers.

Pinehurst Number Two was a totally different golf course now and the ground game was completely eliminated. What remained was a boring layout whose only defense to the modern aerial game was length and high rough.

    The locals were devastated, especially the remaining descendants of James Tufts. Peter did his best to convince Diamondhead executives to preserve the Pinehurst look, but to no avail. *"They just totally ruined it. Just totally ruined it,"* said Peter. *"Broke my heart, but I couldn't stop what they were doing anywhere. They had made up their mind."*

Re-construction of the Ninth Hole of Pinehurst Number Two
(Courtesy: Tufts Archives)

There was no doubt as to where he stood when the dust cleared. He resigned as Vice President of Golf Operations within months.

He also noted how much of Ross's work was eliminated. The intricate contouring of the fairways was rubbed out, many of Ross's hollows and mounds were eradicated, and what remained of the original bunker faces were erased by a bulldozer. In their place was a dull roll of grass slumbering into a flat and lifeless carpet of sand. Remembered Tufts:

> *"Diamondhead went in there with a bulldozer and just flattened out Ross's beautiful architecture around the greens, particularly those where it really showed what he could do. Some of the bunkers had a lip that hung over and you had to get your ball up fast to get it on the green. Otherwise it would hit the lip and roll right back down in the bunker. The faces just disappeared."*

Early 1970's Pinehurst Scene
(Courtesy: Tufts Archives)

According to Tufts, Diamondhead completely rebuilt the greens twice. He recalled:

> *"P. J. Boatwright was a real good friend of mine and Executive Director of the Carolina Golf Association at the time. When he moved to New York he came back four or five months after they had finished the greens. We had gone about eight holes and I said, 'Do these greens seem the same to you'? He said, 'No, they are not the same'. P. J. knew the course as well as I did. For all practical purposes they just totally changed Number Two."*

Mistakenly, Diamondhead's executives felt their changes would attract more guests and make the course easier. What they didn't understand was that their changes made Number Two more like most of the courses in the world. They inadvertently erased the character and tradition that made the course so special in the first place.

Eventually, the new owners realized that they had made a mistake and turned to Tufts to develop a master plan to restore what had been lost. Tufts's plan consisted mostly of re-building sand bunker faces and other bunker repairs. However, the restoration program also included the removal of all love grass and the re-establishment of the wire grass rough around the course. In addition, fairway lines were returned to their original positions. Diamondhead made such an effort to right the wrong they made that the use of carts was temporarily discontinued to help restore the layout to top condition.

Tufts's 1974 master plan was never fully implemented, though. Instead, Diamondhead's executives decided they would walk the middle line between restoration and progress. While touting a restoration of Number Two, they decided to bring in outside design expertise to emulate the popular resorts of the seventies. The plan was to bring in George and Tom Fazio as consultants to work with Peter Tufts on restoration efforts. *"We made the decision in order to restore and preserve the quality and character of the course for which it had become internationally famous,"* quoted William C. Brent, President, in the March 3rd, 1976 *Pilot*. What transpired, however, was a Fazio renovation with very little input from Peter Tufts. In fact, it is very unclear as to who did what during the renovation. The renovation work spanned three seasons.

To be fair, efforts were made to restore some of Ross's intentions, if not actual Ross features. For example, day-to-day maintenance was proposed to shave down grass on mounds near the greens - to a half-inch in height in order to restore pitch shots around the putting surfaces. The sixteenth tee was also extended 50 yards to prevent golfers from flying the bunkers on the left and force them to play down the right side. This was done under the auspices of *"as Ross intended"*. Yet Ross pointed out in his narrative for the 1936 PGA Championship,

> *"I have said that the tee shot must be long and accurate. A tee shot may be penalized either by narrowing the area into which the longer player is hitting or by giving him an advantage for the second shot, according to the placement of the tee shot."*

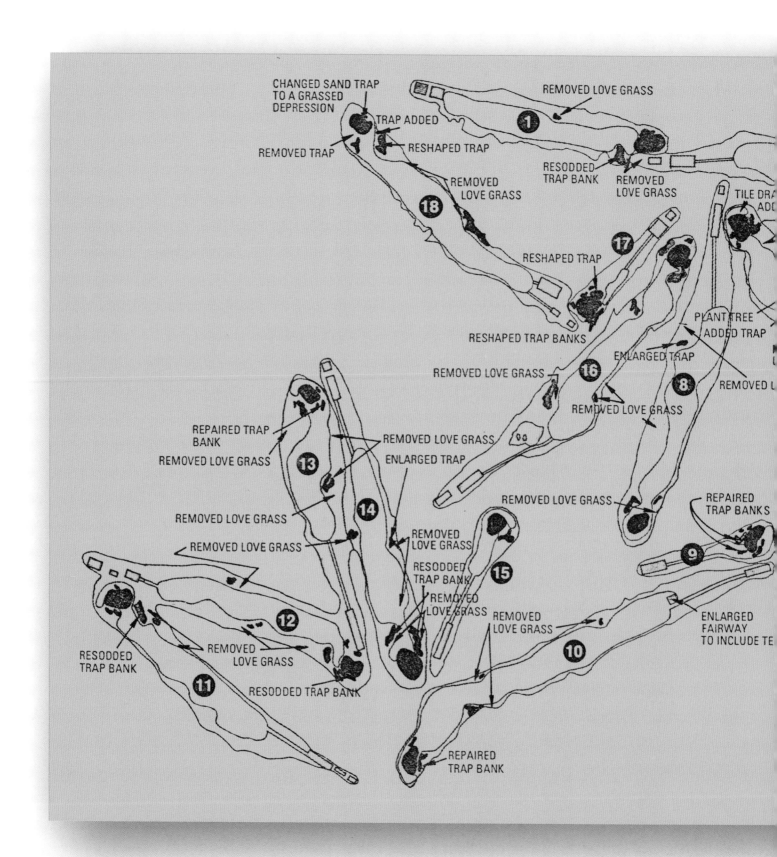

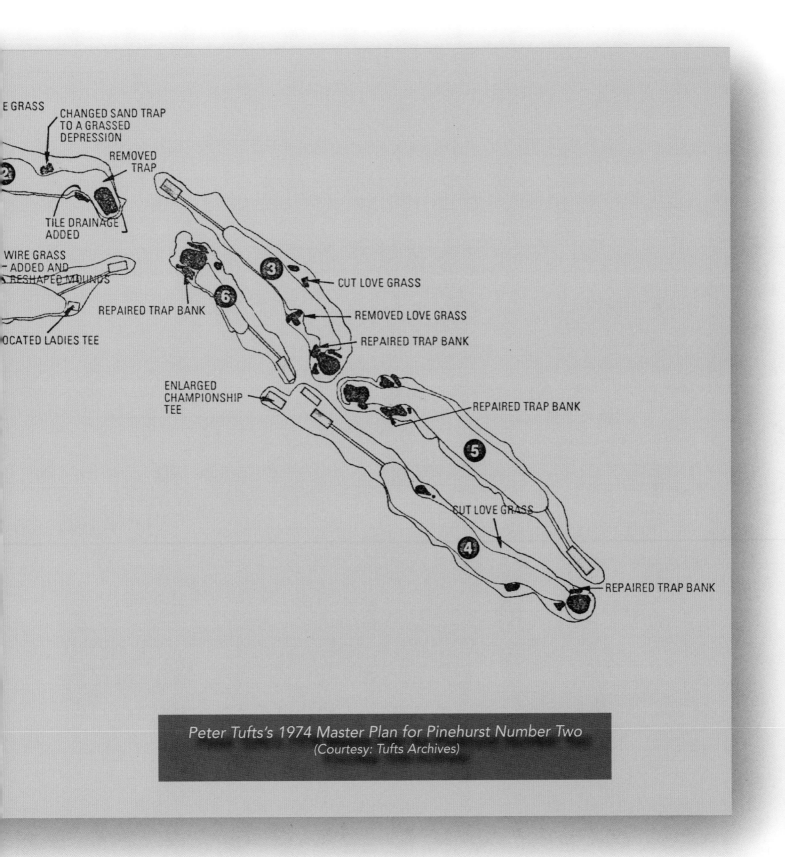

GRASS

CHANGED SAND TRAP
TO A GRASSED
DEPRESSION

REMOVED
TRAP

TILE DRAINAGE
ADDED

WIRE GRASS
ADDED AND
RESHAPED MOUNDS

OCATED LADIES TEE

REPAIRED TRAP BANK

ENLARGED
CHAMPIONSHIP
TEE

CUT LOVE GRASS

REMOVED LOVE GRASS

REPAIRED TRAP BANK

REPAIRED TRAP BANK

CUT LOVE GRASS

REPAIRED TRAP BANK

Peter Tufts's 1974 Master Plan for Pinehurst Number Two
(Courtesy: Tufts Archives)

Ross, a staunch developer of strategic choice, never forced one particular route off the tee. In fact, he placed the original bunker to the left of the fairway on sixteen to promote that route off the tee to gain a more favorable angle and distance into the green.

Other work included restoring the mounds to the corner of the dogleg at number seven. In addition, two trees were added along the right side to force a tee shot twenty-five yards longer to reach the corner of the dogleg. Unfortunately, not all of the attempts to bring back Ross's strategy succeeded. Nor were these changes exactly what Tufts proposed in his master plan. In fact, his reaction to the work is far from friendly:

> *"Fazio did some work out there that I thought was ridiculous after I did my work. He extended the bunkers in the fairway way past the dogleg, which to me ruined the hole. It doesn't bother the good player at all. The guy that it really hurts is the poor player. It used to be a favorite of boys playing in the North and South because they would try to cut the corner and end up with pitching wedge to the green. If they didn't make it they were in trouble."*

The next few years saw implementation of more of Tufts's master plan items to improve strategy, maintenance and drainage. In addition to the continued removal of love grass, wiregrass was planted in the rough and many bunker faces were re-sodded. Other bunkers were removed, enlarged, or added. A series of bunkers installed by Ross down the right side of the second fairway in 1918 were changed to grass depressions.

At the suggestion of Billy Joe Patton, Peter reduced the height of the ridge on the sixth hole about two-thirds of the way down so a player could see the bunkers to the left of the green. Tufts's suggestion to enlarge ten fairway and build new front tees was

Sodding the Eleventh Green of Number Five
(Courtesy: Tufts Archives)

implemented, and bunkers were rebuilt on holes three, seven, and seventeen. Wire grass rough was re-established on four and five and new tees were added on four, sixteen, seventeen, and eighteen. By the end of the decade, Diamondhead wrapped up renovation work with another re-surfacing of the putting greens. This time, they removed the Penncross bentgrass and established Bermuda K-28, again without changing the subsurface.

Diamondhead had already performed its magic on Pinehurst's Number Four and Five courses in preparation for the World Open. Originally Number Five was going to be used (along with Number Two) for the tournament, but because the encroaching condominiums made it difficult for spectators, Robert Trent Jones suggested to Maurer that they use Number Four instead. Although Number Five was out as a tournament venue in 1972. Jones lengthened it, re-built all the tees, and directed a greens conversion from Bermuda 328 to Penncross bentgrass.

That same year, Jones began renovations on Number Four to specifically challenge the tour players. He first combined the sixteenth and seventeenth holes into a longer seventeenth hole and built a longer par-three eleventh to replace the hole incorporated into seventeen. A year later, Jones again lengthened the course by more than seven-hundred yards to 6,905 yards. He expanded both the eighth and twelfth holes into par

fives and rotated the par-three thirteenth hole ninety degrees with a new pond added between its tee and green.

He also added numerous bunkers to the front of many greens, but wasn't allowed to compensate for the carry of a longer, low-trajectory shot with larger putting greens. The professionals had a field day chastising Jones for creating impossible shots into small targets with no way to stop the ball but Jones was simply following Diamondhead's orders.

By this time, just about anything Diamondhead did incurred harsh criticism, especially from the Tufts family. Richard was the first to dole out his aversion to the new attitude and look at Pinehurst. He wrote the following in a letter on May 31, 1978:

Robert Trent Jones's new thirteenth hole of Course Number Four was rotated ninety degrees and toughened up with a carry over water in 1973.
(Courtesy: Tufts Archives)

"Donald Ross was responsible for the architectural design of, at most, seven of the present holes (of Number Four), and about all that is left of his work is their location. Also, of course, he did not build the grass greens on this course. I built the eleven new holes. I built this to be an easy, pleasant course, but judging by what people say and the very vague plan on the

scorecard, I wish the credit could read, 'wrecked by RTJ, golf course architect'. Certainly Mr. Ross (nor I) would not want to be held responsible for anything about the present course."

His son was equally angered by Diamondhead's changes. When asked why Jones was hired, Peter responded: *"The only answer I can give you was that he was a well known architect. They wouldn't fool with an unknown architect in Pinehurst, I think, regardless of the course. They want somebody with a name. It was part of the new theory of Pinehurst."*

By the end of the decade Diamondhead was still in charge of Pinehurst, and despite the constant criticism and anger directed toward them by the locals they moved forward with expansion plans of their own. In March of 1979, the corporation announced plans to break ground on Pinehurst Number Six. Whereas the Tufts often expanded and remodeled for the sake of creating something new and maintain a place in the spotlight of American golf, Number Six was a very different project for two primary reasons: One was that the second home market was taking hold and there was a genuine need (in their eyes) for more golf course inventory. The second difference from the Tufts's expansion efforts was that Pinehurst Number Six was the first course built away from the main clubhouse. It was planned as the centerpiece of a wholly separate residential development three miles away.

Eighteenth Hole of Course Number Six Under Construction in 1979
(Courtesy: Tufts Archives)

Peter Tufts's words regarding a well-known architect proved prophetic when Diamondhead chose the team to design Pinehurst Number Six. George Fazio was twenty years into a design business that he'd started toward the end of his professional career. He'd played on the PGA Tour in the thirties and forties, winning the 1946 Canadian Open and almost beating out Ben Hogan four years later for the U. S. Open title at Merion Golf Club. As a professional at several Philadelphia area clubs, George had first-hand exposure to some of the best examples of golf course architecture, including Pine Valley, where he served as touring professional in 1942 and again from 1952 to 1954.

Noted his nephew Tom:

George and Tom Fazio
(Courtesy: Ron Whitten)

"His design philosophy came from being a very good player and was considered the first player of prominence to be in the golf design business. There weren't many architects who had a playing record. That doesn't necessarily mean that he felt that golf courses should be designed for him in terms of a being a great player, but his philosophy, what I still aspire to today, is very playable golf, not difficult."

George stood out from contemporaries such as Jones or Dick Wilson with a tendency toward a more golden age aesthetic, but with large-scale green complexes and sand bunkers. Not as prolific with heavy earthmoving equipment, Fazio followed the lay of the land a bit more closely in his routings. Tom recalled how his playing style influenced his hole layouts,

"He was a left-to-right player as most good players back then. He was always conscious of how the ball was moving, so that had a lot to do with his philosophy."

Fazio garnered a successful reputation for designing affordable layouts that always stayed within budget but he also became a favorite of clubs looking to create a national reputation by hosting major tournaments, which explained Diamondhead's interest. Tom was George's partner for five years by the time they were hired for Number Six, *"My role was as project director and I was responsible for the design implementation of all the courses."*

Tom was honored to represent Pinehurst at a time when the golf course design business was a struggle for all, *"That was a major project for us at the time. I always refer to it as probably the premier golf course coming out of the downturn of the early seventies and maybe the most premier golf course in the country – certainly in terms of recognition."* When asked about the property for the course, Tom said, *"If you could pick any type of land on which to build a golf course, this spot in Pinehurst would be the ideal type of setting you would select. It is one of the top three sites we've ever built a course on* [and] *we will try to retain as much of the natural terrain of the land as is possible."*

Handed a completed land plan upon arrival, the Fazios stayed true to their reputation despite being tied to the routing. They delivered a golf course that stood out from the other Pinehurst layouts for well under $1 million. *"Number Six was the toughest construction challenge* [for us] *because fitting it into existing conditions and coming out of the recession, budget was a consideration,"* noted Tom. They made at least ten site visits during the shaping of the holes to oversee construction of the course.

The Fazio team developed *"a Pinehurst look"* to tie the new layout to the tradition that had already been set. Upon completion, Tom was asked why the look was indigenous to Pinehurst. His response was simple, *"You cannot build the Pinehurst look on many soils. You need a sandy base that drains quickly and easily. Try to incorporate the Pinehurst look elsewhere and you will likely develop bad drainage problems."*

The Fazios not only relied on the sandy soils to create the Pinehurst look, they also incorporated many of the famous swales and dips that Ross had made such a

Par-Three Thirteenth Hole of Course Number Six
(Courtesy: ® Pinehurst, Inc. All Rights Reserved.)

228

staple in his work at Pinehurst. *"We tried to copy, in places, the rolls and contours of the green areas of Number Two,"* Tom said. "[Its] *such a great course because of the second shots it offers, the bounces and angles of approach."* When delving further into Fazio's Pinehurst look, the real distinction comes simply in its playability, a key element of the other courses. *"We cleared some of the holes wider across the fairway than we would normally in order to make it look more like Number Two,"* Fazio said. They planned to make Number Six a fun, family-type course with small, undulating greens that were typical of the other Pinehurst courses.

Although one goal was playability, a second one was to create a challenge for those looking for top-caliber golf, another characteristic of Number Two. Tom explained:

> *"The better the player, the more trouble he can find. We prefer to design for strategy rather than to penalize the poor player for a lack of talent. We decided on the placement of the fairway bunkers by measuring 280 yards from the back of the tee area to the back of the fairway bunker. Fairway bunkers ought to be used to require strategy for a player and to define a hole."*

Tom once remarked (tongue-in-cheek, no doubt), *"We strive for our courses to be of such caliber that when the architect of any quality course is not known, it might possibly be assumed that since it is such an outstanding course, it must have been designed by a Fazio."* The challenge of blending a functional land plan and a great golf course required considerable compromise not only with the home sites but also from hole to hole. According to Fazio:

> *"We wanted to make the final holes ones to be remembered. But we also had to take the overall course into consideration. In our design of Number Six, we did not sacrifice any other holes to develop our spectacular holes on the back nine. Nature sometimes needs enhancing and some holes needed a great deal of man-made help."*

Although the course opened for play on March 1, 1979, it sat largely unused for the better part of twelve months. Permit issues regarding the final location of the entrance road and a temporary clubhouse meant there was no access to the course for anything except a bulldozer or pick up. Once those issues were finally resolved, Pinehurst Number Six became a roaring success.

The last projects undertaken by Diamondhead were the rebuilding of the greens on the Number One course in 1981 and a complete renovation of Pinehurst Number Four in 1982. The superintendent at the time, Arnold Burns, discovered the original Number One greens eighteen inches below the existing putting surface while excavating the compacted greens-mix layer. Reconstruction was necessary because lower mowing heights and heavy traffic severely compacted the surfaces. The greens were not restored, though. Instead, Burns and his crew enlarged the putting surfaces to an average of 6,700 square feet.

Hole Twelve of Course Number One, circa Early 1970's
(Courtesy: Tufts Archives)

Pinehurst Number Four was closed on July 4, 1982, and the greens were converted from Bermuda to Penncross bentgrass. Rees Jones was brought in to make a number of modifications including the elimination of half of the 70 sand bunkers. Some of the remaining bunkers were relocated to allow run-up shots, eliminating the forced carries introduced by his father less than a decade before. *"My father came in to toughen up the course for the World Open, but they wouldn't allow him to increase the size of many greens,"* reflected Rees Jones in a 1982 *Pinehurst Magazine* article. *"You had people hitting long irons into greens built to receive short irons."* To improve the situation, many greens were enlarged and re-contoured.

When Diamondhead arrived, they strayed far from what they found in terms of golf. But through trial and error, a return to playability and fair challenge was evident as they strove to repair what they originally covered up. This precedent was set long before Malcolm McLean purchased the resort. Even Ross underwent a monumental learning curve from novice to one of the all-time greats. Diamondhead learned from their mistakes as well.

What ended Diamondhead's Pinehurst reign was not the ability to run the resort properly. In fact, the resort was revitalized under Diamondhead. The resort never went bankrupt and neither did the company.

The fatal flaw, though, was Diamondhead's decision to draw all of the profits out of Pinehurst and redirect them to sinking residential developments in Fairhope, Alabama, and Lake Arrowhead, Georgia, among other places. As a desperate SOS, Diamondhead offered Pinehurst to the banks in order to buy time to make their other facilities profitable.

By 1979, Pinehurst was worth an estimated $146 million, including the $30 million in improvements Malcolm McLean poured into the facilities. But Diamondhead faced $5.3 million in interest payments and $113.7 million of bank debt on its other projects. So in order to save his company, McLean restructured the organization to refinance it.

The restructuring included a promise to sell all stock in Pinehurst, Inc. to a group of banks by December 1, 1981 if the debt was not paid off. The cache promised to the banks included 6,000 acres of unsold lots, 100 developed lots, the Carolina Hotel, six golf courses, 24 tennis courts, a gun club, riding club, a 200 acre lake, water and sewer systems, an electricity distribution system and police and fire departments. In March 1982, the Purcell Corporation, Inc. (formerly Diamondhead) turned the resort over to the bank consortium for $31 million in cash plus assumption of all the property's debts ($73 million). The Diamondhead era in the Sandhills was over.

To this day, a majority of residents ruminate about how Diamondhead destroyed the quiet village of Pinehurst. Some of these people have lived in Pinehurst all their lives, others have been residents for less than a decade – long after Diamondhead left town. But the cold, hard, facts are as follows: The original business plan for Pinehurst, as developed by James Walker Tufts, ran out of steam by 1970. Pinehurst was a labor of love for the Tufts family and they treated their guests the same way. Ironically, it resulted in poor management of a business that required cash flow and capital for survival in a changing society.

Pinehurst was worn down and had no funds to compete with the likes of La Costa or Doral. Its future was not bright and seemed certain to end up in the same condition as once-proud grand golf resorts like Bedford Springs in Pennsylvania, French Lick Resort in Indiana, and several others in the Catskills region of New York State were in the seventies. Diamondhead did, however, save the three remaining Tufts children and their partner Bill Sledge from letting Pinehurst slip through their fingers without anything to show for it. By selling to Diamondhead, their families gained financial security. But more importantly, the Pinehurst Resort was saved with an influx of cash.

Was Diamondhead as ruinous as the locals proclaimed back then? Diamondhead did indeed make many mistakes, the most glaring being the failed renovation of Pinehurst Number Two and the overt use of Marshall Park. But Diamondhead tried to make amends as soon as they saw the error of their ways. Pinehurst was the property of Diamondhead and the corporation did with it what they rightfully could, just as the Tufts did for many years. The only way it survived was by adapting to the changing times, something all Tufts generations fully understood and did repeatedly in the seventy-five years under their guidance.

Diamondhead infused the resort with capital, established management practices typical of all successful businesses, and saw the same opportunity in real estate that the Tufts family could not take advantage of without working funds (a little known fact is that the Tufts were actually the first to build condos adjacent to the hotel in the late sixties). Diamondhead's choice to develop its land for residential development was their prerogative and if the Tufts were able, they, too, would have developed Pinehurst in much the same way. In fact, without that decision, many of Diamondhead's critics would not be calling the Village of Pinehurst home today.

The last fact of this matter is that Diamondhead bought Pinehurst for $9 million dollars, put over $30 million into the resort, and created an asset worth close to $146 million. In the business world, that is an unequivocal success. The anger and bitterness directed at McLean and his group (and fomented over these past thirty-five years) was not fair, especially considering the fact that had they not stepped in to buy Pinehurst from the Tufts the resort may not have survived.

Ironically, the demise of Diamondhead came from failed real estate projects elsewhere, without the history and reputation of Pinehurst. But the next savior would not make the same mistake. History would be the foundation for an icon that not even the Tufts could have envisioned.

CHAPTER TEN

CHAPTER ELEVEN
PLOWING AHEAD

"We found a niche in building a community where people could enjoy the game walking on a more comfortable golf course."

- Bob Klug, Knollwood Fairways

BY THE SEVENTIES, THE REAL ESTATE AND GOLF DEVELOPMENT BULL MARKET HAD SLOWED DOWN. Rising fuel costs made development a difficult proposition. Inflation and advances in construction techniques and maintenance practices contributed to the rising costs of golf development. The golf business began its first significant decline since the second world war. Just as the Tufts ceded control of Pinehurst, much of the country turned away from the golf industry and many questionable golf course developments fell into bankruptcy.

Despite escalating costs and a dwindling interest in the game, speculators plowed ahead with new golf course projects, particularly in the Sandhills. Although there seemed to be a lack of players, six new courses opened up in Moore County during the decade. Expansion was on the docket for both Foxfire and The Country Club of North Carolina as well.

Although the Tufts family began the 1970's ceding control of the Pinehurst Resort to an outside corporation, the family did not just walk into the setting sun. James and Albert Tufts continued their quiet existence in Pinehurst, but the same could not be said for their brother Richard and his son Peter. Despite their exit from the resort, they continued to pursue the Sandhills as a viable golf investment. As a direct counter to Diamondhead's capital improvement efforts at Pinehurst, Richard and Peter proposed a 1,000 acre golf course development called Old Yadkin Country Club. It was to be laid out on the site of the failed Montevideo Park development back in 1927.

The site partially consisted of an area called the Pleasants Sandpit and included one large lake and three small ponds as features. Peter designed two semi-private golf courses. Plans for eight tennis courts, a hotel and two residential subdivisions (to be called Pine Valley Estates and Clearwater Properties) were also part of the master plan. The total cost of the project was estimated to be $3 million.

Peter was determined to create a masterpiece dedicated to his Godfather at Old Yadkin. *"I am trying to capture as much of Donald Ross's technique as possible, particularly around the greens, without duplication,"* he said. Peter had studied Ross's approach to field work as a teenager during Number Two's conversion to grass greens in 1935. He was also directly exposed to projects undertaken by both his father and Ellis Maples. In addition to capturing the Ross feel at Old Yadkin, plans called for the creation of three dramatic holes within the Pleasants Sandpit.

Peter Tufts
(Courtesy: Chris Rogers)

Unfortunately for the Tufts, their grand plans were never realized. The financiers behind Old Yadkin – a resident from Southern Pines and three men from Fayetteville – became concerned about Peter's lack of design experience. Although he had done renovation work at the resort, Peter had never designed and built a golf course on his own. As a result, the Fayetteville contingent balked on the entire plan and bought out the Tufts and the Southern Pines partner. Old Yadkin Country Club was never built.

LUCKILY FOR THE TUFTS, OPPORTUNITY LATER CAME KNOCKING IN AN AREA WEST OF PINEHURST KNOWN AS WEST END. To be called Tuftstown Country Club, the original development did not include golf as part of its business plan. But because the property had numerous swampy areas the developer, Fred Lawrence, decided he would be more successful selling homes around a golf course than swampland. He offered to give acreage within the development to Richard and Peter free and clear provided they build a golf course. The development was renamed Seven Lakes Country Club to reflect the seven spring-fed lakes that dotted the property.

The Tufts saw the project as redemption and a new way to challenge Pinehurst Resort after the Old Yadkin project fell apart. *"It will beat anything Pinehurst has to offer,"* Richard said, clearly taking a shot at Diamondhead, *"It will be a course that is fun to play. You have to know golf to design a golf course, especially one with a character of its own."* Peter designed the golf course and his goal once again was a dedication to Donald Ross, *"I tried to put as much of the Ross touch in it as I could with placement and shapes of the bunkers and the greens. One thing Ross did that architects today don't do was go out in the woods and walk it to the point where he was familiar with every bump and swale on the property. I tried to do that at Seven Lakes and I got myself familiar with the spots* [an architect] *tries to avoid."*

A local contractor named Sonny McNeill did the construction with a few backhoes, a bulldozer, and a couple of trucks.

"When I built Seven Lakes I was determined to copy Ross first," said Peter. *"We started with a par five and I got hold of a bulldozer operator that was very good, but not at first. He couldn't grasp what I was trying to do with the bunker or the green. I said, 'Sonny, jump in my car' and we drove over to Pinehurst where I showed him the third hole, seventh*

Seven Lakes Country Club Number Five
(Courtesy: Diane Adams Tufts)

Constructing the Eighth Green of Seven Lakes Country Club
(Courtesy: Diane Adams Tufts)

Seven Lakes Country Club Number Eleven
(Courtesy: Seven Lakes Country Club)

hole, and seventeenth hole where Ross's bunker work was beautiful. Sonny looked at me and said, 'Well why didn't you tell me?' I said, 'Man, I been trying for a week and you couldn't get it'. We went back to Seven Lakes and he had no more trouble."

Despite that breakthrough, Peter knew he still had a major challenge on his hands, *"Unfortunately, it was an awful piece of land to work with. Out of the eighteen holes, only two of them were high and dry. A couple holes were built on a severe slope and the putting surfaces were not my idea of good greens."* Because the site was mostly swampland, drainage was the major issue. So to break up the muddy quagmire, Tufts dynamited both the second and eighteenth holes to create a means of drainage. *"We drilled a hole down about three to four feet and stuck a charge down in there to blow it up,"* Tufts recalled.

Peter's first solo design was projected to open in the summer of 1974. Due to difficult site conditions, however, the course didn't open until July 4, 1976. The course debuted with sixty-two sand bunkers, large greens of 6,000 to 9,000 square feet in size, and ten lakes. Although separated by a road, Seven Lakes Country Club became the centerpiece of a major residential development just a few miles north of Jackson Springs.

MANY MORE DEVELOPERS PLOWED AHEAD WITH PROJECTS BUILT UPON THE STANDARD MODEL OF RIBBONS OF GOLF HOLES FLANKED BY HOMES. New developments such as Woodlake Country Club, Foxfire Village, Oakwood Country Club and Hyland Hills, among others, all fed on the reputation of Pinehurst to garner attention. They benefitted greatly by the new second-home market that Diamondhead spearheaded.

Almost ten years after the completion of Whispering Pines Country Club (1962), A. B. Hardee began another golf course development called Lake Surf. It was located in the small town of Vass, just a few miles west of his Whispering Pines. Hardee built the largest lake in North Carolina at the time (1,130 acres) and planned to include a wave-making machine. The Arab oil embargo and skyrocketing interest rates curtailed his dream temporarily. But it finally opened in 1971 without the wave-maker and with a new name: Woodlake Country Club. Like Whispering Pines, Woodlake was designed by Ellis Maples.

Even though Whispering Pines was highly regarded and Woodlake was up and running, home sales weren't going very well for Hardee by the mid-seventies. To generate more cash flow, he turned to Ellis to design the South Course of Whispering Pines (today called Whispering Woods) with several more prospective home sites on land across Airport Road. It was originally planned to open in October of 1972, but did not open until the following May.

Hardee built another golf course in 1973 adjacent to his Whispering Pines Motor Lodge along U.S. One. Hyland Hills was designed by Tom Jackson, a former associate architect for George Cobb. The exposure from one of the busiest roads along the east coast gave Hyland Hills a step up on the competition. But because the golf course was created solely to sell real estate, it struggled to attract golfers despite the high-profile road frontage. Hyland Hills went into bankruptcy by the end of the decade and was sold to a Raleigh developer named Maurice Brackett.

The difficult economy during the 1970s forced Hardee to use funds from Whispering Pines to cover losses at Woodlake and another Maples original called Middle Plantation Country Club (today known as Ford's Colony in Williamsburg, Virginia). By November 1978, Southern National Bank foreclosed on Hardee and took crucial parcels of land around Whispering Pines as compensation. Whispering Pines Country Club was eventually forced into bankruptcy on October 22, 1980.

Whispering Pines Number Three West
(Courtesy: Avestra Group)

Foxfire Country Club plowed ahead with expansion plans of its own as well. Gene Hamm returned to build a third nine holes in 1974 and a fourth nine in 1976. In between, Foxfire achieved modest attention by hosting the 1975 Atlantic Coast Conference Championship, won by future U. S. Open Champion Curtis Strange. During the seventies, Foxfire evolved into a semi-private country club for golfers from nearby Rockingham and Laurinburg in addition to serving new homeowners and resort play.

Foxfire Country Club Number Fifteen West
(Courtesy: Avestra Group)

Although member play helped pay the bills, the cost of maintaining 36 holes daily and slow home sales led to a new owner and a new business plan. In an effort to attract out-of-state golfers by the new ownership group led by Henry Mayer, condominiums and tree houses were built in 1978 and 1979 to house the golfers. But the resort trade did not respond and Foxfire was soon sold to The Beck Group of Cincinnati, Ohio in February 1983. This company didn't fare much better and lost its acquisition to Carolina Bank through foreclosure that September for $1.5 million. The bank turned a tidy profit three months later when it sold the development to a group called Foxfire Resorts, Incorporated for $1.75 million.

THE DISTURBING TREND OF FORECLOSURES CONTINUED AS WOODLAKE, WHISPERING PINES, OAKWOOD COUNTRY CLUB, AND HYLAND HILLS MET THE SAME UNFORTUNATE FATE, BUT NOT THE COUNTRY CLUB OF NORTH CAROLINA. *"When I came here, the banks had Pinehurst and we were wondering if the area was going to make it because a lot of courses had been foreclosed on,"* recalled George Thompson. *"Then my wife asked Mr. Urquhart if it was solvent. But they never even had a mortgage."* Despite the falling dominoes that surrounded the club, Thompson and the members of CCNC convinced his wife the Sandhills wasn't a sinking ship.

In 1970, seven years after the Dogwood and Longleaf nines opened, Willard Byrd returned to CCNC to design a third nine called the Cardinal. He was the logical choice for the work because of his early involvement with the project. *"Willard did the entire thing and what everybody thought was an extremely credible job for a long time. As time wore on, though, some defects were revealed in the golf architecture,"* recalled Dick Urquhart. Although Willard collaborated with Ellis Maples on the first eighteen back in the sixties, he went solo in 1970. Most of Byrd's holes lacked definition in the landing areas. Many bunkers harmlessly flanked the putting surfaces, providing little excitement for the approach shots. In 1974, Robert Trent Jones finally arrived at CCNC to make extensive renovations to the existing 27 holes. Jones eliminated many architectural oddities and developed shot making opportunities on numerous holes.

In many cases, teeing areas were pushed back and re-oriented to relate better to the golf holes they started. Hazards both in the fairways and around the greens were repositioned to better challenge the good players, and others were modified and made less demanding for poor players. This was evident on the first hole where part of the lake was filled in to provide a wider fairway for short hitters. Conversely, two new bunkers installed along the left of the fairway at 250 yards out tightened the driving area for longer hitters.

Similar changes were made to the Longleaf and Dogwood nines, but the overall strategic character of those holes needed less wholesale adjustment than the Cardinal. Most changes to Longleaf and Dogwood were minor tweaks: Enlarging greens here and shifting the angle of a bunker there. Many tees were also repositioned to provide more contiguous teeing space.

In 1979, Jones's son Rees was brought in to make preparations for the United States Amateur Championship the following year, assisted by his father. No greens were rebuilt, but Rees expanded several in order to create additional cup locations. New bunkers were also added, and others were relocated to help conceal the flagsticks. Minor changes were made on almost every hole.

Country Club of North Carolina Dogwood Course Number Eighteen
(Courtesy: Country Club Of North Carolina)

THE PRIMARY DOCTRINE OF THE REAL ESTATE BUSINESS IS *"LOCATION, LOCATION, LOCATION."* Robert Trent Jones just happened to own property adjacent to the club and found himself in an enviable position. A land swap was agreed upon, Jones laid out a fourth nine, and by 1981, CCNC had two 18-hole courses to offer the elite of the Carolinas and beyond. Combined with Byrd's Cardinal nine, the full 18 was renamed the Cardinal course to complement the original 18, now referred to as the Dogwood course. Byrd's contribution to the Cardinal is the first through fifth holes and fifteenth through eighteenth holes. Jones's nine is six through fourteen. It seemed to be a win-win situation for all involved, but the benefit of working with the most famous golf course architect (and the busiest) of the time had its price.

As president of the club in 1974, Urquhart had the responsibility of representing CCNC's interests while Jones undertook renovations and expansion.

> *"Trent was a little tough for me to deal with. In the first place, he was always in a hurry.*
> *He'd drive in there for one of his periodic inspections and I'd be there waiting for him. As*
> *soon as he would get out of the car he would look at his watch. I'd say, 'Trent, when is your*
> *plane leaving?' He'd say, 'Well, I've got two, one at 4:30 and one at 7:30.' I'd then say,*

242

Country Club of North Carolina Cardinal Course Number Nine
(Courtesy: Country Club Of North Carolina)

'Well you'd better figure on cancelling them because we've got a lot of talking to do about a lot of items here'."

Urquhart also recalled the frustrating design changes that were a staple of the process at CCNC. *"I got mad as hell with him because on the 10th hole* [of Cardinal], *when he redesigned the lake right there in front of the tee, he'd build the lake, go out and look at it, fill it back up, rebuild it. You know, I got the suspicion that Trent is shoving this dirt around for his ten percent, but its costing me 100 percent!"* The lake was removed within months of opening.

One flaw in the final product was a bit of a disjoint between the nine original Byrd holes and Jones' new holes on Cardinal. The difference between both architects' work was found not just in the feature work, but in the routing of the golf holes themselves. Because Jones lacked the freedom of space that Byrd had and was working on rougher terrain, the results were much tighter and hillier golf holes. *"Jones never cleared any type of swath through there – it was all tree line to tree line,"* notes superintendent George Thompson. *"You didn't have to stray far off those fairways on Jones's nine to be in the trees. Byrd's nine was much wider, more open, and easier to play. But the good players liked the Jones nine because it was narrower."*

The better player also took more to the multiple tiered greens that characterized Jones's work and were in stark contrast to Byrd's large, flat surfaces. Although Jones' work was favored by many, it left the club with a bit of an architectural identity crisis.

"LOCATION, LOCATION, LOCATION" **CAN DEFINE THE SUCCESS OF BOTH KNOLLWOOD FAIRWAYS AND MIDLAND COUNTRY CLUB.** By the 1960's, the last of Van Lindley's orchards along the Yadkin Trail had been sold off to speculative realtors, including some of James Tufts's descendants. But through more than just location, both of these courses found a specific niche that other, less successful layouts of the period failed to identify. Mostly because they are both executive-length nine-hole courses, neither Knollwood nor Midland are on any visitor's *"must play"* lists. Yet they are also not the standard real estate golf courses that get lost among the crowd like Foxfire or Woodlake. Both these developments serve specific golfing markets and offer residential choices typically not found around regulation-length golf courses.

The first to be converted from an orchard was Knollwood Fairways. In 1960, a Canadian bridge builder named Charles A. Pitts decided to build a public golf course and lighted driving range at the corner of Midland Road and Pennsylvania Avenue. During construction, workers unearthed the old trolley road bed

Knollwood Fairways Opening Hole
(Courtesy: Bob Klug)

that took vacationers from Southern Pines to Pinehurst. Pitts had the historical find properly marked and integrated into Knollwood.

The concept was vastly different from the Country Club of North Carolina. Unlike CCNC, Knollwood was to be a golf course first with only fifteen, 3/4-acre home sites and three apartment buildings. The practice range was surrounded by a nine-hole par-three course and around that was a nine-hole regulation course. The inner holes ranged from 75 to 150 yards, totaling 1,115 yards. The regulation nine had three par threes, par fours, and par fives totaling 2,760 yards. In the mid-seventies a friend told Bob Kramer about Knollwood Fairways. Kramer was a successful marketing executive in Pittsburgh, Pennsylvania. An entrepreneur by heart, Kramer soon expanded into the real estate business, primarily selling second homes in resort areas.

Although Knollwood had its own niche among the Pinehurst Resort and the Southern Pines courses, the market deficit that was the Achilles heel for these courses made rough waters for Charles Pitts as well. The course had no members, few regular players, and even fewer employees. When Kramer first visited, one person (named John Baldwin) maintained the golf course. He ran from sunup to sundown mowing the fairways, mowing the greens, and running a stripped-down irrigation system. By that time, the par-three course had been shut down and the regulation nine had practically gone to seed.

Kramer saw potential through the weeds and bought Knollwood from Pitts in 1975. The position Kramer strove to occupy was a place for golfers who couldn't handle Pinehurst's difficult Number Two course. *"Our mindset for years was that everything was Pinehurst. Pinehurst Number Two was the draw. But we found a niche in building a community where people could enjoy the game walking on a more comfortable golf course,"* recalled Bob Klug, Bob Kramer's son-in-law and current owner of Pinehurst Area Realty.

The first thing Kramer did was convert the apartments to condominiums. Then his company built thirty-six townhouses. In 1979, he converted the fifth hole of the regulation course into a par four and developed a cul-de-sac of homes on the last hundred yards of the hole. The first four holes of the par three course were preserved as open area but the fifth through ninth holes of the par-three course were also turned into homes.

Kramer's intention was to create a real estate development that would profit not only from it's own golf course, but from the more established courses of the Sandhills as well. Selling condominiums along fairways was certainly a bonus, but the real money was in creating rental properties for golfers.

As for Knollwood Fairways today, the driving range and nine-hole course slowly evolved into the niche Charles Pitts had first envisioned. The par 35 layout and range serve the locals and visitors very well. It even has its own piece of golfing history: Knollwood's extremely tight layout became a quiet practice facility for none other than Gary Player, who at his peak visited Knollwood to hone his skills along the 25 yard wide fairways in preparation for events such as the U. S. Open.

THE ORIGINAL MIDLAND FARMS NEVER CAME TO FRUITION FOR THE TUFTS FAMILY. It is unclear what became of Midland Farms, but its demise did run afoul of the great depression. The land it

Entrance to Midland Farms
(Courtesy: Bob Klug)

was to occupy ran from Airport Road all the way to the Knollwood neighborhood that surrounds Pine Needles Golf Club today. Ninety-two of those acres along Midland Road became a horse farm – coincidentally named Midland Farms.

In 1976, the head professional at Knollwood Fairways, Dave Forbis, convinced the owners of Midland Farms (horse trainers Franklin and Florence Safford) to build a nine-hole private golf course and clubhouse surrounded by forty-eight single-family homes. Forbis continued to serve Knollwood Fairways while developing his new venture, Midland Farms Golf Club. Tom Jackson was hired as the golf course architect, but Forbis ended up doing a lot of the design and construction work himself. Because there wasn't enough land for 18 holes, the nine-hole course was built with two sets of tees and huge greens that featured two flagsticks.

From its inception, Midland Farms Golf Club was a difficult proposition for success. With only forty-eight memberships available, it would cost each member about $6,000 per year to maintain the golf course. In addition to these concerns, the home sites were selling too slowly. By 1980, only six homes had been built and the banks were threatening the development with foreclosure. Nonetheless, Bob Kramer bought the struggling venture from Forbis. For Kramer, a membership for the club already existed across the street at Knollwood as well as at other Pinehurst Area Realty neighborhoods.

Today, the development is known as Midland Country Club and fills a similar niche as Knollwood Fairways. The early improvements Kramer oversaw included a new irrigation system and reservoir, a new pool and an expanded clubhouse. More importantly, a realistic maintenance budget and staff provide a satisfactory playing surface for the senior golfers who frequent the course. From a design standpoint, Jackson's and Forbis's initial work included large putting surfaces and a strong golf course routing that is very playable for older golfers. It also includes strategic choices off the tee to maximize advantage for most golfer's approaches into the greens. The quality of the golf course greatly improved to a standard more befitting a Sandhills golf course.

While new golf course developments were sprouting up all around the Sandhills, the sixties and seventies were relatively quiet for Pine Needles and Mid Pines. At Pine Needles, it was business as usual for Bullet and Peggy Bell. The Bells added tee boxes and bunkers at various points, but refrained from any major changes to Pine Needles. Mid Pines exchanged hands on February 28, 1973 when Quality Inns Corporation bought the property from the Cosgrove family. The company enlarged the pro shop, added air conditioning to the 118-room inn, and built four lighted tennis courts, a swimming pool, and a new shuffleboard court. Very few changes were made to the golf course.

Fifth Hole at Midland Country Club
(Courtesy: Bob Klug)

The same could be said about Southern Pines Country Club as the Elks continued operation of their golf course without incident. The clubhouse wasn't so lucky, though. Long-time member John Sullivan recalls the night in 1967 when everyone got a free steak dinner, but at the cost of the clubhouse:

> *"I was acting manager and we had an awful fire. We had a full house that night for dinner and had just put steaks in the walk-in coolers. Of course, the people took their steaks, and honest to God, they were sitting on the hoods of their cars out there eating and watching the fire. Of course, the fireman all ate very well. We lost the building because we didn't have enough pressure to get any water to put the fire out."*

As luck would have it, the Elks had just completed construction of a new clubhouse and planned to tear the old one down within days of it catching fire.

In 1978, Tom Jackson planned a nine-hole expansion to be combined with the third nine. The new holes were to be south of the main course's eighth, ninth, and tenth holes. Centerlines were located and clearing was begun, but the project was never completed. A few holes were eventually built to replace some of the nine-hole course in an effort to make it longer. As ambitious as Jackson's plans were, nothing compared to the ideas set forth by Rees Jones, who practically suggested reversing the entire layout.

Neither Jackson nor Jones got their way as the existing 18 holes remained status quo, but with one minor subtraction. A transition par-three hole between the fourth hole and the fifteenth hole since the thirties was eliminated at the time of Jackson's work. The tee box sat in the woods to the left of four green and pointed downhill to a green surrounded by two sand bunkers at the foot of the fifteenth fairway. This one-shotter enabled golfers to play a nine-hole loop (the first through fourth holes, the transition hole, and then the fifteenth through eighteenth holes) without having to stray too far from the clubhouse. No one knows why the transition hole was removed and many walkers await its return.

Unfortunately for Sandhills golf, the clubhouse at Southern Pines Country Club was the only element of the golf business to catch fire in the seventies. Although new developments opened, few were very successful. For the first time in the history of the Sandhills area, golf courses were built, but the people did not come. Supply outweighed demand in a way that would take a much larger population to overcome. This led to bankruptcy and frequent turnover because the market for the new courses never really evolved.

Golf was still affordable among the Longleaf Pines, but that was soon to change. Golf course design relied less upon the merits of strategy and challenge that made the first half of the twentieth century a true golden age of golf design. The "*Me*" decade of the eighties brought about a shift in design that focused more on the "*wow factor.*"

CHAPTER ELEVEN

CHAPTER TWELVE
WHAT'S IN A NAME?

UTILIZING FAMOUS NAME DESIGNERS (BOTH TOUR PLAYERS AND PROFESSIONAL ARCHITECTS) WAS THE DEFINING TREND OF GOLF COURSE DEVELOPMENT IN THE 1980'S. The decade started out like much of the seventies, with an emphasis on golf courses whose sole purpose was to sell real estate. As the concept proliferated and more and more golf course developments came on line, owners were forced to distinguish themselves in a more competitive atmosphere.

Although courses have been designed by top amateur and professional golfers for much of the game's history, a new-found emphasis on the *"PGA Tour player as designer"* became the trend. More and more golf professionals began side businesses as golf course designers and prospective golf course developers saw a way to sell real estate reasoning, *"Who wouldn't want to live on a golf course designed by stars such as Arnold Palmer or Jack Nicklaus?"*

However, a famous name designer was not the only attribute to a successful golf course development of this era. Golf courses had to be flashy as well. Golf course construction costs rose in the eighties from intense competition to sell more homes than the next community. The Sandhills was not immune to the challenges. Many new developments opened with pedigree names as designers. Pinehurst National Golf Club and Pinehurst Plantation were the first two Sandhills developments to count on professional golfers for an advantage in the real estate market and leaned on the biggest names in the game: Jack Nicklaus and

Arnie and Jack
(Courtesy: Tufts Archives)

Arnold Palmer. They had an unparalleled rivalry for the hearts of millions of golf fans throughout the sixties, seventies and eighties. Both players-turned-architects were given design opportunities practically next door to each other along Midland Road. Each project was announced within twelve months of each other, seeking to make a splash in the high-end second home market.

In January 1987, Richmond County businessman Claude Smith announced plans for 550 home sites and a Jack Nicklaus golf course along the Pinehurst-Southern Pines border. Six-hundred memberships to the future Pinehurst National Golf Club were available but only one-third were slated for non-homeowners. Upon breaking ground Nicklaus declared, *"We don't want a course that just Jack Nicklaus can play. We want one that all of you can play and that Jack Nicklaus can play."*

The idea came from ClubCorp employee Mike Sanders, who had the vision for an exclusive membership club while working at Pinehurst. He initially teamed up with a Sanford, North Carolina development group that had recently completed The Governor's Club, another Nicklaus project in nearby Chapel Hill. But very early into the project, Sanders and his partner, Allen Jordan, brought Claude Smith in as fifty percent partner while they held the other half.

Design moved quite briskly as Jack made his first visit to the site that March. *"This piece of property, like most of the land in this area,"* Jack said upon walking the site for the first time, *"is just full of natural beauty.*

252

Number Eleven at National Golf Club
(Courtesy: National Golf Club)

When you follow the natural contours of the land, you don't have to move a whole lot of earth. I want to design something that will combine with the natural beauty and stay away from anything artificial."

By the time of that first visit, the majority of the land planning was completed by Ed Pinckney and Associates of Fort Lauderdale, Florida. Jack and his crew reviewed the site a second time on March 18 and made significant routing changes to preserve the character of the property he referred to on his first visit. He eliminated many long walks between holes, and among other adjustments, the decision was made to convert the second hole from a par five to the par three over water that it is today. In addition, Nicklaus moved the first and the tenth tees closer together rather than have the clubhouse sit between them.

But it was a certain *"ugly"* element of the property that truly caught the Golden Bear's attention and cemented Pinehurst National as a Sandhills original. Upon discovering an old sand quarry, Jack remarked, *"It looks terrible but we won't touch it. It's so ugly it's gorgeous and we'd like to keep it that way."* His team did preserve it and today the par-four eleventh hole plays over, around, and through the sandy waste that separates the green complex from the fairway. The green, set at an angle to the fairway, is surrounded by the undisturbed edges of the quarry. Mounds to the front, left, and right delineate the boundaries of the green and the punch bowl putting surface is a foot higher in front than the middle and three feet higher in the back.

Jack's next visit on September 15th was for the purpose of planning the strategy for the golf course and to make additional clearing decisions. He returned in late November to review plans for each hole and made minor changes where he saw fit. Small trees were removed, some greenside bunkers were added (and others deleted), green contours were changed, and tee box positions were relocated. By opening day, only 180,000 cubic yards of dirt had been moved. *"This piece of land that we are turning into a golf course,"* Jack noted, *"has required the least amount of dirt removal of all the courses I have ever designed."*

So well did the holes fit the property, Mike Sanders called Jack's design a tribute to Donald Ross. Sanders based his commentary on Ross's tendency to force the golfer to use all the clubs in his bag. Though this may have been true, Pinehurst National was far from anything Ross ever accomplished. National was a modern golf course for a modern game.

Typical of Nicklaus courses of the period, though, it is a tough layout for the average golfer. Sand bunkers pinch the fairways and water flanks many golf holes. The primary strategy at National is of the heroic type – bite off as much as you can chew. Most green complexes reflect this philosophy as well. They are set at an angle to the line of play and are two- and three- tiered roller coasters with a two- to three-club difference from front to back. Few pin placements are accessible by the average golfer. Even Jack called his National greens *"spicy."*

Number Eight at National Golf Club
(Courtesy: National Golf Club)

Original Charlie Batten Dry-Stacked Stone Wall on National Golf Club's Fifth Green
(Courtesy: National Golf Club)

In a surprise move, a group of Japanese investors bought Sanders and Jordan out on the eve of the ribbon cutting in the spring of 1989, while Smith retained his half. The new co-owners acquired a statement of opulence and difficulty never before experienced in the Sandhills. Nicklaus even imported his own stone mason to create spectacular dry-stacked stone walls to accent green perimeters and other features. Charlie Batten was a sixty-eight-year-old retired farmer and shepherd whose stone work at St. Mellion Golf & Country Club in his native England first caught the Bear's eye. Jack brought Batten to the Sandhills for six weeks to place forty two-hundred-pound boulders in walls along four holes. These were true dry-stacked walls, with no adhesive of any kind. It was Batten's first trip outside of England.

Unfortunately, Pinehurst National struggled to gain a foothold in a second-home market that did not yet really exist in Pinehurst. Although Diamondhead had started selling homes fifteen years earlier, and areas such as Foxfire and Whispering Pines were well established by 1989, National was the first to establish itself along the lines of Palm Beach and other affluent communities. The Sandhills area was not ready for the ultra-rich and it took time for Pinehurst National to develop a clientele. Tired of the struggling housing market, the Japanese sold their half of National in 1992 and Smith assumed one hundred percent ownership.

In May 1995, the membership took over operation of the club. The original development deal specified that the members were to take ownership of Pinehurst National by a specific date, not once the membership grew to a certain size, as most equity transfers are structured. In less than a year, the transaction unfolded because there were not enough members to pay the bills. The course came back into Smith's ownership in June of 1996 and his family has owned National ever since.

National's Midland Road neighbor, The Mid South Club, was originally known as Pinehurst Plantation. The name was in reference to the original Van Lindley orchards that occupied the property one hundred years earlier. In fact, a fruit packing house once was located near the entrance to the club and a Northern & Southern Railroad spur served the house until 1915. During harvest season, trains transported peaches and berries to the Southern Pines train depot for distribution throughout the country. After the orchards were sold off, the land changed ownership often, eventually settling in the hands of a man named Voit Gilmore. Gilmore sold the property in 1987 to the L. F. Rossignol Corporation of Raleigh. Owned by Fred Rossignol, the company was a multi-faceted real estate development corporation specializing in resort, commercial, and residential projects.

Fifth Green at Mid South Club
(Courtesy: Brandon Advertising)

Rossignol hired Arnold Palmer to design the golf course, which was to be surrounded by single-family homes on 536 acres. As in their playing days, once again the comparison to Nicklaus took center stage in the early promotion of the project. National had been open just two months when ground was broken in January 1989 and Palmer was well aware of the positive remarks about Plantation's neighbor,

"I haven't been over to see it and it wouldn't be fair to catch a sneak preview of the course," Palmer said. *"It would be like letting Jack play the final round at Augusta and then letting me go out and play my round. It just isn't done and shouldn't happen in golf competition nor golf course designing."*

Rossignol gave the Palmer organization a simple charge: Make it better than the one next door. But unfortunately for all involved, it went bankrupt a mere eight months into construction. Most holes had been cleared and many had been rough-shaped before the project stalled. The property became littered with Longleaf Pine and Turkey Oak seedlings as the course laid dormant for almost a year. Ragweed and other grasses grew to chest height. In September of 1990, Tri-City, Inc., led by Claude Smith of Rockingham

Mid South Club Number Eleven
(Courtesy: Brandon Advertising)

(owner of National at the time) bought Plantation from Marble Bank of Rutland, Vermont. Smith's plan was to combine National and Plantation into 36 holes of golf and one thousand home sites.

The following July the new owners began work. Two years later, Pinehurst Plantation opened for business. The course had great variety in strategy, even with water in play on eight holes. There was a more prevalent trend toward the utilization of mounding and fewer heroic green sites like those that dominated the Nicklaus project. Within a year, Plantation was doing so well that a company called Golf Communities of America stepped in to buy it from Smith.

Although the founders of both National and Plantation planned to build on two of the most famous names in golf for distinction, it was another of golf's famous names that led to even more turmoil and identity crisis for the burgeoning layouts. In time, both courses were involved in a trademark battle with Pinehurst Resort over the inclusion of the word *"Pinehurst"* in their names. Even though the courses were relying heavily on the attraction of two famous golfers, the resort felt it was the use of *"Pinehurst"* that was the true *"name"* draw and it opposed its use to anyone not associated with the resort. After a few years of litigation, both Midland Road developments were forced to remove *"Pinehurst"* from their names in 1999.

Golf Communities of America held ownership of the Plantation property for almost five years, but home sales lagged and a clubhouse was never built. By May 1999, Golf Communities of America had filed for bankruptcy and the banks put Plantation on the market for $11.5 million. For three years, various suitors came knocking. In the summer of 2002, it was finally bought for $12.3 million by the Mid South Partners. Peter Tufts's son Bob was among nine investors who planned to take the newly named Mid South Club totally private.

Both National and Mid South were planned as high-end golf course residential developments that would break the mold of the earlier golf course developments in the Sandhills. Although it became standard operating procedure for many developments in the eighties and nineties, the high cost of creating opulence sent both developments into a whirlwind of ownership cycles that twenty years later has finally stabilized.

IN JUNE OF 1984, DALLAS-BASED CLUB CORPORATION OF AMERICA PURCHASED THE PINEHURST RESORT FROM THE BANKS FOR $15 MILLION AFTER ORIGINALLY PASSING ON IT BACK IN 1970. Robert Dedman's club management corporation grew by almost twenty percent annually in the fourteen intervening years. At its peak, ClubCorp owned and operated 260 country clubs, city clubs, athletic clubs, and public-fee golf courses worldwide. Among the jewels at the time of the Pinehurst purchase were Inverrary Country Club in South Florida and Firestone Country Club in Ohio.

Dedman was every bit the salesman James Walker Tufts had been and relished the role. *"Salesmen make the world go around and somebody has to make the sale to get the income,"* Dedman liked to say. *"Salesmanship is what built America."* In 1957, he bought four hundred acres in Dallas to develop Brookhaven Country Club and eventually built 54 holes. Brookhaven served as the prototype for ClubCorp as well as an endearing influence to purchase Pinehurst Resort almost thirty years later. Dedman said, *"Since we had the facilities of*

three clubs in one location, we could have three times the normal number of members supporting it yet only one-third the operating costs. It was a good concept and it worked."

The economies of scale allowed him to hire the very best professionals at competitive salaries, yet charge members half as much as a club with only one golf course.

This salesman was born in Rison, Arkansas (population: 1,318) on February 15th, 1926. Along with his parents and three siblings, Dedman grew up in a tiny two-room house with no electricity or running water. After attending Southern Methodist University, he began a career with a law firm in Dallas, where he learned much of his trade representing oil baron H. L. Hunt. His simple ClubCorp sales pitch was *"To allow people who own a house on the fairways of a golf club to live like multi-millionaires on multi-million-dollar estates with swimming pools, indoor and outdoor tennis courts, superb dining facilities, and one hundred-plus servants.*

Robert Dedman, Sr.
(Courtesy: ® Pinehurst, Inc. All Rights Reserved)

They don't have it to themselves, but even the Rockefellers and Mellons shared their estates with friends."

The plan worked and Dedman built one of the largest golf companies in the business. He also became one of the game's most influential people. On a personal level, he planned to make $50 million by the age of fifty and give $1 million away every year thereafter. By 1998, he had made over $1 billion and had given away over $100 million.

After his purchase Dedman talked about his reasons for obtaining Pinehurst, *"First there was this desire to preserve Pinehurst as the heritage of golf in this country, and maybe around the world. Also, it was a business opportunity for us in another division. Pinehurst represented a super opportunity to start a resort division. This was our first resort acquisition and it is one of the superstars in our orbit."*

Pinehurst had begun to deteriorate while the banks searched for a new owner so by the time ClubCorp purchased the resort, there was a lot of work to be done. Dedman recalled his initial visit to the resort.

"The first time I came here, I walked out on Number Two and tears came to my eyes. It's so special and I could see that it wasn't being maintained to the standards that it, the members, the homeowners, the resort guests, North Carolina, and the world were entitled. I had always venerated Pinehurst for its place in the history of golf and when I finally saw

it I knew instantly that we would take this fallen angel and make it not as good as it was, but better than it had ever been."

Many of the same principles the Tufts family instilled in the development of Pinehurst were also part of *"The Concept"* developed by Dedman and the employees of ClubCorp. The concept was a set of principles laid out to all employees in an effort to achieve unparalleled customer service and it was vital to fix this angel's wings. Extraordinary service and enthusiasm were the highest priorities for Dedman and the employees of the resort, just as the Tufts prescribed. *"Every guest is treated like a member, and every member is treated like a king,"* Dedman asserted. The plan included an immediate influx of capital improvements, and not a moment too soon. On September 5, 1984, soon after the closing papers were signed, a staff member fell through the hotel kitchen floor.

Beth Kocher and her husband, Brad, were among the first ClubCorp employees to arrive on site that August. Beth was an Executive Vice President and Brad was Director of Golf Course Maintenance. What they found was a village of failing businesses (the village had about 1,250 residents in 625 homes) surrounded

The Carolina Hotel circa 1970's
(Courtesy: Tufts Archives)

by six golf courses in severe decline. *"I'll never forget when Brad took me out there,"* Beth recalled. *"The golf courses literally had no grass. The exterior was as deteriorated as the interior. The property had been depressed for five to seven years. It took us maybe a year and a half just to determine all the things we owned."*

The goal was to return the resort to the southern grandeur of 1901. The trick was how to eliminate the glitz of 1984. Jim Hinckley was the Executive Vice President of Operations for ClubCorp and his job was to begin the renovations process of both the inside and outside. *"We didn't want our architects and interior designers to be influenced by what was there in place. We really wanted them to go back to the Tufts Archives and see what Pinehurst looked and felt like back at the turn of the century,"* recalled Hinckley. *"We were trying to restore it to what it was originally intended – a turn of the century resort of southern hospitality."* ClubCorp restored fifty rooms per year over the following five years.

When Pat Corso arrived in June of 1986, the resort was in much better shape, but still far from a future U.S. Open site. He was brought in from a resort in northern Michigan to manage the Holly Inn. By October, he became Vice President of Operations. The next January, he was promoted to President of Pinehurst Resort. *"They had done some good things, but the physical asset was still not in great shape. We continued the process of planned renovation and focused on improving the quality of the overall golf experience,"* recalled Corso.

The primary goal with the golf courses was to improve grass quality by any means possible – from simple seeding to rebuilding infrastructure to installing vital irrigation. Although the banks had converted Number Two's original irrigation system to a more modern one a few months before ClubCorp took over, a sufficient water source for Courses One through Five was still an issue. Brad recalled:

> *"In March 1985, we were about to turn the water off to the roughs and the fairways on Courses One through Five because we had no water. We were going to save it just for the greens. So one of the first things we did was put a pump station on Lake Pinehurst to transfer water over to Number Four and then re-pump it to get irrigation elsewhere. The day we hooked up that transfer line was the day we were going to have to turn off everything but the greens and the tees. We were waiting for that water to come flying over the hill so we could have water to over-seed fairways."*

The new water source replaced the holding ponds at the entrance to Number Seven (originally known as Devil's Gut) and served courses One, Two, and Four.

As bold as the Tufts had ever been, ClubCorp had arrived in Pinehurst with expansion plans right out of the gate. Rees Jones had been hired the year before to begin design of Pinehurst Number Seven. *"A former client and friend named Marcus Fields was the manager of the hotel when the banks owned it,"* Jones recalled. *"He brought*

Installing Drainage on Hole Thirteen of Pinehurst Number Seven
(Courtesy: Rees Jones)

me in to do a layout because they wanted more real estate to sell. I was so excited about it, I stayed up all night and did the layout on my kitchen table."

Disappointed by not getting the commission for Number Six a few years earlier, Rees found some redemption with the opportunity to control the entire site, residential areas included. That was something not afforded to the Fazios when they were handed the job of designing Number Six. *"I wanted Number Six badly,"* Rees remembered. *"I was interviewed for it and* [the assignment] *would have made a big difference because I was having difficulty out on my own. But I lucked out and got a better site in Number Seven. Sometimes when you lose, you win. I could do my own routing and control my own destiny."*

The plan was to create a Pinehurst satellite real estate development much like Number Six. With ClubCorp now in place, the project was put on the fast track. The corporation would build and own the golf course but the banks would own the surrounding real estate.

The "*me decade*" required a little more sizzle for Number Seven than what was developed at Number Six a decade before. The original plan was for a low-density condominium community surrounding an 18-hole golf course on 192 acres. A new plan for single-home lots surrounding the golf course became a better alternative in order to attract a high-end market. The hard-hat wearing Diamondhead prospect was replaced by a deep-pocketed millionaire expecting exclusivity.

To expedite the project, ClubCorp brought in a local building architect named Richard Buck to assist Jones in the early stages. Buck worked to maximize land use surrounding the course. "*I did sketches using different layouts and techniques,*" remembered Buck. "*It* [the site] *was totally wooded and very difficult to traverse with a number of streams to cross. Over a period of time, Rees became more familiar with the land and terrain.*" Twenty-four different housing alternatives were drawn up, yet Jones's original routing stayed the same. "*I really wanted to make sure that it wasn't purely a housing golf course,*" Rees noted.

The routing plan was a classic reminiscent of the golden age courses of Ross and others. "*Number Seven is really like an old site built before the depression,*" Rees said later. "*My Dad used to put little x's on the plans at the high spots and it was almost like connecting the dots. You'd go to the high spots, then to the valley, and to another high spot because you didn't move any dirt. We just sort of worked with the natural terrain and used the elevations for*

Eighteenth Hole of Pinehurst Number Seven, circa 1987
(Courtesy: Rees Jones)

both the tees and greens when we could."

He acknowledged that the site was what made the routing spectacular. *"The lay of the land was such that a lot of the holes unfolded in front of us and we didn't need to do that much earth moving except on some of the lower holes. The course may seem long but many of the holes are downhill from the tee, allowing it to play much shorter."*

Fairway Bunkers from Original Employee's Course Along Hole
Four of Pinehurst Number Seven
(Courtesy: Jay Bursky)

The golf course was located at the southwest corner of the Pinehurst traffic circle, with entrances off Midland Road and Route 15-501. Many of the holes front 15-501 on the same property the old employees' course occupied sixty years before. In fact, while clearing a corridor for the fourth hole, Jones uncovered three sand bunkers. Remnants of a large bunker sit to the back-right of the back tee at the fourth with a pine tree growing out of it. The two smaller bunkers are in play about one hundred yards from the front tees. Those two were located at the corner of the dogleg of the Employee's Courses fifth hole and the large bunker protected the right side of the fifth green.

Another feature of Number Seven's design is the diversity of the hazards incorporated by Jones. Large bunkers were set against small pot bunkers. The tenth hole played through a variety of pot bunkers, while the very next hole required an approach over a berm. He even incorporated natural sandy areas as waste bunkers on both thirteen and sixteen. Jones's main goal was to create something completely different from the six existing Pinehurst courses. *"I want the golfer to remember every hole, even the ones they play poorly. Too often, designers try to create a theme on a golf course and when golfers finish their round they don't remember most of the holes because they all seemed the same."*

Of course, Jones also paid homage to Ross. *"Donald Ross was in the back of my mind when I designed the course."* But he intentionally avoided the famous plateau greens of Number Two. That was because plateau greens don't work on such an elevated site like Number Seven as they do on a flatter site like Number Two, where elevation does not contribute to the penalty. Jones purposely built six-thousand square-foot greens with numerous pin placements to balance the elevated locations.

In addition to maximizing both golf and residential development, ClubCorp made a significant effort to save several trees that were scattered about the property. *"The red-cockaded woodpecker was on the endangered*

list and the trees where they lived could not be cut down or disturbed within the complex," Buck said. *"These trees were marked and figured into the overall plan so they would be saved, which took some doing."*

Pinehurst Number Seven had a *"soft"* opening on April 1, 1986. Because the course was grassed with Rye for the spring season and still had to be sprigged with more permanent Bermuda in the summer, Clubcorp had the unique opportunity to test the waters before closing the book on the final design. They decided to make adjustments based upon public reaction as well as daily operations and maintenance. *"Being open for two and half months gave us an opportunity to survey the reactions of all calibers of golfer concerning the playability of the course,"* Brad Kocher explained. *"It's rare that a new course is given the opportunity to make adjustments like these."*

The resulting modifications made the golf course more player-friendly. New tees were added on eleven, twelve, and eighteen. The left side of twelve fairway was widened and a bunker was added to the right. More importantly, a new green was built sixty yards farther from the tee than the original design to utilize the top of a hill for the green site. From a maintenance standpoint, Tifway Bermuda was row-planted on all the fairways and additional drainage was installed on many holes. The course re-opened that fall and has since separated itself from the other Pinehurst courses as a more exclusive option for the members.

For Rees Jones, Pinehurst Number Seven was a jump-start to his career. He had left the comfort of his father's offices in 1965 and had waited twenty years to make inroads in a very competitive business, despite his pedigree. *"It was a very significant golf course as far as my career,"* Jones admitted. *"That period of time was a big turning point, to have a course as part of the Pinehurst complex really helped my career."* Finally, Rees Jones had become a *"name"* in the business.

Less than a year after Number Seven's second opening, Dedman stayed true to his word that he would not only return Pinehurst Number Two to its former glory but elevate it to the top of American golf, where it belonged. ClubCorp recognized the value of returning as much of Number Two's original character as possible and sought to accomplish just that. Unlike Diamondhead before them, there would be no branding to match other facilities. That would come decades later when Clubcorp branded the Pinehurst formula elsewhere.

Like the Tufts before them, ClubCorp understood the importance of holding major professional golf events on Number Two. However, a greens renovation would be vital to the success of attracting the PGA Tour, or – even better – the USGA. It would be the first step in a twenty-year path back to the top. Although the type of grass had been changed twice in the previous decade, the native soil remained intact since Ross and Frank Maples' work back in 1935 and 1936.

So in 1987, Number Two's greens were rebuilt and sodded with Penncross bentgrass. The fairways were converted, too, from Common Bermuda to a new hybrid Bermuda 419. It was a far cry from the days when Leonard Tufts discovered a lone patch of native Bermuda growing in the dairy fields.

Jack Nicklaus' design firm assisted Kocher and the Pinehurst maintenance staff in the renovation efforts. Because there were no construction drawings from when Ross created his masterpieces, an effort to preserve the existing contours was undertaken by a subcontractor named Ed Connor. Connor's firm,

Golfforms, mapped them using a Theotolight (a computer digital terrain modeling device) so they could be put back to the exact specs Ross intended.

Although the plan was well-intentioned, the greens had already been changed three times and were not exactly as Ross had left them, a detail overlooked by Nicklaus' team. Annual top dressing also meant that the greens were not even at Henson's original elevation. Although the original Ross greens had significant undulation, the intervening years had added a few inches of top-dressing in spots. Unfortunately, those few inches generated a lot of speed, especially with the lower mowing heights that were achievable in 1987.

Nonetheless, the greens were cored out, rebuilt to USGA specifications (drain tile, a four-inch gravel layer, two inches of coarse sand, and fourteen inches of a sand and peat moss mixture compressed to twelve inches) and sodded with Penncross bentgrass. Load after load of cored material had different layers of soil, sand, and organic matter. Kocher recalled the excavation of geologic history beneath the famed greens as well as concerns about the actual elevation of the new greens. *"When the greens were cored out, it was just old native sand. When we got it cored out and looked against the wall in there you could see layers. There was no effort to lower or raise the height of the greens when we did them in 1987."*

The result of the greens renovation was less than ideal because faulty construction techniques slowly made themselves apparent. The decision to sod the surfaces was a mistake as well and Kocher later expressed his frustration. *"Everybody was in a hurry and I think some of the grass varieties at that time were just not real pure. The grasses segregated so badly and so quickly. We could never get it healthy."*

Eleventh Green of Pinehurst Number Two, circa 1991
(Courtesy: Frank Pierce)

Although the greens were sodded in an expeditious manner, the seeds were literally sown for the future because Pinehurst Resort was finally infused with the amount of capital that was vital for survival. Not only did Pinehurst survive, it thrived under the watchful eyes of the Dedman family and the rest of ClubCorp. When the Resort was purchased, it was losing one million dollars per year. But after the first twelve months, the resort turned a $2.7 million profit.

That success was primarily from ClubCorp's customer service and the redefinition of a better club and resort experience, but it was also an industry-wide effort. *"We had great support from anybody and everybody you could think of – from the golf writers who started to write good things about what we were doing, the* [golf] *manufacturers and vendors were trying to help, the USGA, the PGA Tour,* [the members and the Village]," said Hinckley. *"Everybody wanted Pinehurst to be successful."*

Within four years of ClubCorp's purchase, Pinehurst generated an operating profit of $10 million. *"Robert had this great opportunity where everybody wanted you to win,"* said Hinckley. Dedman's vision indeed made Pinehurst Resort better than it ever had been, just as he predicted (or maybe expected).

Sunrise on Ten at National Golf Club
(Courtesy: National Golf Club)

CHAPTER THIRTEEN
A LEGACY AND A STRUGGLE

"Purchasers could have a Ford, chickens, a cow, a hog, and live for half the cost of living in Southern Pines or Pinehurst."

- A Tufts brochure for Midland Farms

ALTHOUGH THE MAPLES FAMILY HAD NO MORE CONNECTION TO THE PINEHURST RESORT BY THE TIME CLUBCORP ARRIVED, ITS SANDHILLS LEGACY STILL CONTINUED WITH A NEW GENERATION. Frank's grandson, Dan, grew up under the watchful eye of his father and continued the tradition of active Pinehurst golf architects just as Ellis did upon Donald Ross's death. When Ellis passed away in 1984, Dan took full rein of the design practice and quickly established his own name in the Sandhills, ultimately crafting three original layouts in Moore County.

The first of his projects was the Pit Golf Links, just a few miles south of Pinehurst in and around an old sand quarry. The Pit was the third attempt to develop a golf course on this property, ironically beginning in 1928 with his grandfather's only solo design effort named Montevideo Park. Forty-four years later, J. P. Riddle and two partners joined forces with Richard and Peter Tufts to develop the Old Yadkin Country Club project on the same property. Cold feet led J.P. to back out for more than a decade before another Sandhills twist of fate led Dan to Riddle.

Andy Page, the longtime head professional of Southern Pines Country Club (and a descendant of the very same Page family who sold the original Pinehurst land to James Tufts), had seen the sand pit and told Dan about the property in passing one night at dinner. Dan recalled:

"Joyce [Dan's wife] *and I were out eating one night at The Barn with Andy Page. He asked me if I had ever been over to look at the sand pits on Highway Five. So I rode over there the next couple days, looked around, and just fell in love with the place. It was so massive."*

He immediately contacted Riddle and a deal was struck in which Maples would build a golf course surrounded by four hundred acres of residential development owned by Riddle. Two main entrances were planned, one on Highway Five and one at the Town & Country Shopping Center off U. S. One.

Almost one hundred years before construction at the Pit commenced, a sand operation began at what was known as the Pleasants Sandpit. Upon closing, the operators left behind depressions and dunes of sand as well as numerous mounds of topsoil along the perimeter, some of which stood over sixty feet tall. What laid before Dan was an opportunity to create something the Sandhills had never seen. Neither Ross nor his Father ever had a site like the one at his fingertips and he knew it.

Dan Maples
(Courtesy: Dan Maples Design)

In some ways, very little dirt was moved for the Pit, yet technically more than a million yards had already been relocated. On the one hand, Maples routed a golf course on a virgin piece of property. On the other, the golf course was literally a hundred years in the making as Dan utilized the unique land features left by the sand operation.

Maples walked the property finding numerous green sites and then decided how to string them all together. Just like Ross, Dan used a combination of topographic maps to gain a general feeling for the site, but relied more on first-hand reconnaissance to finalize the routing. *"We used topos and aerials to a great extent, then routed the course on the ground following the lay of the land. The pit areas were largely unchanged, and there was a pattern of ridges across which the course follows. We continued to walk it over and over again moving the center lines back and forth to use the terrain in a way we believed was best."*

One thing the topography did not show was the quality of the trees on the site. *"The golf hole centerlines didn't show you where the pretty trees were and I wanted to preserve them as much as possible,"* said Maples. The

Number Fifteen at The Pit
(Courtesy: Dan Maples Design)

site was peppered with towering hundred-year-old pines thriving in the topsoil cast aside by the sand operation. *"Some of the trees are like those at Augusta National. But when you get out of the topsoil, the trees are half the size."*

The original sand pit ceased operations around 1890 and wasn't touched again until Dan and his crew sought out logical tee and green sites. The area at the extreme northern corner of the property is where he began carving out the golf course, routing the third and fourth holes around and through sand piles, ridges of spoils, and huge Longleaf Pines.

Dan described the design process in a very matter of fact manner: *"Basically we just went in there, walked it and found those features by hand before we started taking any trees out. There is a huge thirty-foot-high mound behind* [the fourth green] *that is a hundred years old. That was the kind of feature I wanted to surround the green. We started back up from there to find a tee, trying to leave the biggest trees."*

What evolved was a very long, narrow hole with barely twenty yards from tree edge to tree edge. The tees were built by literally knocking the tops off spoil mounds. A green of less than three thousand square feet sits at the base of the topsoil with huge pines towering overhead. It literally requires threading a needle from more than two hundred yards away.

The second pit was more than 200 acres and closed in 1972. Dan located the clubhouse on a bluff overlooking this pit and the driving range plays into its bottom. The tenth hole follows the pits' left edge, creating a heroic strategy. The eighth hole plays from the opposite corner of the pit down into the bottom. The golfer can gamble with the sand ridges to the right of the double-dogleg if he chooses or take the longer route down the left side.

Although Maples moved about 250,000 yards of dirt (not including the million from the sand operation), many holes on the back nine were created with little earthwork. He relied on topographical

The Pit Number Four
(Courtesy: Dan Maples Design)

The Pit Number Eight
(Courtesy: Dan Maples Design)

The Pit Number Ten
(Courtesy: Dan Maples Design)

maps to rough the holes in, but freelanced them once he staked them out. Walking the property resulted in completely turning around three holes from the original plan, a good example of leaving the drawings behind and designing by instinct. *"Fifteen, sixteen, and seventeen were routed backwards from where they are now. But if you played sixteen that way, all you would see are huge power lines. Now you don't see the lines at all."*

THE SUCCESS OF THE PIT DID NOT COME WITHOUT CHALLENGES OR CONTROVERSY. Although flexibility in design and construction allowed for great field changes, the weather and the site's history weren't as cooperative. One challenge when building in pure sand is the inevitable rainstorm and resultant erosion. Where most washes on golf course projects require hand shoveling and a few well-placed hay bales, erosion at The Pit required heavy machinery. *"We had a couple of blowouts during construction,"* Dan remembered. *"By the time somebody found them it would take two or three tandem loads of trucks to fill the holes."*

Another unforeseen circumstance Maples encountered was the discovery of a series of trenches filled with toxic chemicals to the right of the sixth hole. Uncovered during the summer of 1984, three trenches were filled with bags from the Taylor Chemical Company dumped over a forty-year period. Nine chemicals were found, including DDT and other insecticides. They were covered by six feet of dirt and were not considered a threat to the groundwater. Dan had no idea of their existence until construction of the hole.

Nonetheless, a necessary cleanup operation was administered under the Comprehensive Environmental Response Compensation and Liability Act of 1980 (aka, Superfund). Cleanup began in the summer of 1985 but as costs approached $1 million, the project slowed to a halt in 1988. The remaining contaminants sat covered by a plastic tarp and surrounded by a locked chain-link fence. For more than a decade following the course's opening in 1986, golfers teed off in full view of a twenty-foot-tall tent of bad dirt. Finally, in July of 1998, the remaining material went through a special procedure called low-thermal desorption and it left behind harmless soil.

Upon its opening, The Pit Golf Links was a revolutionary design accomplishment in a period when golf courses either relied upon name recognition or settled for the standard. The property contributed greatly to the Pit's reputation over the years, but it was also Maples' ability to lean on the teachings of Donald Ross and recognize the value that sandy soils and special site features can have on a project.

THE PROPERTY THAT LONGLEAF COUNTRY CLUB SITS ON TODAY HAS A VERY DIFFERENT HISTORY FROM THAT OF THE PIT. Peter Shaw originally acquired 3,200 acres of land in grants and bought another 1,280 acres (at $0.25/acre) on both sides of the Yadkin Trail in the mid 1800's. Once the land was stripped of all its lumber and naval stores, he sold 1,800 acres to J. Van Lindley in 1891. Van Lindley planted fruit orchards and watered them from a tank near where the first tee of Longleaf sits today.

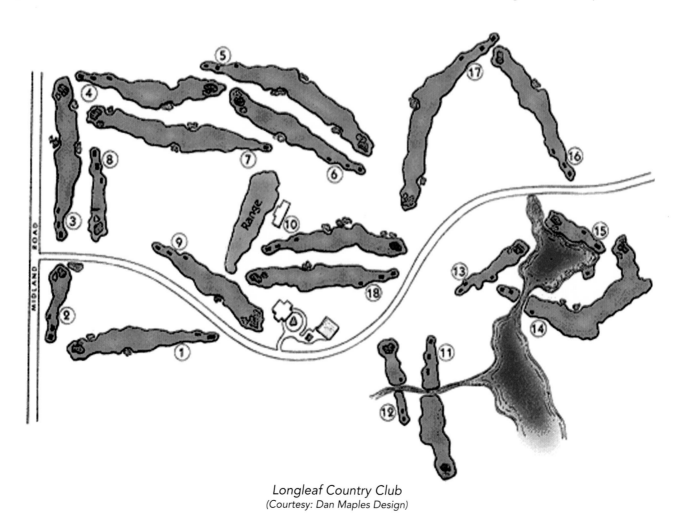

Longleaf Country Club
(Courtesy: Dan Maples Design)

Starland Farms in 1954
(Courtesy: Tufts Archives)

In 1920, a coalition of Pinehurst men led by Leonard Tufts bought the property and divided it into seventy-one 4.6-acre plots (selling for $1,500 each). Their development was called Midland Farms and marketed as an affordable alternative to the established towns of the area. In fact, "*Purchasers could have a Ford, chickens, a cow, a hog, and live for half the cost of living in Southern Pines or Pinehurst,*" (according to an early brochure). For Leonard, Midland Farms offered the opportunity to create an in-fill development connecting Pinehurst to Knollwood. James Barber acquired the property a few years later as part of a 3,400 acre tract and leased the land for a steeplechase course in the thirties. New fencing, stables, grandstands, paddocks, and a jockey house were all built and a fruitful history as a horse farm was born.

From 1935 to 1942, a mid-March equestrian event drew 15,000-20,000 spectators annually where the Governor of North Carolina presented the "*Sandhills Cup*" to the winner of the three-mile main event. The Cup was kept at Dr. Neal's veterinary hospital, a small white building that sat just yards west of the racetrack. Today that building still stands and happens to be this Author's storage shed, complete with dog runs and a floor which slopes to one corner to most efficiently hose the animals down (just a beagle named Scout today).

As a child, Dan Maples watched the races with his Uncle Henson, who lived on a hill overlooking the racetrack across Midland Road. All those years ago, Dan envisioned a golf course around that track. In 1948, a well known local golf pro named Leo Walper and his wife bought one Midland Farms lot and leased a few others for a golf range. The Walpers built a house, grass tees, three target greens and night lighting. Golfers hit balls away from Midland Road onto the property where Longleaf's third fairway sits today.

Parhaven Golf Range didn't last very long. Before the year was out, Anne Cannon Reynolds (the textile heiress) and her husband, L. P. Tate, bought 457 acres (including the Walper's range) and built a horse training center and new racetrack. It was named Starland Farms, in reference to Mr. Tate's star performers (the horses). The entrance was off Midland Road directly behind today's second tee.

The Tates ran the Mid South Horse Show at Starland Farms on March weekends in the 1950's with about one hundred jumpers. By 1974, the farm had a one-mile flat track along the original steeplechase track and a three-quarter mile turf race course with a center show ring. Many great thoroughbreds were boarded there, including 1956 Kentucky Derby participant Jean Baptiste and Disputed Testimony, winner of the 1983 Preakness.

Dan Maples' vision became reality in early 1988 when the plan to build a residential golf course development on 319 of Starland Farms' acres was announced. The new project called for 454 home sites on 149 acres with a golf course to occupy the remaining 170 acres. The development was a joint venture between Maples and General Investment Developers of Boston (GID). Dan was to be responsible for the design, construction, and operation of the golf course.

Longleaf Country Club was fast-tracked to open eighteen months after it was first announced. Coordination between GID and Maples' team was crucial to the success of the project, yet the final site plan wasn't even agreed upon before the start of construction. First, the Town of Southern Pines required GID to build a connector street that bisected the property from Midland Road to Airport Road. To make matters even more difficult, the developers strongly considered buying additional land adjacent to the site. Maples not only had to route a golf course and residential development on very difficult terrain split with a spine road, he also had to plan for three hundred more acres (including 18 additional holes) that may not even be included in the final product.

The Original One-Mile Racetrack Runs Through the Seventh Green of Longleaf Country Club
(Courtesy: Dan Maples Design)

The way he approached the expanded project was to locate the clubhouse as centrally as possible. He routed most of the Longleaf holes behind the clubhouse to the west, allowing for 18 holes on the additional property to be accessed from the front. If the land was never acquired, there would be no effect on the Longleaf eighteen.

The layout is two distinct nine-hole loops with very different characteristics. The front nine is fairly open on gently rolling property where the horse farm sat. The small size of the property and its property line configuration minimized the number of lots Dan could lay out along the holes, so he broke away from the conventional "*double-loaded*" fairway system to route a partial core golf course (no homes along the holes). The result gave homeowners multiple fairways as a backyard.

The wooded property for the back nine had much more elevation change, as well as wetlands and fifty trees that were protected habitat for red-cockaded woodpeckers. Each of these trees were off-limits to clearing. If even one was cut down, a $20,000 fine would be handed down by the U.S. Fish & Wildlife Service. To Dan, this meant more opportunity to create an interesting set of golf holes. The site constraints created so many obstacles that Maples was forced to make holes twelve, thirteen, and fifteen par threes. "*With a small site, you want to have eighteen good holes and try not to compromise,*" stressed Maples.

Dan's childhood memories watching horse races from his uncle's yard were never far from his mind in designing Longleaf. The most fascinating characteristic of the golf course is the preservation of the mile-long horse track that was built in the seventies as the centerpiece of Starland Farms. Dan implemented the track throughout numerous holes of the front nine in a variety of ways. In his estimation, three-fourths of the track is still intact.

The racetrack acts as the landing area for number one fairway and also runs along the right side of holes three and eight. Off the fourth tee, the track must be avoided down the left side because it crosses the fairway twice. Most golfers do not even realize that the seventh green sits on the track itself. Maples simply removed the track fencing from one side of the green to the other. "*On number seven green the track gave us the fill material to build up the green,*" said Dan. Original hedges and water jumps are still in place on the first fairway, eighth fairway, and near the ninth tee. Incorporating the track was a great example of utilizing the features of the site to create the character of the golf course. Typically contours and land forms accomplish this task, but in this case, a cultural icon of the Sandhills gave Longleaf Country Club its flavor.

As speedy as the design process was, it did not compare to the fast track the development team charted for construction. Bulldozers cranked up in March of 1989, seeding commenced that September, and the course opened just two months later. "*From day one we never stopped moving. It is all sand and ideal to work on with no down time,*" said Maples.

The sandy soils were key to expeditious construction, but they also wreaked havoc when the inevitable summer thunderstorms rolled through. Because he was the contractor as well as the architect, Dan's recollection of fighting both time and the weather is vivid. "*We got the back nine planted in three weeks but then had a thunderstorm in July, which just absolutely blew everything out with three inches of rain. Just washed holes in the*

The Fourth Hole at Longleaf Country Club
(Courtesy: Dan Maples Design)

fairways so big you could put trucks in them. We could have just shut down and waited until the next spring, but we skimmed grass from some areas that had survived, did a lot of seeding and sprigging, and then prayed another storm didn't catch us. Pure construction experience put the golf course back together in about three weeks."

Longleaf made its fall 1989 opening day and has become a busy residential community with a golf course that is tailor-made for the homeowners. The layout is very playable for the members yet has hosted a variety of regional events over the years. The Maples style is evident with flashed sand bunkers and greens complexes more similar to the way his father created features than from the Donald Ross look. Although few people would say that Dan's design style is reminiscent of Ross's, the methodology is a carbon copy. Utilizing natural features to determine the routing and working around natural drainage patterns is as old hat to Dan as it was to Ellis and Donald Ross.

Maples and GID accomplished their initial goals with Longleaf Country Club, but decided against adding the 300-acre parcel to the east. They weren't the first group to pass on what was known as the Savin property. Bob Klug's Pinehurst Area Realty passed on an option for the land when it purchased Knollwood back in 1975.

When the Diamondhead Corporation bought Pinehurst from the Tufts, they bought the Pinewild property from Richards with plans to develop Pinehurst Number Six, Seven, and Eight. But once ClubCorp took over, the property was sold to six developers in November of 1985. Fred Lawrence, who was the original developer of Seven Lakes, joined forces with Tommy Albin, William Lawrence, Roy Register, Kenneth Wilkerson and Dr. Bob Foster to build Pinewild Country Club and the surrounding neighborhood.

Golf Course Architect Gene Hamm (Sitting) With Pinewild Partners (L-R) Tommy Albin, Ken Wilkerson, Dr. Bob Foster, Bill Lawrence and Roy Register
(Courtesy: Tommy Albin)

The original plans for Pinewild were very ambitious. The group was brought together by Albin, who had been in the golf business for fifteen years and dabbled in real estate as well. Albin recalled the pure beauty (and great location) of the land right from the start, "*I couldn't believe there were 2,100 acres one mile from the Pinehurst Hotel. Horse trails running through it, a beautiful little lake called Lake Pinewild, beautiful magnolia trees everywhere. It just looked like it was waiting for somebody to build golf courses on it.*" In fact, when Albin first rode the property he found where Diamondhead cut out a few holes around the lake. Convinced they found a gold nugget, Albin and his partners bought the property for six million dollars (less than $3,000 an acre).

The group hired Gene Hamm to design two golf courses called the Magnolia and the Holly. Hamm got the pick of the entire acreage to lay out the Magnolia course. Albin told Hamm to make sure the hole corridors were twenty percent wider than the average hole. "*I didn't want to feel like you had to shotgun it every time.*" The first phase, which included the back nine and all the lots around Lake Pinewild, broke ground in November 1985. Don Thomas Construction (the same contractor for Seven Lakes Country Club) built all the lakes and installed all the drainage. They also brought in people from Bruce Devlin and Robert von Hagge's golf course architecture firm (based in Texas at the time) to do all the shaping and feature work (tees, bunkers, greens) to expedite the project.

Like many first time developers, the Pinewild partners ran into financial stumbling blocks once construction began. "*I opened three different board meetings to tell the partners we need a million bucks and we need it by next Friday or we are in a little trouble,*" recalled Albin. "*Thankfully, I had the partners who saw the need and the potential so we sailed right through some of the hard times.*" The first roadblock was financing of the

Pinewild Country Club Magnolia Course Eighteenth Fairway
(Courtesy: Pinewild Country Club)

water and sewer lines. Although the funds were secure in the bank, the partners didn't realize the Village of Pinehurst required an equal amount as security until construction was complete.

Another problem arose when personal financial difficulties for Fred Lawrence forced the remaining partners to buy him out. His replacement turned out to be a familiar player in the Sandhills golf scene. Albin's group sold sixteen percent of the project to ClubCorp and signed it to a management contract as well. Albin remained the primary on-site manager and ClubCorp brought their own manager to work hand-in-hand with him. *"I can say nothing but great things about ClubCorp,"* Albin stated. *"We were proud to have them. We had a lot of expertise that made it very successful."* He also made a lifelong friend in Robert Dedman. *"He taught me a lot about win-win situations. It's not a good deal for him or it's not a good deal for us unless you have a win-win deal."*

Right from the start, Dedman and ClubCorp brought a new perspective to the project as well as collaborative advice from some familiar names. *"Mr. Dedman flew in one day and said, 'Tommy, pick me up at the airport'. I went out there and the first man off was Rees Jones, second man off was Ben Crenshaw, third*

man off was Pete Dye." Jones had nothing but great comments about the natural appearance of the layout and Crenshaw gave some strategic advice in regards to bunker placement. *"His philosophy is you don't have both sides of the fairway at the same length for the trouble. You give them one out or the other out,"* recalled Albin. A specific example of his guidance was the dogleg-right ninth hole. His suggestion to move a fairway bunker from the outside of the dogleg to the inside stressed challenging, aggressive play instead of just framing the fairway.

Hamm's Magnolia layout opened in 1989 with some minor construction difficulty and a price tag of less than three million dollars. One curve ball was the discovery of two graveyards on the site. The first was found just beyond the Linden Road entrance to the property where ten wooden posts marked the remains of old turpentine workers. Albin embraced the discovery as an asset at the cost of two home sites. He then discovered a second *"asset"*, this one for horses near the twelfth tee.

Wetlands presented another challenge. According to Albin, the eleventh and thirteenth holes couldn't be built today due to environmental restrictions. Back then they could, but it was costly. *"We lost bulldozers,"* Albin recalled. *"I remember one night they tied a bulldozer to about six trees to keep it from going under."*

Initial plans for the Magnolia course included a warm-up hole numbered *"0."* In addition, there were plans for a Cayman golf course (a reduced-length golf course where golfers hit shorter-flying balls with regulation clubs) that was to double as a par-three course (with regulation golf balls). The short course was laid out by Dedman himself and completed in 1989. Similar to Augusta National's par-three course, it was named Azalea with holes from 99 to 192 yards long.

THE SUCCESS OF LONGLEAF, THE PIT, AND PINEWILD CREATED AN EXCITEMENT IN THE SANDHILLS THAT WAS CONTAGIOUS BY THE END OF THE DECADE. Even the Bell family considered expansion. For most of the family's ownership of the course, Pine Needles sat quietly on the sidelines and watched the competition roll in – and sometimes roll out. Other than building a new clubhouse and the lodge, little was done to the resort. But in September of 1988, the Bells saw an untapped opportunity. Having noticed the influx of name architects arriving in recent years, they signed up another golfing family to build a second course. Pete Dye and his son P.B. were asked to design eighteen holes on 300 acres next to their Donald Ross original. A legend in his own right, Pete had never designed anything in the Sandhills, but had fond memories. Back in the forties, he played the Pinehurst courses many times while he was stationed at nearby Fort Bragg. He even had the opportunity to spend a day with Ross, which helped sow the seeds for his own future in golf course design.

Construction was slated to begin the spring of 1990 with the opening of the semi-private course the following year. *"P.B. and I are certainly looking forward to working with the Bells and designing a course in one of America's most spectacular golfing areas,"* stated Pete. *"It will be a labor of love."* Regrettably, the Bells soon realized the buzz of the late eighties had turned to recession by the early nineties. The golf course was never built due to environmental challenges, the downturn of the economy, and a quickly saturated golf market.

AS THE EIGHTIES CAME TO A CLOSE, EIGHTEEN NEW GOLF COURSES HAD OPENED THEIR DOORS IN THE PAST TWENTY YEARS, MORE THAN DOUBLING THE NUMBER OF LAYOUTS IN THE SANDHILLS. It was a dangerous time to build and the Bell family was wise to step away. Unfortunately, the same could not be said for many other golf course owners. Not every new development of the eighties was lucky enough to have the name Ross, Nicklaus, Palmer, or Maples attached to them, and many struggled to gain a foothold in the Sandhills. Neither did their owners have the deep pockets that the Country Club of North Carolina and ClubCorp possessed.

In 1983, Deercroft Golf Club opened in the town of Wagram. Designed by a man named Gardner Gildey, it not only lacked a recognizable architect it was ten miles south of Pinehurst. Another course named Oakwood Hills was designed by regional golf course architect Russell Breeden in 1986 to serve as a manufactured home development for local builder Oakwood Homes. Like Deercroft, it was also a bit isolated from the golfing center of the Sandhills.

A third golf course on the outskirts of Pinehurst was the sister development of Seven Lakes Country Club called Beacon Ridge, located across Route 211 in West End. Although Seven Lakes did well to survive the difficult seventies, it took more than a decade to break ground on Beacon Ridge. Just as he had done across the street, Peter Tufts completed the routing. The design details and day-to-day construction, however, were handled by Gene Hamm.

The course was routed around Lake Auman, an 820-acre spring-fed lake that served as the backdrop for the entrance road and numerous home sites. Hamm supervised the clearing, staking, and grading of the

Whispering Pines West Course Number Six
(Courtesy: Avestra Group)

golf holes, and his son Gary shaped all the greens, sand bunkers, and other feature work with the intention of eliminating every flat spot on the property. Gary stayed on to be the first golf course superintendent once the fairways were planted in the spring of 1988.

THE COUNTRY CLUB OF WHISPERING PINES BEGAN THE EIGHTIES ON VERY SHAKY GROUND. A resident named Lowell Newmeyer became the "*debtor in possession*" to keep the club out of bankruptcy. More than four hundred members pitched in to keep operations running and the Village of Whispering Pines maintenance crew kept both golf courses in shape. On December 29, 1981, the members (thirty percent ownership) joined forces with two men from Connecticut named Roland Beausoleil (fifty-

Whispering Pines East Course Number Ten
(Courtesy: Avestra Group)

one percent) and Sheldon Buffeld (nineteen percent) to take the club out of bankruptcy. The plan was that the members would take full control of everything except the Whispering Woods course within six years. Beausoleil would cover any budget deficits until that time.

His plan was to sell forty homes per year to cover operations and increase club membership. By 1985, the membership had risen to pre-bankruptcy levels but home sales lagged severely behind Beausoleil's goal. With no capital to maintain the facilities, the courses again fell into disrepair and Beausoleil found himself at a $250,000 deficit. He refused to contribute any more money to the cause, leaving the members no choice but

Whispering Woods Number Eleven
(Courtesy: Whispering Woods Golf Club)

to sue for ownership rights. On November 27, 1985, the members successfully took control of Whispering Pines Country Club and a $1 million loan was secured to pay off the existing debt and help restore both the East and West course.

Beausoleil still owned Whispering Woods across the street. Although the course was making money, his real estate ventures continued to fail and he was forced to look for a buyer. Before he could sell, Beausoleil was forced into bankruptcy and in March of 1989, Buck Adams, the head professional at Country Club of North Carolina, successfully bid on the course and obtained ownership.

Woodlake Country Club was also under control of the banks by the start of the eighties, but was purchased by Henry Mayer, the owner of Foxfire. In 1983, it was acquired by the Ingolf Boex and Thomas Radner families of Germany for $2.5 million after Mayer sent the club back to the banks. Originally a financial supporter of A. B. Hardee's efforts, Boex planned to turn the facility's lake into an international yacht club. He also planned bridle paths and private riding stables. In 1989, he hired Dan Maples to build a third nine as a complement to Ellis' original eighteen (Dan also built a practice hole). Boex wanted Dan to not only design nine great golf holes, but focus on bringing the lake into play as much as possible. Most golfers agree that Maples accomplished his task.

In some ways, the eighties was a period of positive growth for the Sandhills as new golf courses with nationally-recognized connections proved there was more to the area than the Pinehurst Resort. But in other ways, the decade also proved the opposite was true: There was not enough attraction beyond Pinehurst to maintain a vibrant and profitable golf region. Deercroft, Oakwood Hills, and Beacon Ridge struggled due to their location far from Pinehurst and found stiff competition for golfers and home buyers alike. Woodlake, Foxfire, and Whispering Pines continued to battle ownership changes and a lack of capital. They struggled with increased competition from the newer courses as well. Another course on the outskirts of the Sandhills, called Legacy Golf Links has fared better though. A high-end daily fee model opened in 1990, it was Jack Nicklaus, Junior's first design.

For the Pinehurst Resort, the eighties brought about a golfing renaissance and true financial security for the first time in its history. The nineties would once again see Pinehurst take its rightful place as the Home of American Golf.

CHAPTER FOURTEEN
THE TURN OF ANOTHER CENTURY

"I envision Number Nine to be a lot like Pine Valley."

- Gary Player

BACK IN THE TUFTS'S DAY, THE GOLF SEASON LASTED FROM NOVEMBER 1 TO MAY 1. They rolled up the sidewalks and tee boxes and took them up to Maine until the heat broke in late fall. As recent as 1990, the golf season was still broken into two sub-seasons. Spring season began in March and extended into May, while the fall season typically started in early September and continued into November. The intervening summer months were so quiet you could hear a putter drop and a round of golf could be found almost anywhere. Local superintendents took advantage of the down time to protect their greens from the heat by growing them visually shaggy.

Today there is no season because the Sandhills is a year-round golf destination as well as a thriving business and retirement community. Although recession slowed the golf business at the onset of the nineties, the country quickly recovered from this small hiccup to experience economic prosperity, leaving a surplus of old and new money for discretionary spending. Moore County experienced strong population growth, particularly in many of the older golf course communities. Foxfire, Woodlake, and Whispering Pines grew in numbers, providing stability to their neighborhoods.

The Sandhills experienced very little slowdown in golf development. In fact, almost every year of the nineties experienced a new opening, major renovation, or expansion. The Country Club of North Carolina and Pine Needles underwent extensive renovations, Pinewild and Woodlake expanded their facilities, and even more golf courses came on line to provide additional real estate options.

In 1991, the original Pinewild developers came to a crossroads. Faced with the commitment (to the members) of building a second course and the clubhouse, it was time to either sell or continue building. According to Tommy Albin:

> *"We were building roads all over the place and water and sewer lines with budgets that were pretty considerable. Our monthly budget was $3.5 million and we were going through it as quickly as we could by selling enough home sites. We had to decide if we wanted to spend another ten or twelve million dollars on a second course and clubhouse or consider somebody finishing the job for us."*

The decision to sell was made and within thirty days, Albin had three potential buyers.

The development was sold for $13.5 million to the Pinehurst Project Limited Partnership, a joint venture between a real estate development company from Tokyo called Lieben, an arm of the Tohato Corporation (which is Japan's version of Nabisco), and ClubCorp Realty Holdings Inc., a subsidiary of ClubCorp. Lieben controlled seventy-five percent of Pinewild and the ClubCorp subsidiary owned the remaining twenty-five. ClubCorp's interest was mainly in a management role and to utilize Pinewild for overflow golf from the main resort. It was generally accepted that Gene Hamm's Magnolia course would become Pinehurst Number Eight and the proposed course would become Number Nine.

The new owners decided to follow the big-name architect trend established in the late eighties for the next course, which meant that Gene Hamm was out as the golf course architect. Instead, Gary Player beat out Robert Trent Jones Sr. and the teams of Tom Weiskopf and Jay Morrish and Bill Coore and Ben Crenshaw for the new Holly course. *"We wanted to have an internationally recognized designer who wasn't already represented in Pinehurst,"* noted Pinewild Superintendent Bill Sessums.

Pinewild Country Club Holly Course Number Eighteen
(Courtesy: Pinewild Country Club)

Player was equally excited to contribute to the growing list of notables to design courses in the Sandhills. *"Nature has spoken for itself at Pinewild. The terrain and soils almost immediately guarantee a picturesque and attractive golf course. It is hard not to build a super golf course on a piece of property like this because it won't require moving a lot of dirt. I envision Number Nine* [Holly] *to be a lot like Pine Valley."*

Oddly, Pine Valley is one of the toughest courses in the world yet Player established his desire to make the Holly course as playable as possible for the average golfer. He deliberately cited the difficulty of Number Two as a prototype to avoid. *"Playability is the thing with this golf course. As great as Number Two is, it can be too tough for some golfers. I intend on making the greens flat so that the average golfer who only hits six greens in regulation will have a chance to make birdie. There* [also] *won't be any of those nine-thousand-square-foot greens like some architects like to build that causes the average golfer to four-putt several times a round."*

The resulting product was indeed far from Pine Valley. The Holly developed into a traditional member's course with turf aplenty, much different from the islands of turf bounding through the sandy wasteland of Player's prototype. Greens with modest contours, a minimal number of sand bunkers, and proper placement of the forward tees meant a very playable Holly course for a growing retirement community.

The second Sandhills development to expand in the nineties was Woodlake Country Club. In 1996, Arnold Palmer combined eight new holes with Dan Maples's ten to create the Palmer eighteen.

The following year, Palmer arrived in the Sandhills for the third time to build the first golf course in Whispering Pines in more than a quarter of a century. Working to capitalize on his Woodlake operation,

Number Fourteen at The Carolina
(Courtesy: Richard Mandell)

Ingolf Boex brought a new project to A. B. Hardee's old neighborhood. In fact, his golf course community broke ground on land owned by Hardee's son Andy.

Across from the Moore County Airport, the new golf course on 166 acres was christened simply The Carolina on June 15th, 1997. Eighteen holes traverse one hundred feet of elevation change. Despite a few blind shots, the golf course is typically Palmer-playable. Chock full of the standard Sandhills features (sandy pine straw roughs, towering Longleaf Pines), The Carolina also weaves through wetland pockets and numerous sandy waste bunkers offset by classic cape and bay bunkers.

AS NEW COURSES WERE BEING BUILT FROM SCRATCH AND OTHERS EXPANDED, THERE WAS INCREASING PRESSURE ON OTHER SANDHILLS COURSES TO REMAIN COMPETITIVE (WHETHER IT WAS FOR NEW MEMBERS, RESORT PLAY, OR REAL ESTATE SALES). Regional golf course management company GolfSouth bought Foxfire Resort in 1997 with plans for a five million dollar facelift. Past days of watering all 36 holes by hand were over because the renovation included double-row irrigation, new sand in all the bunkers, cart path resurfacing, a new 8,000 square-foot clubhouse, and six rebuilt holes. Improvements were also to include new Penn G-6 Bentgrass greens and a driving range.

Foxfire Country Club West Course Number Twelve
(Courtesy: Avestra Group)

Optimism was high because GolfSouth brought much needed experience to Foxfire. Before much work could be accomplished, however, GolfSouth principal Barton Tuck sold the company and its course portfolio to a Minnesota technology entrepreneur named Rick Born in 1999. GolfSouth became GolfMatrix and the renovation work didn't miss a beat. But the optimism quickly waned as Born's new venture resulted in $31 million of debt spread over many different courses, including Foxfire and Beacon Ridge. In December of 2002, Woody Davis's Avestra Group bought Foxfire out of bankruptcy once again. Avestra instituted a sensible agronomic program, focusing less on real estate and more on golf.

WITH INCREASING COMPETITION FROM NEW DEVELOPMENTS FOR THE HIGH-END PRIVATE CLUB MARKET AND AN AGING INFRASTRUCTURE, THE COUNTRY CLUB OF NORTH CAROLINA DECIDED IT NEEDED SPRUCING UP AS WELL. Other than minor work to one hole in 1990 by Dan Maples and renovations to the fairway bunkers by John LaFoy in 1999, neither course had been significantly touched since the seventies.

Despite positive response to LaFoy's work, the club members eventually felt they needed a complete facelift for Dogwood and a big-name architect to do the work. The club decided a fresh spin on things was

Country Club of North Carolina Dogwood Course Number Thirteen
(Courtesy: Alan Van Vliet Photography)

necessary so they hired Toledo, Ohio-based golf architect Arthur Hills. Originally a landscape architect, Hills broke into the golf architecture field in 1966 and worked on over two hundred new projects and renovations. He was excited about the opportunity to work in Pinehurst and personally spent several weeks on site.

By the time Hills began his work in 1999, the Dogwood greens were thirty-seven years old and showed signs of poor condition. This was mostly a result of the aging greens construction materials and techniques of the sixties. The sand came out of a tobacco field and was only slightly modified to conform to USGA guidelines of the era. Some greens were entirely layered with gravel, yet others had none. Drainage pipe consisted of old clay tile covered by tar paper to keep the sand out and its installation was as random as the gravel.

Club members also wanted faster green speeds, which meant not only new construction materials but the most modern grasses as well. George Thompson studied demonstration plots of twenty different bent grass cultivars with North Carolina State University turfgrass experts for four years. The best performer was A-1 and it became the grass of choice for Dogwood.

The club was very protective of Dogwood's design, so they limited Hills' architectural freedom. His two primary tasks were to soften the greens' slopes to provide the new A-1 surfaces (particularly from back to front), and extend the greens in places to accommodate additional cup locations. Hills also adjusted the grassing patterns around the greens complexes to promote short game choices, similar to what was found at Pinehurst Number Two. For the most part, the putting surfaces were cored out and rebuilt along these guidelines (with the exception of the fifteenth green, which was completely rebuilt).

Hills rebuilt all the green-side bunkers, but only a few of LaFoy's fairway bunkers. He pulled the slopes down a bit but reincorporated the flashed capes and bays of the original Ellis Maples bunkers. He also eliminated all the sand bunkers behind the greens. This decision promoted chipping after an aggressive approach instead of blasting out of sand to a putting surface sloping away from the golfer. The new bunkers resulted in increased hand work for the maintenance crew and somewhat of a challenge for the golfers to get in and out, but created a unique hybrid of the Maples look and the standard grass faces of Hills.

In addition to the green and bunker work, many tees were raised to improve visibility and the third, fifth, fifteenth, and sixteenth greens were all shifted to incorporate water hazards. The fourth fairway was moved ten yards to the left, fourteen tees were elevated to bring the adjacent lake more in play on the tee shot, and eighteen fairway was reshaped and moved to the edge of the lake as well.

Firmly satisfied with Hills' work on Dogwood, the club asked him back in 2002 to renovate the entire Cardinal course. This time he was given permission to create a completely different eighteen. To contrast with the grass-flash hybrid of Dogwood, Cardinal's new bunkers were mostly flat sand with grass faces, giving it a character more associated with Charles Blair MacDonald or Seth Raynor. The grass faces are intricately shaped in the form of mini-mountain ranges, but are lost to the naked eye when covered with rough.

Upon completion of the Cardinal renovations, the only deficiency lay in the club's practice facility, which went largely ignored. The driving range was a flat expanse with rudimentary push up targets, a simple

Country Club of North Carolina Cardinal Course Number Two
(Courtesy: Alan Van Vliet Photography)

Country Club of North Carolina Short Game Practice Area
(Courtesy: Richard Mandell)

chipping green and bunker, and not enough tee space. In 2005, the club hired Richard Mandell to design a completely new practice facility on the site of the existing range.

The first task was to ensure the club of almost two acres of tee space. Although two acres is an incredible amount of tee space, it was recommended specifically by the USGA as a requirement of a club the size of CCNC. In the process of carving out the fairway, we sculpted four target greens with bunkers that remained at the original elevation, leaving a dramatic view from both tees. A short-game area on the adjacent parcel included two practice greens with a variety of undulations in between both targets. The shaping of the features and the placement of the bunkers and hollows each got their cue from both the Dogwood and Cardinal courses. Not only do the members have a completely modern set of golf courses, they now have one of the premier practice facilities in the Carolinas.

THE SECOND SIGNIFICANT WHOLESALE RENOVATION OF THE NEW CENTURY WAS AT THE PINE NEEDLES RESORT IN 2003. But before the Bell family undertook that project, fate intervened. When the Bell family passed on building a second eighteen in the early nineties, their cautious attitude resulted in a much better opportunity a few years later. In 1994, they were offered the chance to purchase the Mid Pines Resort across Midland Road. For Peggy Kirk Bell, it was a sentimental move because of her past with Pop and Masie Cosgrove, who purchased Mid Pines after they sold their shares in Pine Needles in 1955.

Almost forty years later, the Bells rescued Mid Pines from the very hands that had purchased the resort

Mid Pines Number Eighteen, circa 1980
(Courtesy: Tufts Archives)

from the Cosgroves back in 1973. Mid Pines Development Group, LLC was composed of the Bell family, Stuart Ridenhour (of Winston-Salem), Jack Campbell (Winston-Salem) and Jim Marsh (High Point). They purchased Mid Pines from Manor Care Inc., the parent company of Quality Inns. The new ownership group set about to restore the hotel to its former glory and repair an aging and neglected Donald Ross golf course.

Although few were made, the architectural changes at Mid Pines during the seventies and eighties were done to suit the needs of Quality Inns. With little golf operations experience, it was apparent the owners didn't recognize the gem in their possession. The changes made by Quality Inns were strictly for ease of play and convenience of operation. For instance, cart paths were rerouted to go from the tees directly down the center of the fairway before allowing carts to fan out in all directions. In addition, a new sand bunker was built behind the eighth green. Although blind from the tee, the purpose was to corral mishit tee shots to maintain pace of play. They also rebuilt the ninth green larger to grow grass more efficiently. The change to nine green is a good example of forgoing strategic challenge (a small target on a short par four) for maintenance concerns.

Chip King was hired by the Quality Inns group in 1984 and was the head professional at Mid Pines until 2007. He recalled that his first employers did not really capitalize on one of the few intact Ross courses. *"They never really had a true vision for the golf course and weren't doing the detailed things that should be done to keep it at the highest level."*

Mid Pines Number Fourteen
(Courtesy: Pine Needles/Mid Pines)

The state of confusion at Mid Pines was immediately changed once the Bells took over in 1994. In addition to an infusion of capital and maintenance expertise, cart paths were rerouted as far from the fairways and greens as possible and continued conditioning brought Mid Pines back to respectability. Today Mid Pines is arguably the most well-preserved of all of Ross's Sandhills courses. The routing remains unchanged, as do the majority of the greens complexes. In fact, only three greens have been rebuilt since 1921. In addition to eight and nine, Director of Maintenance Dave Fruchte rebuilt the fourteenth green to improve the turfgrass quality in 1995. The 1921 Mid Pines yardage of 6,393 yards has only increased to 6,528 yards.

Mid Pines Number Seventeen
(Courtesy: Pine Needles/Mid Pines)

The new fourteenth green at Mid Pines was not Fruchte's first foray into renovation, though. He and his boss, General Manager Kelly Miller, made numerous changes to Pine Needles back in 1990. The course had largely been left untouched from Ross's day, except for a few changes by Miller's father-in-law, Bullet Bell. From 1959 until his death in 1984, Bell made minor tweaks to the golf course, mostly in response to a lack of irrigation water. In addition to expanding the third and fifth greens toward the front, he added tee boxes on ten, eleven, and eighteen and built new sand bunkers on three, ten, eleven, and thirteen. In 1981, Bullet teamed up with Pete Dye to install a group of mounds in the corner of the dogleg on fourteen. Miller and

Pine Needles Number Five, circa 1992
(Courtesy: Richard Mandell)

Fruchte then set about a modest program of returning the course to what they interpreted as Ross's design ideals and completely re-seeded the greens in Penncross bentgrass.

Over the previous seventy-five years, the accumulation of sand in the bunkers elevated the floors above the putting surfaces. A stark example was the left greenside bunker on the first hole, which sat a full one foot higher than the putting surface. They re-established the edges and lowered the floors to rectify the oddity.

In addition to the bunker work, three greens were revised by the removal of the extra putting surface added by Bullet Bell. Two greenside bunkers Bell added on the third hole were also eliminated. Miller and Fruchte also expanded the fifth green to the left, and took almost fifteen paces off the front of a very narrow sixteenth green.

The Pine Needles team got the renovation bug, and for good reason. Partially as a result of their successful work (but mostly because of Peggy Kirk Bell's reputation), the USGA awarded the 1996 U. S. Women's Open to Pine Needles. So successful was the event (won by Annika Sorenstam) that the resort was awarded a second Open an amazing five years later. Additional changes were necessary in preparation for the 2001 event and the Pine Needles staff quickly obliged.

In 1999, Miller and Fruchte continued what they began in 1990, but with much more experience in design and in the day-to-day consequences of their work. The original tenth hole was a sharp dogleg-left par four that Bullet Bell converted to a five with a new back tee in 1959. Over the years, Bullet had let one of Ross's sand bunkers at the corner of the dogleg revert to a natural state yet kept a second bunker intact. Miller and

Peggy Kirk Bell
(Courtesy: Pine Needles/Mid Pines)

Fruchte moved both bunkers uphill thirty-five yards to help keep today's golfers from cutting the corner. They also restored two bunkers in front of ten green and a series of fairway cross bunkers about fifty yards in front of seventeen green while reworking the greenside bunkers. Once again the USGA held a flawless event, this time won by Sorenstam's main rival, Karrie Webb. Once again they made plans for a third Women's Open in 2007.

In preparation for the event, the Pine Needles team laid out their most ambitious plans yet, much to the chagrin of family matriarch, Peggy. *"I was really upset about changing, but it's progress and* [today's] *ball. People are younger and stronger."* The club became the first to attempt a complete restoration in the Sandhills.

This time, Miller brought golf course architect John Fought from across the country to attempt his very first Ross restoration. On the surface, the designer choice seemed odd. However, Fought had played

Annika Sorenstam Winning the 1996 Women's Open
(Courtesy: Pine Needles/Mid Pines)

The Par Five Opening Hole at Pine Needles
(Courtesy: Pine Needles/Mid Pines)

college golf at Brigham Young University and on the PGA Tour with one of Peggy's sons-in-law, Pat McGowan. To Fought, the Pine Needles restoration was a dream job. He revered Ross as an architect and Fought was eager to uncover many interesting, lost features he recalled from twenty-five years of playing Pine Needles.

Fruchte obtained aerial photographs of the golf course taken in 1939, 1950, and 1966 from the North Carolina Division of Soil and Water Conservation. The photos showed the size and shape of the greens and the positioning of tees, bunkers, and fairways. Fruchte had access to a routing as well. Over the years, the greens had lost their original contours and dimensions and had became smaller and more oval-shaped.

The project included completely rebuilding the greens complexes as well as lengthening some holes to recapture landing areas. Miller made much-needed length a primary goal, *"A major focus was to restore shot values. If Ross were alive today, he would be making changes. He would want to restore the shot integrity."*

Ross's routing philosophy often dictated laying out golf holes with landing areas located on top of hills. As technology enabled golfers to hit the ball farther, however, Ross's targets were easily carried, providing even greater distance advantages off the tees. Many greens that were reachable with a long iron in the thirties were reached with a pitching wedge by the late nineties so new back tees on six, seven, eleven, and twelve restored the lost landing areas. Additional tees were built as well, stretching the course to over 7,000 yards.

The New Tenth Green at Pine Needles
(Courtesy: Pine Needles/Mid Pines)

Pine Needles Number Fourteen
(Courtesy: Pine Needles/Mid Pines)

This Hole Began Life as the Fourth Hole of Pine Needles...
(Courtesy: Tufts Archives)

...Today it is the Third Hole
(Courtesy: Pine Needles/Mid Pines)

1950 Aerial Photograph of Pine Needles. Midland Road Separates the Course from Mid Pines at the Northeast Corner of the Aerial
(Courtesy: Moore County USDA)

The Pine Needles team also returned the fourteenth and fifteenth holes to their original pars (four and five respectively). *"At some point, houses were built behind fifteen tee and that made them move the tee up,"* Miller pointed out. *"There was plenty of room to pull the tee back to accomplish this task."* The new tee also brought a grassy swale and a sand bunker in front of the green back into play for most players.

The new tees and other changes were big improvements to Pine Needles, but the most memorable aspect of Fought's restoration efforts was his greens complex work. The course's Penncross greens, seeded in 1990, were replaced with a combination of Penn A-1 and Penn A-4 bentgrass. These grasses produce a very dense and upright growing leaf that thrives at a tight mowing height in hot weather. Because of these attributes, they were the logical choice to handle the warmer temperatures of early summer (when the Women's Open is held). All the greens were kept in their original positions except the tenth, which was relocated sixty yards behind the old green.

The results of the Pine Needles restoration garnered great praise from the national media despite fundamental variations to some of the Ross features and an over-reliance on conditioning (which created a discrepancy between restoration and modernization). This is where the divergence between a *"pure"* restoration and the modern game exists. The new bunker work at Pine Needles did not truly reflect Ross's design tendencies. Almost every bunker on the course now has flat sand and grass faces that often obscure a golfer's view of the sand from the landing areas.

The design team chose to incorporate Zoysia grass on the bunker faces for maintenance purposes as well as to create an aesthetic contrast for the eye. Unfortunately, the grass choice is the only thing the golfer can rely upon to locate these hazards. Ross never had the luxury of using grass types to distinguish the presence of a hazard. He specifically relied upon flashing enough sand where necessary to catch the golfer's attention. Another issue with the bunker work was the lack of variation in bunker style beyond the flat bottom style. Ross utilized a variety of bunker types, incorporating concave bottoms in many forms with most of his bunkers. Yet despite these minor issues, the goal of re-introducing the world to a Donald Ross original was accomplished.

ANOTHER COURSE THAT LOST ITS IDENTITY OVER TIME IS SOUTHERN PINES COUNTRY CLUB. There is very little information regarding the original course design available. Neither are there any drawings at the club (many were lost in the clubhouse fire of 1971) nor at the Tufts Archives. In fact, there is no concrete evidence of Donald Ross's involvement with the golf course. Either his contribution was legend that has grown to fact over the years, or he deliberately kept his name off of the project because it was in conflict with his employers' business. He freely discussed Pine Needles and Mid Pines (which were Tufts developments) over the years but the same could not be said about Southern Pines Country Club.

Perpetually in the shadows of Mid Pines and Pine Needles, Southern Pines Country Club sits on one of the most scenic golf properties in the Sandhills. Mostly due to a lack of capital, very few changes had ever been made to the golf course until 1989 when the Elks Lodge brought John LaFoy in to renovate the greens.

Along with Tom Jackson, LaFoy learned the golf course design business from George Cobb, who practiced in a completely different era than Ross. By the time Cobb was at his busiest, design trends moved away from golden age principles and more toward heavy earthmoving and a focus on playability.

LaFoy's new design for the Elks course incorporated tiered greens for visibility and numerous mounds in clear contrast to the subtle contouring achieved by Ross and his contemporaries. In 1996, the driving range was renovated by in-house staff, prompting a few changes to the third (now known as the Cardinal) nine. These alterations included converting the sixth hole from a par three to a par four and the seventh hole from a four to a five. Also, the ninth hole was relocated to south of the driving range.

Still owned and managed by the Elks Lodge, Southern Pines Country Club is a hidden gem. For years, the club's struggles came from tight control by the National Elks office, which limited advertising and outside play. Budgetary constraints led to deteriorating facilities and hampered daily maintenance to the point that the Cardinal nine was closed in 2004. Even with such a drastic cost cutting move, the staff struggles to just keep the existing eighteen fairways and greens mown on a regular basis.

The Elks are working feverishly to create a new image and expand the layout's notoriety. Richard Mandell was hired to work with the golf committee and the Elks Exalted Ruler to develop a renovation

The Fifth Hole at Southern Pines Country Club
(Courtesy: Jay Bursky)

business plan for the golf course. My vision for the future of Southern Pines Country Club is a microcosm of the future of golf not just in the Sandhills, but across the country. Supplemented by an aerial photograph of the course from 1939, my goal is to return the site to a rough-hewn and natural state more associated with Sandhills golf of the early twentieth century. Controlled underbrush burns, the clearing of woods to expose dramatic sand dunes, and the elimination of all non-Ross features will establish this course as a Sandhills jewel at a very reasonable cost. Southern Pines Country Club's character will come from the lay of the sandy land. As dramatic as the site it sits on, the course will challenge players based on thoughtful choice and not pure strength. A great example is the fifth hole which will be widened to the left to give the golfer two routes: Along the ridge on the left or the valley to the right. Rotating the first greenside bunker on the right towards the center of the fairway will necessitate even more thought. The final product will be an early twentieth-century experience for the twenty-first century golfer.

hole number

detailed grading and perspectives

100 0 200
200 50 100

MICHAEL
STRANTZ
STUDIOS

CHAPTER FIFTEEN
MINIMALISM RETURNS TO THE SANDHILLS

"Jack and his people were fairly emphatic that if they were going to do the golf course, they would do the golf course."

- Terry Brown, Forest Creek Principal

MANY OF THE SANDHILLS COURSES BUILT DURING THE LAST DECADE OF THE TWENTIETH CENTURY (SUCH AS PINEWILD'S HOLLY COURSE OR THE CAROLINA AND WOODLAKE) WERE NOT BIG-MONEY, EYE-CANDY PROJECTS LIKE PALMER'S MID SOUTH OR NICKLAUS'S NATIONAL GOLF CLUB OF THE EIGHTIES, MOSTLY DUE TO A LACK OF AVAILABLE FUNDS COMING OUT OF THE RECESSION. As the recession signaled a dangerous precedent in overspending, the response was a changing landscape of golf architecture in America.

By the mid-nineties – in terms of design – almost everything had been tried in reaction to the previous era's trends. Architects as a whole had readily accepted the idea of not reinventing the design wheel. Just as Robert Trent Jones shook up the status quo of the golden age and Pete Dye altered the face of golf design in the eighties, a new movement established something completely different from the excesses of the late eighties and early nineties.

This new movement of golf course design is known as the age of minimalism. Minimalist golf courses are defined simply as layouts which had very little movement in their features and mimicked the natural contours of the land just like architects had done during the golden age – but with one difference: Architects of many mid-nineties minimalist tracks simply moved an excess of dirt to create softer features (hardly a true minimalist approach). Nonetheless, the results were an improvement from the artificiality that plagued the art since large-scale earthmoving equipment was introduced in the fifties. Minimalism sparked a renaissance in golf architecture and was clearly evident in the newest Sandhills project called Forest Creek Golf Club.

Taking a page from the successful business plan of The Country Club of North Carolina, Forest Creek Golf Club focused on the upper echelons of the wealthy for membership. Like CCNC, Forest Creek also had plans for 36 holes. Pointed out club founder Terry Brown:

> *"If we were going to do a golf course, we wanted to do a private golf course. Our family has always been involved with private golf courses. We wanted to have a very high-end and exclusive club so we retained a company in New York to give us a feasibility study as to what our dream would be and whether it would work. The conclusion was that we could be successful if we followed the pattern of being truly a private club with a high-end golf course and high-end architecture."*

Like many of the courses built in the Midland Farms area between Pinehurst and Knollwood, the Forest Creek site was previously an orchard. Part of the land sat on the old James Barber estate. The rest of the property was owned by George T. Bilyeu and originally called Bilyeu Farms. Bilyeu grew grapes and dewberries on the land until he sold it to G.M. Cameron for $12,500 in 1928. In November of 1931, George E. Turnure of Lenox, Massachusetts took possession of the land and turned the old homestead into a shooting lodge. A 22-room farmhouse was also built. Charles Louis Meyer bought Bilyeu Farms in 1942 and it ended

Bilyeu Farmhouse
(Courtesy: Tufts Archives)

up in the hands of his three grandchildren: Terry Brown, his brother Louis Meyer Brown, and their cousin, Heidi Hall-Jones.

Terry Brown first visited his grandparents in Pinehurst as an infant in 1948. *"Back in the early days, all the activity for people was either horseback riding or golf. We did do a fair amount of quail shooting on this property,"* said Brown. *"Besides that, any evening activities were at The Carolina Hotel. There really wasn't anything else with the exception of The Dunes Club* [a type of speakeasy along Midland Road]."

What started as a 500-acre farm for the Meyers expanded to more than three-thousand acres. *"Over the years, anytime a piece of property came up for sale that was on our border, my grandfather bought it,"* Terry related. *"He was a horseman and loved fox hunting. The more land he could get, the more fox hunting he could do, which was his passion. My grandmother's passion was golf."* At the time Forest Creek was started, the property stretched almost to the Moore County Airport.

In the early nineties, a simple sign advertising *"Bent Creek Country Club"* sat along Airport Road across from Longleaf Country Club and Sandhills Community College. Rumors persisted around town that Pete Dye was to be the architect for the project, but when Pete was approached to do the design, he turned the Browns down due to his commitment to Pine Needles. By the time Pine Needles shelved their project, Dye came back to the Browns only to learn Tom Fazio had already routed 36 holes. Terry recalled:

> *"We actually went under contract with Fazio in 1987. He wasn't a real well known architect at that particular time. He had done some things, but his uncle George was the famous guy. We interviewed Jack Nicklaus, Desmond Muirhead and Robert Trent Jones. We also talked with* [Ben] *Crenshaw at one point. He had not done anything at that point, but being a classical architecture kind of guy, he was interested in Pinehurst."*

According to Brown, Nicklaus did a layout first but they couldn't agree on a final plan, so the Browns went back to the drawing board and chose Fazio. *"We had a very good idea of what we wanted to do relative to the golf course. Not that we wanted to design the golf course but we wanted to have input into it. Jack and his people were fairly emphatic that if they were going to do the golf course, they would do the golf course. I guess we had enough ego ourselves that maybe we should just keep looking for somebody else."*

Of the architects the owners seriously considered, Fazio was the only architect who spent time understanding the client's goals, particularly in terms of course type, difficulty, and appearance. *"The other architects were more apt to try to impress us with what they had done, how good they were, and that their name and credentials would make the project successful,"* said Brown. *"They never really sat down and said 'it's your property, what do you want to do with it?' Fazio picked our brains as to what we wanted and he has done exactly what we wanted."*

The original development team was a joint venture between the Brown family and Wingfield Properties of Greenville, South Carolina, led by Barton Tuck (who later started GolfSouth). Terry gave Fazio free reign of the whole acreage to find the best golf holes.

Eighteenth Green of Forest Creek's South Course
(Courtesy: Forest Creek Country Club)

For the most part, Fazio's initial routing stayed true to form once construction began, but with one significant exception. Originally, the eighteenth hole was to be a par five with golfers hitting their approach over an existing lake to a green at the base of the clubhouse. After walking the hole early on, it appeared too difficult for the average player as a par five so the design team shortened it to a par four. The green was set on a peninsula in the lake.

But with design challenges came design opportunities as well. Because the shortened hole now remained on the far side of the lake (away from the clubhouse), the only way to get from the green to the clubhouse was by a circuitous cart path route around the lake or with a bridge. It was agreed that a bridge would be an eyesore. A longer route back to the clubhouse was the lesser of two evils.

The owners were now left with the extra land from the shortened hole. Recounted Brown:

> *"One night over a little bit of wine, Barton and I said maybe we should build a nineteenth hole. Barton went to Tom, told him what we were thinking about and that we recognized it wasn't traditional. If he wanted we would design it ourselves. His response was, 'you know I think that could be a fun idea, but I'll design it – you guys won't."*

So the Hog Hole was born, a par three over water that plays from 86 to 169 yards.

One reason that few changes were made from the original Fazio routing was because there were few environmental constraints to overcome. The site was primarily Longleaf Pine forest with some wetlands. The only other changes from the initial routing were a relocation of the seventh green and eighth tee, as well as minor adjustments to the driving range. From the beginning of the design process, eighty-nine red-cockaded woodpecker trees were preserved.

The Forest Creek team expected to begin construction in the late eighties, but the recession delayed the project until November 1994. By then, sixty-five founding members pledged $90,000 each (totaling $5.5 million) to begin construction. In addition, because the Browns owned the property outright, they had the luxury of choosing the right time to break ground without any pressure from the banks.

Construction of the South Course went very smoothly for all involved, including golf course superintendent Bill Patton, who arrived on site in the spring of 1995 with nine holes already shaped. A hallmark of the Fazio organization is the production of very few construction drawings, a concept that requires on-site involvement on a regular basis. Instead of producing grading plans, a field representative from Fazio's office works in concert with the shaper, often relying on him to develop conceptual ideas into detailed golf course features. Despite the seemingly free reign the shapers were given, the Forest Creek owners weren't concerned with the project getting out of hand. *"It wasn't as though we weren't there everyday seeing what was happening and throwing a little input in here and there,"* recalled Terry Brown. Fazio made about twenty-five site visits during construction himself, despite having his project manager on site just as often.

The South Course wanders through one of the finer pieces of Sandhills property. The golf course features resemble classic golden elements, with a combination of grass-faced and flashed-sand bunkers. The greens complexes have numerous hollows and swales.

A Cross Bunker on Forest Creek South Number Three
(Courtesy: Richard Mandell)

The par-five third hole particularly stands out with a cross bunker cut into the middle of the fairway about 150 to 200 yards away the green. Almost any decent tee shot will leave golfers with a dilemma on their hands for the next shot. One may lay up, carry the bunker, or play to either side. The golfer who plays conservatively short has a long, uphill approach to a partially blind putting surface.

On the surface, the wide fairways and minimal number of hazards give the golfer a false sense of ease, yet by the time they reach the last few holes it is readily apparent that the subtle putting surfaces and deceiving targets can wreak havoc for all talent levels.

IN 1949, EUGENE AND SHEILA DEPASQUALE BOUGHT ONE OF THE TUFTS'S DAIRY FARMS, ITS VAST ROLLING PASTURES AND ITS TWO HUNDRED ANGUS BROOD COWS. Beginning in 1952, the newly-named Little River Farm (named after the Little River that runs through the property) became one of the largest quarter-horse breeding farms in the south. Covering 850 acres, the farm had plenty of pasture land and three-hundred stalls for horses to board during the winter months. By 1977, Little River had half-mile and five-eighths mile tracks with blacksmith shops and eleven barns.

Arguably the best property for a golf course in the Sandhills, Little River Farm has all the variety a golf course architect seeks in a piece of land. The site has a great balance of woods and pasture with long vistas. The property has more elevation change than most sites in Moore County (with a variation of more than one hundred feet). Most sites with that much elevation include unusable steep slopes. Yet at Little River, the rolling pastures and easy slopes allow for playable golf holes whose character evolves from the lay of the land. Little River, Wads Creek, and a good amount of wetlands were perfect natural features for a golf course routing. One more feature was an old quarry operation (from 1969 to 1975) that left two crystal clear lakes and spoil areas reminiscent of the Pit.

Since the early eighties, plans for a golf course development at Little River had been on the periphery of becoming reality. Dan Maples was impressed with the site from the start. *"We tried to get that property before we got The Pit, but it didn't work out. I thought it was a great location. Great water, great distance, good timber. It is right on the edge of the Sandhills so there is clay and a sandy gravel mix."* At one point, Tom Doak was hired to develop a golf course routing as an enticement for potential joint venture groups.

Tired of waiting for a viable development partner in the project, developer Bobby Blanche (son-in-law of the DePasquales) donated 190 acres to the Town of Carthage to build Little River Farms Golf Course in 1995. He held onto 520 more acres to build a hotel, single-family homes, condominiums, and townhouses. The town turned to Maples to design and build the course. Immediately, the parallels to the former Starland Farms came to mind. *"It had great facilities like Longleaf,"* Maples said. *"That's a lot of heritage and a lot of vertical beauty you don't get right away."*

The same drive to build Longleaf quickly was also true at Little River for the Maples organization. With Dan again acting as his own contractor, the construction process had a major influence on the golf course design. At a site like Little River, though, it didn't really matter that much. *"We cleared it, grubbed*

Little River Farm
(Courtesy: Tufts Archives)

Little River Golf Resort Number Eight
(Courtesy: Little River Golf Resort)

Little River Golf Resort Number Six
(Courtesy: Little River Golf Resort)

it, moved all the field material, and installed the irrigation in three months. Then we got twenty-two inches of rain, yet still got it back on time that same season." Just as he did at Longleaf, Dan incorporated the horse tracks at Little River into the design of the golf course. The tenth hole plays from one corner of the half-mile track to the opposite corner, and the driving range sits inside the larger track. Dan placed one tee for the range on top of a hill and another tee at the bottom of the hill. He used the old barns for the pro shop and maintenance facility.

Like at Longleaf, where to begin construction had a bearing on expediting the process. At Little River, the holes in the pasture were built first. *"We started in the open where we could start moving dirt right away,"* Maples remembered. *"We must have had thirty-five pieces of heavy equipment out there running at one time."* Although construction lasted only a few months, the process was not an easy one. *"I'd say the toughest holes to build were the ones around the quarries and back over to thirteen, fourteen, and fifteen. They were the wettest and hardest to deal with."* The wooded, back nine holes wrapped around Little River and were the last ones built because removing timber and building haul roads were the biggest challenges. By the end of construction, despite a great natural piece of property, Maples and his crew managed to move almost 300,000 cubic yards of dirt.

In 1996, the town sold the course back to Bobby Blanche. The deal was worth more than $5 million, including the assumption of Carthage's initial $3.9 million construction loan. Blanche decided it was in his best interest to control the whole piece of property to protect his future real estate interests. So he began another search for a joint venture partner to develop the real estate, this time with a much more valuable amenity to work around. In 2005, he sold the property to an investment group from New Jersey.

THE LAST TWO MOORE COUNTY GOLF COURSES TO BE BUILT MAY VERY WELL BE THE TWO MOST STRIKING AND DRAMATIC IN THE SANDHILLS. Tobacco Road Golf Club and the North Course at Forest Creek may also best reflect the stark desolation that characterized the original Pinehurst courses and can make a case for authentic minimalism in that regard. In the early 1900's, the reason for a course's rough-hewn edges was the inability to grow grass. But one hundred years later, the reason was intense competition on a local scale and rankings on a national level.

Rough-hewn edges don't begin to describe Tobacco Road Golf Club. Gigantic dunes, enormous pits, and ragged, eroded tree lines existed long before the first bulldozers began clearing fairways. In a previous life, the site was a sand and gravel pit excavated by the Lee Paving Company, which has been responsible for paving most of the roads in Lee County (north of Moore) since 1957. Lee Paving principals Mark Stewart and Tony Woodell first contemplated the idea of being golf course developers while on a golf trip to Myrtle Beach. The simple joy of golfing with friends inspired the two to develop a daily-fee golf course. *"The more we looked at it we realized we already owned probably one hundred acres of an old sand pit that was perfect for a golf course,"* Stewart said.

The pit Stewart referred to had been continuously mined by his family since 1962. With such a unique piece of land, Stewart and Woodell found an equally unique golf course designer to create Tobacco Road. While interviewing a variety of candidates, they repeatedly heard the same name mentioned from industry sources. In the mid-nineties, he had not yet become the recognizable force he would a few short years later.

Not knowing much about this hot talent, they ventured back to Myrtle Beach to visit Caledonia Golf and Fish Club and were finally introduced to its creator, a former Tom Fazio shaper by the name of Mike Strantz. Stewart recalled:

> *"We convinced him to come take a look at our project. There are a lot of great golf courses in the Sandhills and we did not need another Donald Ross golf course. Mike had an artistic flair and we felt the nature of the course was something we could market. A designer [who did] one project at a time would be a unique approach as well."*

Not a formally trained architect, Strantz approached design with more of an artist's perspective. This artistic vision was another aspect that appealed to the Tobacco Road team. Typically after completing a golf course's routing, Strantz would visit each tee and landing area to draw the exact view of what he wanted built. This was something Stewart did not see in the other candidates for the project. Recalled Stewart:

> *"He visualized what he wanted to happen on the hole, sat out there with his sketch pad and took a couple of hours to draw the view. Mike would show the perspective off the tee and then he would ride down to the hinge point in the fairway and say, 'Here's what I want the golfer to see when he finds his ball right here'. He really tried to plan every shot of every hole."*

Mike Strantz Sketch of Hole Six at Tobacco Road Golf Club
(Courtesy: Tobacco Road)

Hole Six at Tobacco Road Golf Club
(Courtesy: Impact Golf Marketing 2006)

At Tobacco Road, Strantz completed a routing plan but didn't necessarily commit to the bunkering or the hazards until after each hole was cleared. He sketched one hole at a time, gave the drawing to the shaper, and then moved to the next hole. In the process, he averaged four days per week on site.

While the individual golf holes may have been easy to come by for the artist in Strantz, his routing was the real challenge because the property was oddly-shaped and included 35 acres of wetlands. Although he was far from a Donald Ross disciple, Strantz also utilized high points for his tees, landing areas, and green sites while playing over extreme topographical changes and natural watercourses. Every one of the 220 acres was needed to create a golf course that plays just 6,554 yards from the tips.

Many of the more memorable holes were routed with very little earthwork even though most people think the topographic drama was created by Strantz' team. A perfect example of this erroneous presumption is the very first hole, where golfers stare at mammoth 60-foot-tall ridges from the tee. The first reaction is that

The Opening Tee Shot at Tobacco Road Golf Club
(Courtesy: Impact Golf Marketing 2006)

these mountains are the product of an over-zealous designer. The reality is that Strantz directed his crew to enhance a pair of existing thirty-foot spoil piles to define both sides of the fairway. Pits and spoil piles also gave birth to the seventh, eighth, ninth, thirteenth, fifteenth, sixteenth, and eighteenth holes.

A product like the opening tee shot has the tell-tale signs of a Mike Strantz design. *"Architects at some golf courses want to ease you into the round, but he didn't want to do that at Tobacco Road. He wanted to challenge you on the very first tee shot,"* Stewart points out. Clearly making a big statement (natural or not), Strantz believed in 18 signature holes on every project. He wanted those signature holes to look hard, yet play easy. At Tobacco Road, golfers may say that no hole plays easy, but most play easier than they look. Ample fairways

Tobacco Road's Seventh Green
(Courtesy: Glenn Dickerson Photography)

Mike Strantz Sketch of the Seventh Hole
(Courtesy: Tobacco Road)

Tobacco Road Number Thirteen
(Courtesy: Glenn Dickerson Photography)

are obscured from view on many holes, creating a sense of unease for golfers. Wildly undulating greens are still large enough to handle multiple-foot elevation changes and are some of the most enjoyable putting surfaces in the Sandhills.

The most controversial hole at Tobacco Road is the thirteenth. A par five stretching to 573 yards, the 13th is a double dogleg that begins with a tee shot into a pit. The second shot is squeezed by two spoil mounds to the point where golfers can see just a sliver of the second landing area (with no evidence of the green). The gambler can blindly play as far left as desired, but greed will make the approach to the putting surface much more difficult. The green is just sixteen yards deep and almost completely obscured by a large spoil pile from the old sand pit days. Stewart is caught off guard with the amount of criticism Strantz received regarding thirteen, most of it undeserved: *"The thirteenth green complex gets a lot of publicity and comments, but a lot of that was already there. Mike really didn't construct it, it's something he left."*

Ironically, the one hole that appears the most natural is the one hole that was completely fabricated. Number eleven is a 531-yard par five dogleg-right which plays over a wetland area to a wide fairway. The putting surface is perched almost at a ninety-degree angle to the fairway but separated by a chasm. Thirty feet below the green sits a combination sand bunker/waste area which to the naked eye is clearly another pit from the mining operation. But Strantz dug the bunker completely from scratch to create the ultimate in risk-reward strategy. The golfer can bite off as much as he chooses, regardless of the length of the tee shot. In many cases, the shorter tee shot is the safer choice. The longer the tee shot, the thinner the neck of fairway becomes for the second shot.

Tobacco Road Number Sixteen
(Courtesy: Glenn Dickerson Photography)

Clearing of Tobacco Road began in August of 1997 and the first greens were grassed the following July. Tobacco Road Golf Club epitomizes the original Pinehurst look more than most other courses in the Sandhills. The success of Tobacco Road lies mostly in the site, but also because strategic marketing plans and calculated real estate feasibility studies were passed over in favor of creating something special for pure enjoyment and the chance to be different. *"We didn't do it to win any awards. It was a labor of love; to have some fun and make a little money,"* said Stewart.

In addition to a great concept, Stewart and his partners also have one of the very few Mike Strantz golf courses in the world. *"At that time, Mike was talking about doing maybe twenty golf courses in his career, but unfortunately he didn't make that. We felt it would be a limited edition so to speak, but we are sad it's as limited an edition as it is."* Tragically, Strantz passed away from throat cancer in 2005. Yet in a very short period he created many memorable layouts, including a sand pit masterpiece in the middle of tobacco country.

FOREST CREEK GOLF CLUB ESTABLISHED ITSELF AS ONE OF THE PREMIER PRIVATE COUNTRY CLUBS IN THE SANDHILLS WITH A WORLD-CLASS TOM FAZIO GOLF COURSE, AN EXCLUSIVE MEMBERSHIP, AND IMMACULATE CONDITIONING IN A VERY SHORT TIME. Rivaled only by The Country Club of North Carolina, Forest Creek clearly secured its identity and had the capital influx to avoid the struggles and potholes so many other Sandhills courses found.

Forest Creek North Course Number Eleven
(Courtesy: Bill Patton)

Unlike developments such as Mid South and National, Forest Creek wasn't heavily burdened with bank debt. Because Terry Brown and his family owned their property free and clear, there was no need to build up a membership just to recoup initial capital. Forest Creek's solid financial grounding allowed its owners to weather unforseen circumstances such as economic recession, international affairs, or natural disasters. *"The chances of failing (and failing rather quickly) are a lot smaller if you have a piece of property where you really don't have debt, because you can control costs. We have never gone out and built all of our road systems, surveyed all our lots, or put up the big clubhouse until such period of time as we really needed it,"* Brown confided. He waited six years after the South course was completed to finalize the North course.

One facility with two golf courses is always a design challenge, especially when the same golf course architect is chosen for all 36 holes. To make matters more challenging for Tom Fazio, the North

(L-R) Terry Brown, Bo Elling And Tom Fazio Survey Construction on the Tenth Hole of Forest Creek's North Course
(Courtesy: Bill Patton)

course was built in five different phases over a nine-year period. Staying true to his word, Brown and his partners built only what they absolutely needed to build and only when they absolutely needed to build. In their case, the forward progress was driven purely by residential home sales. As golf-front home sites were sold, more golf holes were needed to sell additional golf lots.

When the South course was built, the first three holes of the North course were also completed and they (the future first, second, and eighteenth holes) served as a temporary practice-hole loop for the members. Ground was broken on six more holes in 2001 (three, four, five, twelve, thirteen, and fourteen) and ten and eleven were added two years later. An irrigation lake was needed by 2004, so construction began on the three holes surrounding it (fifteen, sixteen, and seventeen). After another six months, the North course was finished as the sixth, seventh, eighth, and ninth holes came on line.

The silver lining in the lengthy schedule was that the club could experiment with ways to distinguish the new course from the South course. The original North course design concept distinguished the sand

Forest Creek North Course Number Eighteen
(Courtesy: Bill Patton)

bunkers with a high-flashed, clean-edge sand line that resembled the bunkering at Augusta National. The high bunker lines simply bled into the horizon line and weren't framed by a grass face like the more golden age bunkers of the South course.

During the few years the practice holes were up and running, the membership came to the conclusion that the Augusta look wasn't what they wanted for the North course. Brown and Superintendent Bill Patton approached Fazio about a more rough-hewn look such as one might encounter at Pine Valley. Tom agreed and as the remaining holes were built, the golf course features took on a shaggier look and bunkers receded into the landscape.

With the completion of the North course, Forest Creek Golf Club boasts two distinct world-class Fazio courses on a piece of property which is tailor-made for Sandhills golf. The common thread through both courses is the native sand that provides both character and playing conditions for Forest Creek. The natural vein of *"Pinehurst sugar"* helped to transition the formal sand bunkers on the South course into native waste areas along its edges. Yet the North course possesses nothing but native sand waste areas as hazards.

From a conditioning standpoint, nothing lends itself better to a fast, firm playing surface than the native sand and Patton is very thankful. *"That's one feature of this club that makes my job a little more satisfying. We have members who want good playing conditions and I can't really get it too firm or fast enough for them."*

Although both courses have a strong golden age design character, the South course plays the part of traditional Pinehurst and the North course is the ragged landscape which harks upon a long-past era of Sandhills golf. *"I am proud of the fact that we were able to develop two distinctively different appearances on the same piece of property,"* Brown said. *"We wanted to have two different-looking, different-playing, and different-feeling golf courses of equal quality. That combination of variety and the fact that we pay a lot of attention to conditioning makes a wonderful golfing experience for people of all levels."*

Forest Creek North Course Number Thirteen
(Courtesy: Bill Patton)

CHAPTER SIXTEEN
THE HOME OF AMERICAN GOLF

"Don Padgett's job was one assignment: Bring major championship play back to Pinehurst."

- Pat Corso

HISTORY REPEATS ITSELF OFTEN IN ALL WALKS OF LIFE, BE IT GOLF OR ANYTHING ELSE. In 1901, James Tufts's act of bringing Donald Ross south to serve as golf professional changed the landscape of golf not only in Pinehurst, but across the country. Pat Corso's first act as president of Pinehurst Resort was bringing his own golf professional south to serve as Director of Golf and the results were close to the same. *"The first thing I did was bring Don Padgett in,"* Corso remembered. *"I called his son Don II,* [Professional at Firestone Country Club at the time] *and said I needed a Director of Golf. Don asked, 'Have you talked to my Dad?' I said, 'Hell no, I thought he was dead.' So I called him up, flew him in, and he took the job."* From the start, Corso and Padgett's singular goal was to bring the U.S. Open to Pinehurst and the 1987 greens renovation on Number Two was the first step in attracting notice from the USGA.

The USGA did take notice, but also thanks to Padgett's fifty-four years of friendship-building in the golf business (including a stint as PGA of America president). *"Don Padgett's job was one assignment: Bring major championship play back to Pinehurst. He and I defined that as to bring the U.S. Open to Pinehurst,"* said Corso. He and Padgett carefully set about building a relationship with the USGA. They, in turn, awarded Pinehurst Number Two the 1989 U. S. Women's Amateur.

The PGA Tour then successfully brought the Tour Championship to Pinehurst in 1991. Because Pinehurst proved the resort could handle a sizable event, the USGA awarded the 1994 Senior Open to Number

Two immediately after Craig Stadler's victory (the Tour Championship returned the following year, won by Paul Azinger). According to Brad Kocher, Pinehurst Number Two provided a much better playing field as compared to when the Tour hosted the Colgate Hall of Fame Classic there from 1977 to 1983. *"It was a good test of the top thirty players at the end of the season. We could let the course get really firm and dry, even with the old penncross greens. They* [the PGA Tour] *did not want a golf course that was going to have soft surfaces."*

Yet Corso, Padgett, Kocher, and the rest of Pinehurst were not satisfied because their eyes were on a bigger prize: the United States Open Championship. Although the course held up well to the Tour, the greens weren't firm enough for the USGA. *"The reason why we got the Open in 1999 is*

Don Padgett Served as Director of Golf Operations at
Pinehurst from 1987-2002
(Courtesy: ® Pinehurst, Inc. All Rights Reserved)

because we agreed to rebuild the greens on Number Two," recalled Corso. *"We made that promise to them in 1992 at Pebble Beach when we presented our case to the Championship Committee. David Fay always told me, though, 'Pat, if it doesn't work, we could do it on Bermuda.'"*

The official announcement that Pinehurst Number Two would be the last U.S. Open of the millennium came in January 1994. ClubCorp had five years to complete another greens renovation as well as numerous other modifications. But they first had to get through the Senior Open just a few months away. Although they were ahead of the curve because they had lengthened the eleventh and sixteenth holes in preparation for the first Tour Championship, it was agreed that any greens renovation would wait until after the Senior Open. The focus for the first USGA event in thirty years was limited to a badly-needed tree removal program.

A by-product of years of maturity was tremendous overgrowth of the pine trees and subsequent narrowing of Number Two's hole corridors. When the Pinehurst courses were originally built, the Longleaf Pine was non-existent at the resort. Over the years new pines took root, created shade and air circulation problems, and provided a backdrop to many of the green complexes. Not only did they provide depth, they also changed the wind patterns. From his days at St. Andrews where he learned about wind from Old Tom Morris to his early years in the Sandhills, Ross knew a lack of depth perception and swirling winds was an important component of his strategy, especially on Number Two.

Third Green of Pinehurst Number Two Course, circa 1991
(Courtesy: Frank Pierce)

In July of 1995, David Eger (of the USGA), Padgett, Kocher, Bob Farren, and Scott Lavis (superintendent of Number Two) evaluated every tree on the course to determine how it affected the health of the greens and the strategic merit of each hole. They were also interested in spectator viewing. Their work resulted in partial removal of trees from behind three, twelve, and sixteen. The clearing was validated by the success of the Senior Open later that year (won by Simon Hobday).

1995 WAS ALSO THE ONE-HUNDRED YEAR ANNIVERSARY OF THE PINEHURST RESORT AND THERE WERE MARKETING OPPORTUNITIES TO BE ADDRESSED BEFORE ANY RENOVATIONS TO NUMBER TWO. What better way to celebrate the Pinehurst Centennial than by construction of an eighth golf course for the resort?

Like Number Six and Number Seven, the Centennial Number Eight course would have its own clubhouse separate from the main clubhouse. But unlike its older siblings, Number Eight was strictly pegged to be a resort golf course.

Pat Corso pointed out the challenge ClubCorp faced in introducing another golf course at Pinehurst: *"Number Eight was a big decision for us. We wanted to create a private club experience in a resort environment. That was our goal."* To accomplish it, the resort handed Tom Fazio more than 420 acres two miles from the hotel. In Corso's mind, Fazio was selected by ClubCorp because he and his firm represented the best in contemporary golf design. Fazio's past experience with Pinehurst and a deep respect for its heritage made the decision an easy one.

An opportunity to become part of the Pinehurst story can even make one of the top golf architects in the world giddy. Fazio remembered the excitement (and surprise) when he got the call to design Number Eight: *"Mr. Dedman Sr. and Don Padgett left me a voice mail when I was at the Masters because they had something very important to talk to me about. I called Mr. Dedman back and he said, 'Tom we are going to do Number Eight and we want you to do it and get started immediately.'"* Tom was equally anxious to pursue the challenge set forth by his clients. *"As a designer, there are only a very few names that are synonymous with great golf. Pinehurst is one of them,"* said Fazio.

The Par Three Eighth Hole of the Centennial Course

Even though Number Eight was a separate facility, it was important for Fazio to capture the Pinehurst look, especially for the resort golfers. *"You want to give people the Pinehurst feel, you don't want to design a different golf course.* [Most people] *put Number Two in* [their] *mind. Not necessarily the elevations, but the pine trees, sand on the edges, gentle rolls around greens and roll-offs. That's what I call the Pinehurst look, and that's what we tried to incorporate on Number Eight."*

The Centennial course debuted in 1996 to rave reviews. Fazio took advantage of the sandy soils much like he did with Forest Creek, exposing vast waste areas along the fairways. At strategic points, he challenged the golfer to cross the sand. Some of the course (holes four and nine) was built on the old Pinehurst Gun Club where Annie Oakley and others gave resort guests shooting lessons.

Number Eight was the first course ever to try a new bent grass called Penn G2 on its greens. This was a huge gamble for such a high profile project, not only because it was untested, but because the USGA was breathing down the resort's neck to come up with a new putting surface for the 1999 Open. Pinehurst decided that the use of G2 on Number Eight would determine its viability for Number Two. If it failed, David Fay may have been forced to return Number Two's greens to Bermuda. Fortunately, G2 was a huge success.

With number eight now in the rotation, clubcorp returned its focus to preparing number two for the open. In discussions with the USGA, it was apparent to Kocher and his staff that the greens would have to be rebuilt due to the errors from the 1987 reconstruction. Many construction techniques from the eighties were of the experimental type and forced many clubs into additional renovations soon thereafter. Pinehurst Number Two was no different. The errors from 1987 included a deficiency of sub-surface drainage, poor grass seed quality (a more accurate description may be: not as advanced as the nineties), and an ill-conceived use of plastic liner to separate the green from its surrounds. *"The drainage was impounding water against the fronts due to a lack of perimeter drainage so we had to go in and rip the plastic out,"* Kocher recalled. *"We dug down around the green and you had to back up for about a half a day because it was septic. It smelled like a sewer."*

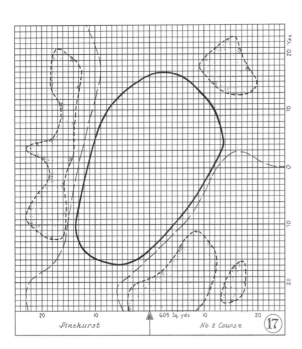

Rassie Wicker's 1962 Drawing of the Seventeenth Green of Number Two
(Courtesy: Tufts Archives)

For the 1996 renovations, the goal was to again maintain the integrity of the slopes as Ross intended. As-built maps from 1962 recorded by long- time Pinehurst surveyor, Rassie Wicker, were used to return perimeters and restore sizes of each green. A local engineering firm, Hobbs and Upchurch, recorded all the existing contours on a three foot by three foot grid and ensured they were put back the exact same way by the contractor. Modern technology allowed for an accuracy of two-hundredths of a foot in elevation, far from the mule and drag pan technology of Ross's time or bulldozer blade accuracy of Henson Maples' era.

The greens were then painstakingly rebuilt following the most recent USGA greens construction recommendations. For Brad Kocher and Paul Jett (Superintendent of Course Number Two), this was a vital step in order to replicate the firm and fast playing conditions Ross was more apt to provide rather than the over-watered grounds most modern courses accept in chasing *"the perfect green carpet"*. The finished product was a milestone. The 1999 Open was the first to be played on USGA greens.

The greens reconstruction was just phase one of preparations for the Open. Additional changes were made to ensure the course met not only the USGA's high expectations but Kocher's and Jett's expectations as well. With Rees Jones as consulting architect, the team went about final tweaking of Number Two. Double-head irrigation was installed around the green complexes to ensure proper coverage for both the putting surfaces and the surrounding slopes, which were converted from common Bermuda grass to Bermuda 419.

The standard practice of preparing Number Two for a national event meant the course was lengthened yet again. Holes five, six, nine, ten, twelve, sixteen, and eighteen were all extended, bringing the course's total length to 7,175 yards. In addition, many tees were raised to improve visibility (including five, six, nine, and seventeen). The biggest change was moving the eighteenth tee to the left (behind seventeen green). Interestingly, this was the tee's original location prior to 1923.

The project expanded into a full-blown bunker renovation as well, but was scaled back when Jones suggested a more archaeological approach. *"The USGA wanted to deepen the bunkers and I said let's just see what we've got. We found two to three feet of sand from previous years that we just dug out. This deepened them pretty much where Donald Ross had them,"* said Rees.

Picking up where they left off in 1994, the Pinehurst team continued it's tree thinning program, only this time on a more aggressive scale. As was their goal when they began tree removal, restoring some of Ross's design intentions was foremost in their plans. Every tree behind the third green was removed, providing stark contrast to how the hole's backdrop appeared in the early nineties. Tree removal behind thirteen created depth perception problems for the players, yet improved crowd control. The remaining work was limited to individual trees for sunlight and crowd circulation, but with one exception. Taking a cue from Peter Tufts twenty-five years earlier, Jett insisted upon the removal of a lone remaining tree at the corner of the dogleg on the seventh hole.

Looking Back Down the First Fairway of Pinehurst Number Two

Seventeenth Green of Pinehurst Number Two
(Courtesy: ® Pinehurst, Inc. All Rights Reserved.)

WITH RENOVATIONS TO NUMBER TWO COMPLETE, ALL PINEHURST HAD TO DO WAS MASSAGE THE GOLF COURSE INTO PERFECT CONDITION OVER THE NEXT TWO YEARS AND PREPARE FOR THE WORLD TO ARRIVE. But instead of just sitting and waiting, the resort saw an opportunity to provide not only a venue for the biggest golf tournament in the world, but to showcase their other golf courses as well. The decision was made to renovate courses One, Four, and Five before the Open. The logic of such a decision was the economies of scale in multiple renovations. What seemed illogical was that the projects were such a huge undertaking with the Open just around the corner. Regardless of any outside concern, Kocher and his staff were well up for the task. To make matters more challenging, they oversaw the renovations on One and Five themselves.

In August of 1997, plans were laid forth to renovate the greens of the Number One course, replacing the old Penncross bentgrass with Penn G2. All the sand bunkers were rebuilt and irrigation was upgraded around the green complexes. Tees were added to the fourth, fifth, ninth, twelfth, and sixteenth holes.

Right on the heels of Number One's renovation was a similar project for the Number Five course the next year. Kocher led the efforts there, but with a little help from his friend Fazio, golf course builder Bill Sessums (the former golf course superintendent at Pinewild), and Five's golf course superintendent Kevin Robinson.

The changes to Number Five started simply enough with a new irrigation system, but escalated into

Hole Number Five of Course Number One

rebuilding all the greens to USGA specifications, a new set of forward tees, and new bunker sand. Many holes were lengthened and bunkers were adjusted accordingly. In the process, Kocher and Sessums redesigned some green complexes to improve playability.

As in almost all greens renovation projects, softening of the putting slopes was of prime importance. When Number Five opened in the early sixties, putting surface slopes regularly exceeded five percent. But modern grasses require much softer contours in the (1.5 to 3.5 percent range). The putting surfaces were changed to move surface water off the greens in two or three directions. To Kocher, the results were subtle movements accentuated by faster putting speed. "*We tweaked the greens complexes so they would receive a shot and softened slopes that were a little severe*," he said.

The most significant changes to Number Five were on holes eleven and thirteen. The eleventh hole had a blind tee shot that pigeon-holed many golfers into laying up for fear of not carrying the water on their approach. Not only was the water a detriment to strategic choice, it also had no relationship to the green, which sat about twenty yards behind the pond edge along a severe slope.

The solution to this problem was a sensitive give-and-take situation for golfers of all abilities. Kocher and his team made the conscious decision to shorten the golf hole and lower the fairway in the process, providing full visibility of the fairway and water hazard off the tee. This change significantly allowed more golfers the opportunity to carry the water on their approach (provided they played the correct tees) without being forced into a lay up. But that gift was balanced by bringing the green complex down the hill, forcing golfers to sink or swim on their approach. The new green design by Fazio's team was protected by water in front and to the right.

That same design thought repositioned the putting surface of the downhill par-three thirteenth hole closer to a pond. By twisting the green complex slightly, Kocher fit it into the surrounds a little more comfortably as well. The new green became a more heroic target set at an angle off the tee instead of the old left-to-right orientation.

Eleventh Fairway and Green of Course Number Five
(Courtesy: Jay Bursky)

Although the project did not have the sizzle the Centennial Course possessed, the project was intended to accommodate member play more than anything else. But surprisingly, Number Five gets more play from members and resort guests than any other course. With professional assistance from the Fazio organization and input from his builder, Kocher was more than satisfied with the results. *"Five is a course that you could put anywhere in America and have a good membership course."*

KOCHER WISELY LEFT RENOVATIONS TO NUMBER FOUR IN THE HANDS OF TOM FAZIO. His challenge was to create another showcase property for the resort, distinct from his work on Number Eight

The Cathedral Hole in 1935 was hole six on Course Number Three.
(Courtesy: Tufts Archives)

In 1953, the hole became the fifteenth of Course Number Four.
(Courtesy: Tufts Archives)

Beginning in 1961, it became number fifteen of Course Number Five.
(Courtesy: ® Pinehurst, Inc. All Rights Reserved.)

and the other courses yet eminently playable. *"My design philosophy has never changed from day one: it's always about enjoyable, playable, dramatic golf for all levels of players,"* said Fazio. *"The philosophy is that no two golf courses ever look alike."*

Fazio didn't see any concern with creating distinction among his Sandhills courses. *"You take the land that you have and you make it fit to what your client has programmed in terms of the land uses. It is not an idealistic 'I'm going to design a golf course and this is what it's going to look like.' It doesn't happen that way – never did – never will."* To Fazio, repetition wasn't a problem.

The consensus among the principals at Pinehurst was to undertake a complete blow-up of the existing Pinehurst Number Four course, replaced by something James Walker Tufts could never have seen coming. His grandson Richard would probably have met the vision with the same disdain he had for RTJ's changes back in the seventies. Somehow, many of the members were up in arms about the potential bulldozing of a Donald Ross original.

But history clearly shows Donald Ross's Number Four course was long gone by 1999. In fact, more than sixty years before Fazio's *"new"* renovation, Leonard Tufts directed the closing of Ross's original 1919 layout. When a new Number Four appeared in 1953, only six of the original Ross holes were part of the new layout. These few holes were remodeled at least three times before ClubCorp brought Fazio back in 1999.

There were many other reasons why Number Four was chosen for a complete makeover. Course Number One and Course Number Three were just too short and Number Five was too tight (with the encroachment of houses) to become the premium facility Pat Corso envisioned. Because Number Four had the length and no homes along its fairways, it was the only candidate. Number Four also had topography, existing lakes, and extra acreage to reroute the course where Fazio saw fit.

Among the routing changes Fazio's team undertook included combining the old first and second holes into a new opening hole, converting the old third hole corridor into the new second hole, and utilizing the existing seventeen and eighteen corridors for a new par five and four. In addition, holes four, seven, eight and fourteen were relocated. The remaining golf hole corridors were left intact. Fazio kept the central lake in play

Fifteenth Fairway of the New Pinehurst Number Four Course
(Courtesy: ® Pinehurst, Inc. All Rights Reserved.)

with two golf holes as before, but the new thirteenth hole heroically followed the lake edge to the left. Unlike the old twelfth hole in this same spot, the new hole was entirely visible from tee to green.

Fazio's team completely modernized the golf course features of the new Number Four. Fazio associate Tom Marzolf called upon Pine Valley Golf Club, Royal Dornoch in Scotland, and Pinehurst Number Two as primary design influences for those features. The new course had convex plateau greens like Number Two, over 15 acres of sandy waste areas that echoed the fundamental character of Pine Valley, and a plethora of pot bunkers with uneven bottoms that one might find in Ross's hometown of Dornoch in the Scottish Highlands. The renovation work also included the expansion of the practice facilities and a new teaching center in anticipation of the Open. In order to create enough space for such an effort, Fazio's team moved the par-three eighteenth hole of Number One fifty yards to the left.

BUT THE RE-OPENING OF NUMBER FOUR HAD TO WAIT AS THE OPEN TOOK CENTER STAGE IN JUNE OF 1999. The months leading up to the event were dicey for the maintenance staff as unseasonably cool weather slowed the growth of the Bermuda rough, a vital element of any U. S. Open. Although renovations to Number Two returned the course as close to Ross's version since his death, the course setup was all USGA. The heat finally kicked in and kicked up three-inch-high rough surrounding twenty-eight to thirty yard wide fairways just for the occasion. The thirteenth hole was only twenty-five yards wide and the third was three feet tighter than that. The emphasis was on narrow and straight.

But the 1999 U.S. Open was not won with accuracy off the tee. In fact, it was won with putting and the short game. Ross's genius was a major factor in the success of this Open. Despite the typical USGA fairway width and rough heights, Paul Jett was afforded the freedom to mow the greens' surrounds down, similar to the way Ross envisioned. Options other than the standard USGA flop shot inserted doubt into the player's minds as they stood over recovery shots around the greens.

As a result, the pro's usual short game didn't garner much reward that week. Only the players who kept short shots low to the ground were the most successful in getting up and down. The lasting memories of the event were not only Payne Stewart's winning putt, but also the havoc the greens complexes wreaked on the player's games all four days. Who can forget John Daly behind the eighth green as he repeatedly hit up the slope, his apathy growing with each mishit stroke?

Stewart's final putt to edge Phil Mickelson for the Open trophy helped place Pinehurst Resort at the pinnacle of the golf world just as Robert Dedman had assured years earlier. *"What he allowed to happen here was an extraordinary willingness to supply the resources for the resort to return to its rightful place as one of the few remaining great American resorts,"* said Corso.

Within a few months of that final putt, after all the tents were put away, the completed Number Four course debuted with a bang. The entire Pinehurst staff breathed a sigh of relief as they tirelessly completed one of the most ambitious long-term renovation efforts in history, yet still pulled off the U. S. Open without a hitch. For their

Payne Stewart Statue

reward, the USGA awarded a second Open in 2005 (the six years in between was unprecedented).

Never one to rest on its laurels, it seemed that as soon as Stewart's putt dropped, ClubCorp announced plans to develop a 275-acre site with plans for a golf community, a 50-acre mixed use village, hotel space, and golf schools led by David Leadbetter and Dave Pelz. ClubCorp initially considered a site on Route 211 near Foxfire Village but settled on a location just a few miles from the main resort along Highway Five toward Aberdeen.

The land was formerly owned by an old Pinehurst friend, Robert Trent Jones. Although he passed away a few years before, an agreement had long been in place requiring a member (or members) of the Jones family to design the golf course if Trent had sold the property for a certain price. After evaluating their options, ClubCorp closed on the property with the intention of using Rees for the new Pinehurst Number Nine. At the same time, there were initial discussions with Jack Nicklaus to design Number Ten. Corso had every confidence in the world the time was right for expansion, *"The resort was growing. We didn't think we had enough golf and there was a demand at that time."*

The entire project was a more intimate, high-end approach than the existing business model at Pinehurst. The new layouts were to have completely separate memberships but with access to the other courses. The relative isolation of the project was intended to create a corporate retreat atmosphere with a small, one hundred-room inn. *"We thought the approach was to add totally new products and align them with the existing product so that they shared the heritage* [of Pinehurst]," recalled Corso.

The projected opening of the ambitious project was sometime in 2002, but it never happened. On September 11, 2001, Pat and his associates were en route to the corporate offices in Dallas to sell the final details of the project to ClubCorp founder Robert Dedman Sr. By the time they landed with plans in hand, everyone knew the project was not going to happen for a very long time.

September 11th brought the golf business to a screeching halt and the resort felt its own reverberations for the next few years. But terrorism had no place on the agenda for ClubCorp as plans for the 2005 U.S. Open were well in motion along with numerous related projects. Just as they had prior to the 1999 Open, ClubCorp was about to wrap up the twentieth century and begin the next one by undertaking renovations to their remaining courses (three, six, and seven).

For the second time since its initial debut back in 1986, Rees was invited back to Pinehurst in 2003 to supervise a complete renovation of Pinehurst Number Seven. Corso saw a clear need for change. *"We knew we had to do something with Number Seven. It had become kind of a stepchild and was being diminished by what we were doing with Four and Eight."*

Rees wholeheartedly agreed and was eager to begin, *"It's seventeen years later and I'm a whole lot more knowledgeable. It was time to make changes."* This time, Jones was afforded the luxury of bringing along his own construction crew, something he learned from his father when he started on his own way back in 1965.

Par Three Sixteenth Hole of Pinehurst Number Seven
(Courtesy: Larry Lambrecht)

"Dad had his own construction crew and I sort of carried that on, too. I learned that it was best to control your own destiny and not have to rely on somebody else's interpretation of your ideas."

The chance to oversee his own shapers allowed for much more intricate green surfaces. *"Green contours are a form of hazard. Donald Ross proved that probably to the greatest degree ever at Number Two and that's what I tried to accomplish."* In addition to greens renovation (with G2 for the putting surfaces), Rees decided to replace many of the mounds surrounding the greens with grass hollows. *"When we first designed it in 1986, there was a tendency toward framing. Now we're back to a more classic look."*

He also changed the bunker style. *"Back in the eighties, pot bunkers were really in vogue,"* Jones pointed out. *"Now that style is gone and we decided to do something completely different. We built them almost like Alister Mackenzie-style bunkers."* New bunkers were added as well as more distance to stretch the course to 7,200 yards. In the process, he rebuilt all the tees in a more traditional square style. The final product returned Number Seven to its elite private stature among the Pinehurst courses and continued the update of the entire resort.

As a continued effort to maintain grass-type consistency on all the Pinehurst greens, the decision was then made to re-grass the greens of Course Number Three in the summer of 2003. The greens were stripped of the old Penncross and reseeded with G2 Bent.

The final course to undergo changes was the Number Six course. Pinehurst Number Six always held a special place in Fazio's heart because it was one of the first golf courses he did with his Uncle George and ClubCorp never considered anyone else for the job. They began renovations in 2004. As with all the other Pinehurst

Rees Jones's renovation of Number Seven in 2003 moved away from the pot bunkers and more to what he refers to as Alister Mackenzie-styled bunkers. Above is the fifteenth green in 1986 (left) and the same green prior to grassing in 2003.
(Courtesy: Rees Jones)

Eighth Green (With Ninth Green in Background) of Pinehurst Number Three
(Courtesy: ® Pinehurst, Inc. All Rights Reserved.)

renovations, the putting surface slopes were softened and G2 was established. But a large part of the project focused on fixing the basic drainage flaws of Six. Given no choice as to their location, many of Fazio's original holes were placed in low lying areas of the property. As a result, the land plan left numerous green complexes deficient in a variety of components, from a lack of proper drainage to poor growing environments. To make matters worse, original construction was outdated and twenty-five years later, the golf course features had started to break down.

Fourth Hole of Pinehurst Number Six
(Courtesy: ® Pinehurst, Inc. All Rights Reserved.)

One of the primary fixes identified by the design team was to eliminate situations where runoff from adjoining property came onto the putting surfaces. Eight green complexes were completely renovated and the remaining ten were cored and rebuilt. The total cost of the renovation work was $1.5 million (more than two times Fazio's entire 1979 design/build contract of $650,000).

ALTHOUGH CLUBCORP HAD ONLY A SHORT TIME TO PREPARE FOR THE 2005 OPEN, THERE WAS NOT VERY MUCH TO DO TO NUMBER TWO EXCEPT MAKE IT EVEN LONGER AND NARROWER. Thirty-nine yards were added with new tees on holes two, four, eleven, and fourteen. Just like during the '99 Open, the par-five fourth and sixteenth holes played as par fours for the pros. The USGA's reasoning was part of their general philosophy and not specific to Pinehurst Number Two. *"If you have a choice between a borderline ho-hum par five and a very stern par four, we will go with the par four every time. It is good in today's game where you see players using a long iron and maybe an occasional wood into a par four,"* noted USGA Executive Director David Fay.

In June of 2005, Pinehurst Number Two played 7,214 yards long and once again had three inches of rough. But this time around, the rough was more of a factor because Kocher and his team added approximately 400 sprinkler heads to the perimeters of the golf course in 2000. *"We had a difficult time getting consistent rough in 1999 because we had to drag hoses along the tree lines,"* explained Kocher. *"We now have a system where*

Hole Eleven of Pinehurst Number Two
(Courtesy: ® Pinehurst, Inc. All Rights Reserved.)

there are heads going down the perimeter throwing [water] *in* [to the fairways]. *The rough was incredibly thick, incredibly dense, incredibly upright, and incredibly consistent. The ball dropped to the bottom every time."*

The thick rough, added length, and the narrowing of the fairways (four yards less than 1999) resulted in an Open with less aggressiveness on the part of the players. It was more a matter of survival as Michael Campbell of New Zealand ran a steady stream of pars on Sunday's back nine to a two-shot victory over Tiger Woods. The final score was the highest total (even par) in an Open since 1974's *"Massacre at Winged Foot"* yielded a seven-over-par winner in Hale Irwin.

That June week saw 42,000 spectators walk the course daily, shop more than 38,000 square feet of merchandise space, and socialize in 300,000 square feet of hospitality tents scattered throughout the grounds of Pinehurst Country Club. More than just a seven-foot-high fence was required as security focused on much more than a bunch of razorback hogs. In fact, eleven miles of green chain-link fence surrounded the facilities.

James Walker Tufts just wanted to provide a relaxing getaway in 1895. But a grand vision by many led to the completion of the 2005 United States Open Championship and the Pinehurst Resort established itself once again as the Home of American Golf.

Ross' plateau greens confounded the greatest golfers in the world in 2005.
(Courtesy: Frank Pierce)

word to best describe Ross's greens, "*Fun golf is Pinehurst* [Number Two]. *Fun golf is learning how to maneuver the ball on the ground and give yourself options.*" Jack Nicklaus shared a similar sentiment in a losing effort before Tiger was even born. Said Jack, "*I never enjoyed playing a golf course more. I learned about five things about design this week on a course fifty years old.*" This came after he (and others) lost to Johnny Miller in a playoff at the 1974 World Open. He was a fast study: Jack beat Curtis Strange the following year.

The Spirit of Pinehurst
(Courtesy: USGA)

Every day, an architect is designing (or redesigning) a green in a far away corner of the universe, trying to emulate the various hollows and dips and rolls that surround a putting surface whose appearance does not match its size. Whether you are a resort visitor playing the dream round of a lifetime or competing against the world's best in the U.S. Open, the shots required are so varied that many golfers have not the wherewithal to execute them properly. Amazingly, the game starts for most not on the tee but within twenty yards of the hole, even for Tiger Woods: "*Pinehurst* [Number Two] *is so different from any other U.S. Open because it so much more relies on the short game than pure ball striking.*" The fun and challenge lay in those confounding greens.

So how will Number Two maintain its integrity in the future? Brad Kocher thought about that back in '97: "*When we did the greens, I kept a copy of all those transit shots and placed bench marks in the ground so when somebody redoes these greens fifty years from now they will know where they are supposed to be located. They can go back and find a spot in the ground and find that reference point and elevation stored on a computer chip the size of my fingernail.*"

Pinehurst Number Two does not rely on costly waterfalls, rock walls, or acres of water and sand. Just simple high points and low points connected by grass. There is a lesson in that thought.

EPILOGUE:
THE FUTURE OF THE SANDHILLS

PINEHURST HAS OFTEN BEEN NICKNAMED THE ST. ANDREWS OF AMERICA. Although there is a strong fraternal relationship between Pinehurst Resort and the St. Andrews Links Trust, that connection stops with the actual golf courses. Layouts in St. Andrews and the North Carolina sandhills are carved out of sandy soils yet the sand golf features characteristic of Scotland are seldom replicated in the sandhills. Instead of a links strategy and rough conditions, the American ideal of perfectly controlled golf conditioning dominates the sandhills.

Unfortunately, most current golf course design and management trends in the United States are based on controlling the golfer's playing environment. Each golf hole has perfectly manicured landing areas, fully in view from the tee and waiting to catch everything like an oversized first baseman's glove. Putting greens have emerald-colored putting surfaces and always stand at attention to the golfer with a welcoming back to front slope. The bounce and roll which helped make golf such a gift in the first place are some of the qualities missing on many of the sandhills area golf courses today. The elements of randomness and mystery have been effectively removed from the game in the process.

For me as a golf course architect, great golf is all about creativity and inventiveness in shotmaking, two golfing traits which have become non-essential in today's golf design. The future sandhills golf course should be dominated by the one site characteristic that truly separates great golf courses from all the rest: SAND. Sandy soil is the defining mechanism of the sandhills area and is the best medium for creativity and inventiveness in golf course design. Yet many golf course designers ignore the freedom sandy conditions provide in golf course design. The future of Pinehurst is a golf course that maximizes the playing characteristics of sandy soils with golf course features that are reflective of conditions found in the links courses of the past.

The compact, spongy underlayment of thatch and native grasses on firm, sandy ground gives links golf its flavor. Undulation, in the form of ridges, ripples, rills, hollows, and knolls, is the primary defense found on a links course. Contours deflect one's ball from a desired path and at the same time may direct that same ball into bunkers and hollows. Today's golf should be played along similar links conditions in keeping with the origins of the game and to promote the art of shotmaking.

Sandy Pinehurst soils allow the golf course architect to use undulation to create strategic challenges for those golfers seeking out a birdie, yet still allow the lesser-skilled an opportunity to enjoy the game. The incorporation of undulating ground will result in specific targets to gain a considerable advantage. For example, natural ridges can provide landing points for bold tee shots, a stiff downslope shall give the golfer hope of gaining extra yardage, and out of a natural rise a sandy hazard can emerge to entice the golfer with an alternate (yet riskier) route. Features can be plateau fairway areas that provide better angles or views to the next target or specific quadrants of a putting surface for the aggressive player looking for a short birdie putt. Yet because undulation is truly a hazard which promotes challenge and does not unduly penalize, the disadvantaged can play at a fair pace without fighting their own physical limitations. As baby boomers get older, they will appreciate the ground game. The days when they may have once welcomed a carry over water seem less and less appealing.

With the ability to develop the rolling sand dunes of Pinehurst into dramatic links-type features, the golf course architect can correctly develop authentic rolling golf course features that more resemble the waves created by thousands of years of erosion found throughout the British Isles. Many architects fail to accurately replicate natural land forms to use as hollows and mounds. Often times it is a result of poor soil conditions, but more often than not it is the inability to recognize the merits of nature and translate them to the ground. The deficiency in mounds and hollows do not come in the high or low points which most people first recognize. It is in the inability to create broad waves between two high points or two low points. The resulting products are choppy, out of scale chocolate drops or pots.

The future of golf in the sandhills is in creating a golf course that takes full advantage of sand's ability to sustain low-profile, well-draining golf course features and hazards full of variety and strategy. Sand bunkers can appear simply as extensions out of the ground. They should mimic nature unlike artificial hazards that must be built on top of heavier soils. Sand soils also afford the opportunity to move away from the perfectly manicured fairways and re-introduce the rub of the green – sandy rough areas which bleed out of the pines and creep into the fairway.

By making a conscious effort to develop strategy on a hole by hole basis, the golf course architect can develop enough options to provide a myriad of choices for the golfer. Of course, choices on any soil can only become reality through proper fairway width. Enough of it will blur the black and white choices that render many holes boring after only one or two rounds. Instead, a wide fairway provides enough alternatives that the golfer must ponder a gray area of choices. It is this variety in strategic choice that will create memorable experiences and repeat play.

The practicality of width can provide broad golf course corridors which, in turn, can provide an expansive backyard for the homeowner who may choose to live along this golf course. Moving away from the age-old trend of double-loaded fairways and maximizing home sites, the future of Pinehurst will lay in the creation of premium lots of sufficient acreage. Minimizing the density of homes will create a sense of open space between adjacent homes and across the broad fairways of the golf course. The result will be a more private and natural setting for the homeowner.

A sandhills throwback to the golf courses from one hundred years ago will show a new generation of golfers that the simple thrill of hitting a golf ball over, through, and around nature's wonders is much more entertaining than a perfect lie within a painted picture. A memorable round will result from the architect's ability to provide strategic options from hole to hole. In turn, these options will allow the golfer to make choices – some correct and some not so correct. Undoubtedly, the golfer will yearn for the prospect of another chance to make the right choice and the golf course developer will reap the benefits of repeat play. The future Pinehurst golf course will not only possess these essential ingredients of great sandy golf, but also be more sensitive to the ground, more environmentally-friendly, and most importantly, affordable to construct and PLAY.

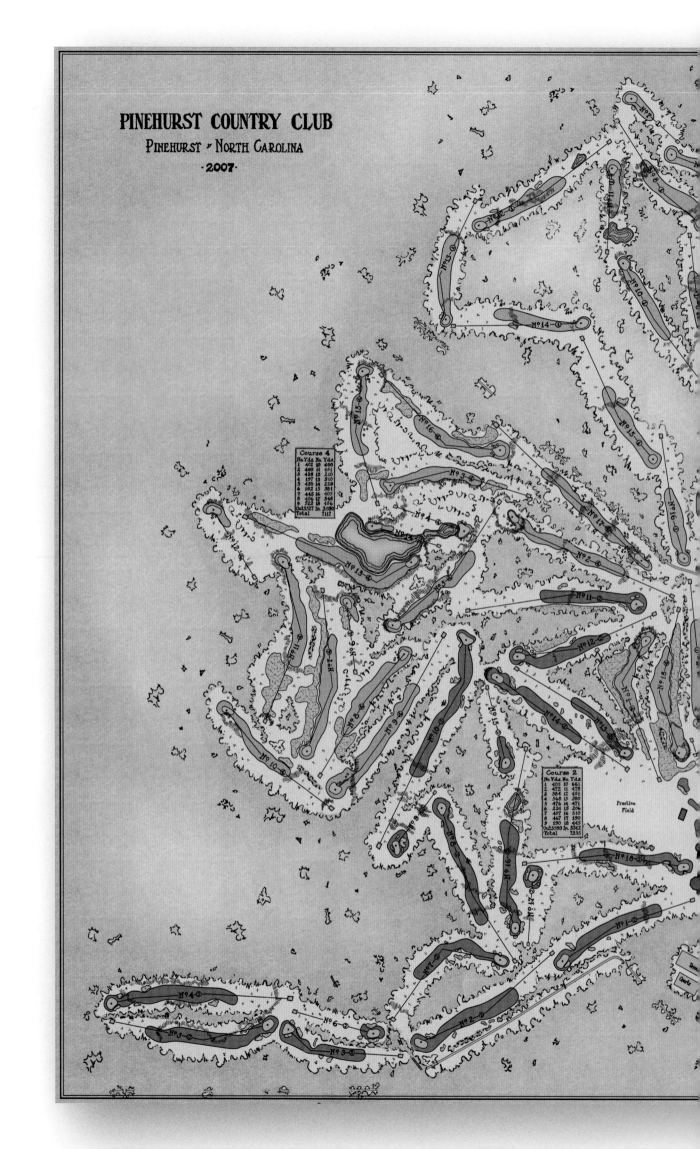

PINEHURST COUNTRY CLUB
PINEHURST ~ NORTH CAROLINA
·2007·

Course 4			
No.Yds.		No.Yds.	
1	402	10	400
2	495	11	491
3	428	12	210
4	197	13	310
5	450	14	228
6	182	15	381
7	445	16	405
8	406	17	346
9	522	18	456
Out 3527		In 3590	
Total		7117	

Course 2			
No.Yds.		No.Yds.	
1	405	10	661
2	472	11	478
3	384	12	451
4	548	13	380
5	474	14	471
6	224	15	206
7	407	16	510
8	447	17	190
9	190	18	445
Out 3593		In 3742	
Total		7335	

Practice
Field

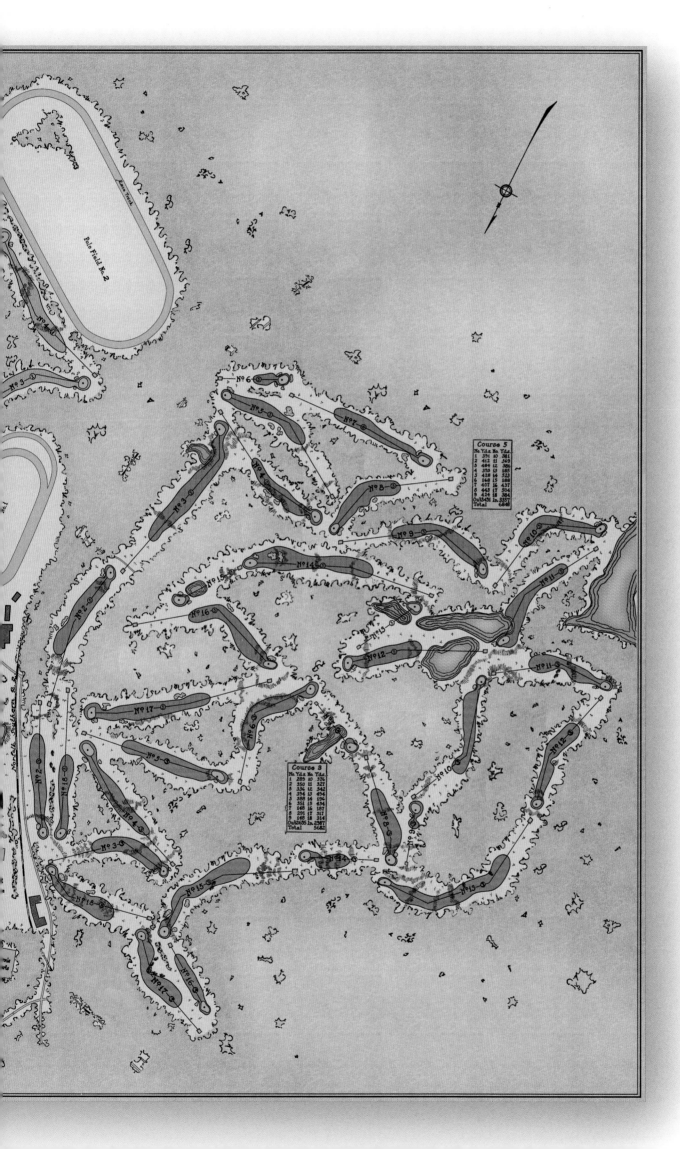

Polo Field No. 2

Course 5

No.	Yds.	No.	Yds.
1	391	10	361
2	412	11	369
3	484	12	386
4	353	13	185
5	428	16	521
6	168	15	188
7	407	16	437
8	443	17	504
9	424	18	384
Out	3491	In	3357
Total		6848	

Course 3

No.	Yds.	No.	Yds.
1	289	10	376
2	350	11	327
3	334	12	342
4	394	13	454
5	388	14	494
6	351	15	434
7	148	16	187
8	291	17	311
9	148	18	314
Out	2695	In	2387
Total		5682	

THE COUNTRY CLUB
GOLF AND TENNIS
Donald J. Ross, *Manager*

(4 Eighteen-Hole Golf Courses and 5 Tennis Courts.)

Golf

Charges for use of course:

Season	$75.00
Month	40.00
Week	15.00
Day	3.00
Season member's wife or children	45.00

Locker charges:

Season	$ 7.50
Two	10.00
Month	4.00
Two	6.00
Week	1.50
Two	2.00
Day	.25

Caddy fees:

18 holes, carrying 1 bag	$1.00
18 holes, carrying 2 bags	1.25
9 holes, carrying 1 bag	.60
9 holes, carrying 2 bags	.75
1 hour's practice	.50
½ hour practice	.30

Caddies are engaged in their regular order through the Caddy Master only. No caddy can be engaged for more than one round. When engaging caddies you will be handed a card giving caddy's number and fee to be paid. Please hand card to Caddy Master with amount due caddy on completion of play.

A minimum fee of $15.00 will be charged those entering Pinehurst tournaments who are not Pinehurst cottagers or guests of the Pinehurst hotels.

ACKNOWLEDGEMENTS

THERE ARE NO TWO PEOPLE MORE IMPORTANT TO ME THAN MY WIFE AND SON. They are the ones who have sacrificed the most in this four-year odyssey of book writing. A few weeks before wrapping up the design of this book, while viewing the first few chapters in their final form on the computer, **MARY** remarked, "Boy, someone sure has put a lot of effort into this!" There was nothing to do for both of us but laugh at the irony of her statement. The fact is, she put as much effort into it without writing a single word. She is the one that has made this book possible, as well as my career. I thank her for the love, patience, and support she has given me these past eleven years. Without her, I couldn't follow my dream of being a golf architect. I'd probably be flipping burgers somewhere.

I first sat down to begin research on this book about a month after Mary and I found out we were expecting a baby. My son, **THOMAS**, is now three years old and has never known his Daddy when he wasn't writing this book. We could all keep going like this and he would never think that wasn't a part of what every daddy does. He has sacrificed without even knowing it. I have tried my best to be there for him as much as possible while also writing this book. One reason this book took as long as it did was my need to walk away from it at times when Thomas wanted to play. I love you T-Bone. Now, let's go play golf (Whoa, Nelly!). You're my Knock Around Guy.

If not for **JANICE** and **AL SOLLE**, Thomas wouldn't be potty-trained and my house would have fallen apart surrounded by a jungle. I owe this wonderful couple my deepest gratitude for keeping my family fed and clothed while I continued to type away.

WALT YOUNG is my Design Associate and the artist of many of the maps of the Pinehurst courses found within these pages. When he interviewed for his job, he said he was used to eighty-hour work weeks. He certainly lived up to his billing and put in countless hours during and after work drawing these fantastic layouts and creating all the wonderful overlays that set this book apart.

I finalized the manuscript for the last time on March 1, 2007. At that point I decided to self-publish this book out of desperation to be done for the U. S. Women's Open at Pine Needles. On March 2nd, I purchased my first book on bookmaking. A week later, I purchased Adobe Indesign CS2. After two weeks of studying the user's guide and a tutorial followed by one very frustrating Saturday trying to figure out margins, I called **JAY BURSKY**. Even though he arrived late to this game, I would be far from finished without him. He was dropped into my life with a one month window to help me design this book and gave it his all. His attention to detail and dedication to the project as a whole were the only things that could have made it a reality. There is not another person out there that could have pulled this off, without sweating a drop. Thanks Jay, for everything.

In addition to Walt in the office, I also want to thank **SUSAN WILSON**, who ran gopher for the past year, chasing down the most minuscule details either online or in her car. She is my biggest cheerleader and took God's lead in pushing me to finish this book without any worries. I also must thank Walt's predecessor, **SAM BASSETT**, who laid much of the groundwork for this book before Walt arrived.

Although my parents, brothers and their families all live away from Pinehurst and aren't around on a day to day basis, I wish to thank all of the **MANDELLS** for the support they unknowingly gave me as I pursued this book project.

I want to thank **DANNY FREELS** to agree to edit this book for a penance. His work was invaluable at two critical junctures in constructing this treatise to Pinehurst. The number of errors he found and suggestions he made had my head spinning, but I'm glad he was there. Too bad he burned through a full box of pencils in the process.

This book would not exist without the **TUFTS ARCHIVES** and its Curator, **AUDREY MORIARTY**. Thanks for the support throughout this process and thanks for giving me free reign of the joint for the past four years. A special thanks must go to **JOHN ROOT** at the Archives, who searched excitedly for any needle I needed in that great big haystack of folders, boxes, and drawers. Thanks also go out to **MELISSA BIELBY**, **LIZ DOWLING**, and the countless volunteers at the Tufts Archives and Given Memorial Library who dedicate so much energy to a timeless treasure of Pinehurst, one that more and more people must discover. Without history, we have no future. The Archives is history preserved.

Thank you to **Margaret Pleasants** and **Jomara Dunn** for transcribing the countless hours of interviews I conducted for this book and patiently rewinding through barking dogs, planes, trains, call-waiting, and any other interruptions they found on those tapes.

Ran Morrissett was there for me from the book's inception as my *"push the envelope muse"*, always challenging me to stay away from the fluff piece. He was the critical eye that made sure I didn't miss a part of history or an opinion on design that needed to be shared.

Tom Stewart was another great cheerleader who always inspired me to continue the project whenever I stopped by Old Sport Gallery to talk when I should have been writing. The place smells of books and history and Pinehurst. Being there pushed me to contribute to the history of Pinehurst and to become part of golf literature with this book. I hope it is worthy of space on its shelves among the giants of the subject like Golf Architecture In America and Scotland's Gift: Golf. I must also thank Tom for leading me to Jay Bursky.

Ted and **Carol Thomas** have been supportive on many different levels throughout this process, from friends to mentors, from editors to spiritual leaders. Ted kept me up when my business was struggling. Now that we have turned the corner, he is a part of RMGA as my sales and marketing arm. Carol, at the drop of a hat and because her husband can't read, gave the manuscript a once over in less than two weeks time, despite not being a golfer. She had great input. Thanks also go out to **Tracy Parks**, **Wink Kinney** and **Robbie Farrell**, who all gave the book a critical look as well. Thanks and love go to the entire **Congregation of Page Memorial United Methodist Church** for all of their support throughout this time in my life and for watching over Mary and Thomas for me.

Thanks to **Janeen Driscoll**, **Cindy Reed**, **Steve Cryan**, and everyone else at the **Pinehurst Resort** who wondered if I was actually writing this book all this time. Thanks for providing everything I needed (and more) to properly document James Walker Tufts's (and ClubCorp's) vision.

Thank you to **Caleb Miles** and the **Convention and Visitor's Bureau of Pinehurst, Southern Pines, Aberdeen Area** for working with me graciously and allowing me to highlight *"The Home of American Golf"*.

The first bit of research I conducted in writing this book was a call to **Paul Daley** on the other side of the world. His insight into the publishing world helped me set focus on day one. For more than three years, his charge to get this book published at all costs lingered in the back of my mind. Amused by his call to arms, I never thought much of it, but here I am a publisher.

Thank you **REES JONES** for making this book as important to you as it is to me, for your efforts with the foreword and contributing your insight and experiences to the book. I am greatly honored and flattered that you have taken such an interest in me, my career, and this book. I just hope it lives up to your expectations. Thanks also go to **DIANE JACKSON** and **VICKI CARUSO** in Rees's office for helping to push him along.

Thanks to **PETE GREER** and the people at **JOSTENS**, who put this to print and hit a demanding deadline, despite dealing with a first-time book publisher. Jay and I thank you for your guidance throughout the publishing process. I hope this book is something Jostens can boast about.

BRAD KLEIN said I was crazy for thinking I could have this thing done in time for the 2005 Men's U.S. Open Championship. Shows how much he knows! Thanks for your early insights and the inspiration your book, *Discovering Donald Ross*, was to my efforts. I also thank **FORREST RICHARDSON**, a fellow architect/writer from the other side of the country. Your guidance and support two times a year was more than valuable.

Thanks to **JIM MORIARTY** for pushing me along and encouraging me whenever I saw you at the Java Bean Plantation. Thank you for providing professional references such as Danny Freels as well. I also must thank the **FOLKS AT THE JAVA BEAN** for keeping me awake all these many days.

I want to thank everyone who allowed me to interview them for this book. Without first-hand experience, this book is just a history. But with your contributions it is a living, breathing story. Thank you to **BRAD** and **BETH KOCHER**, **TOM FAZIO**, **BILL PATTON**, **TERRY BROWN**, **DAN MAPLES**, **DICK URQUHART**, **BILL SLEDGE**, **JERRY SLADE**, **JIM HINCKLEY**, **CHIP KING**, **PEGGY KIRK BELL**, **KELLY MILLER**, **BOB KLUG**, **TOMMY ALBIN**, **MARK STEWART** (for also giving Thomas his first set of golf clubs), **GEORGE THOMPSON**, **ANDY PAGE**, **WOODY DAVIS**, and **PAT CORSO**.

A very special thank you goes to two people who were gracious enough to grant me interviews in the last months of their lives, **JOHN SULLIVAN** and **PETER TUFTS**.

The opportunity to include personal remembrances of Donald Ross makes this book more special than any other books about Donald Ross. I am forever grateful for the opportunity to interview both Rod Innes and (again) Peter Tufts. Peter Tufts was Donald Ross's godson and watched Ross convert Pinehurst Number Two's greens from sand to grass way back in 1935. First-hand knowledge from someone's own eyes help make this book stand out.

ROD INNES worked for Donald Ross here in Pinehurst and his Father grew up with Ross in Dornoch. It is amazing that there can be such a connection directly to Ross's homeland within this book.

Thank you to all who have helped me fill in a few blanks along the way, like those already mentioned above as well as **RICK MCDERMOTT, BOBBY HANSEN, JEFF DAWSON, DAVE FRUCHTE, JOHN ELLIS, JEFF DOTSON, SUE POCKMEYER** and the **MOORE COUNTY HISTORICAL ASSOCIATION, TONY PARKER, HEATHER HAMBRICK**, and countless others. Thanks also go to **BEN CRENSHAW** and **SCOTT SAYERS** for their generous contributions to this book.

The research and the manuscript took more than three years to complete, but collecting drawings and pictures took just a few months and I thank all of those people who quickly and expeditiously delivered some of the best photography around: **ROBBIE** and **JULIE WOOTEN** of **IMPACT GOLF, JOE GAY, STUART TAYLOR, BRANDON LIVENGOOD, DOUG THOMPSON, BARRY MATEY, HOLLY BELL, DIANA TUFTS, MIKE SPAYD, DEAN ALLGEYER, ASHLEY TURNER, JEAN MCAFEE, KEN CROW, MARVIN WATERS, LARRY LAMBRECHT, JEFF DOTSON, GLENN DICKERSON, ALLEN VAN VLIET, BILL GLASS, JOHN MCDOUGAL, REES JONES, JANEEN DRISCOLL** and **ABBY PINTER** of **CLUBCORP, BOB KLUG, TOMMY ALBIN, CHRIS LITTLE**, and especially the **TUFTS ARCHIVES**.

Thank you to the **MOORE COUNTY HISTORICAL ASSOCIATION** for supplying many key images of the sandhills. The Moore County Historical Association was founded in 1946 and is one of the oldest non-profit historical associations in North Carolina. The MCHA has been recognized as a pioneer in preserving the history of everyday life of the 1700s and 1800s in North Carolina. Among the homes they maintain are the historic properties of the Shaw House, Garner House, and Sanders Cabin in Southern Pines and the Bryant House and McLendon Cabin in Carthage. The Association also maintains a Photographic Archives located at the Shaw House. I urge anyone interested in history to get more information about the MCHA at their website: www.moorehistory.com.

Thank you **CHRIS KOLTYK** and the **MOORE COUNTY GIS DEPARTMENT** for providing the aerial photography of Pinehurst Resort which serves as the basis for the many overlays in this book. Without your gracious contributions, the reader would never know where the fourth hole of the old Employees Course could be found today.

A special thanks to **DONALD ROSS** and the **TUFTS FAMILY** for providing such a great story and a home for me and my family.

Lastly, and most important, I want to thank God for giving me all that I have.

A SPECIAL THANKS

JOHN HEMMER
Photographer

Many of the great photos found in **PINEHURST: HOME OF AMERICAN GOLF** were taken by Mr. John Hemmer. Hemmer was the official photographer for Pinehurst from 1926 until the seventies. His photographs were art because of his ability to create the perfect composition, not just take a picture. His mastery of light with less than sophisticated equipment far outshines many pictures today taken with even the most advanced technology. He was truly an artist and is responsible for much of the success of this book.

Thanks, John

TUFTS ARCHIVES

THE MAJORITY OF THE INFORMATION CONTAINED IN *PINEHURST ~ HOME OF AMERICAN GOLF* WAS DISCOVERED IN A PLACE CALLED THE TUFTS ARCHIVES, LOCATED IN THE HEART OF THE VILLAGE OF PINEHURST. As much as this book recounts the history of Pinehurst, it is a standard bearer for what historical preservation is all about and how important the Tufts Archives is to its history.

The Tufts Archives was built as an expansion of the Given Memorial Library in 1975. Its creation was spurred by Richard S. Tufts. Richard created the Tufts Foundation to fund construction of the archives and as an endowment for its continued operation. Richard Tufts provided the archives with historic family records, including thousands of copies of correspondence dating back to the founding of the village and the earliest days of American golf.

The countless hours spent in the Archives told me one thing – the Tufts Archives is a fascinating place. If I had the time I could spend days in there with little more than bread and water. The displays are full of personal items donated by hundreds of people over the years which tell the story of the Tufts family, Pinehurst, and the numerous characters which define this golf destination. At one point, I decided I needed to stay out of the archives for fear of never finishing this project. In fact, a few days before sending the book off to the printers, I found myself waiting for someone at the Archives and stumbling into yet another fantastic photograph that just had to be part of the book. I had over 100,000 images to choose from for this book.

Archives displays include not only the history of Pinehurst but a Tufts marble 19th century soda fountain and items from the Tufts silver plate business, horse training track memorabilia, displays of early artifacts from the Carolina Hotel, the Holly Inn and artifacts from Annie Oakley, who served as a shooting instructor at the Pinehurst Gun Club from 1916 to 1924. Behind the displays is a full wall of boxes and boxes of the most interesting stories about not just the Tufts family and Pinehurst, but about the countless golf tournaments and players who frequented the golf courses.

The boxes also include the most in-depth collection of golf architecture documents from all eras. But, of course, the primary focus is on Donald Ross. Over 300 of his original field sketches and course layouts are housed at the Tufts Archives. In addition, many of his personal letters and other special Ross items are preserved. The most special of these are his original sketches he did for George Thomas's 1927 seminal work, *Golf Architecture In America*.

The Tufts Archives is a private institution and open to scholars and the public. The Archives continues a quest to preserve the thousands of artifacts and photographs for years to come. Thousands of images must still be converted to digital format before time damages them beyond repair. At the same time, numerous other items continue to arrive at the archives, needing immediate attention. The Tufts Archives is a not for profit organization that relies solely on gifts and donations. It is a must-visit that deserves support.

FACING PAGE EXHIBITS

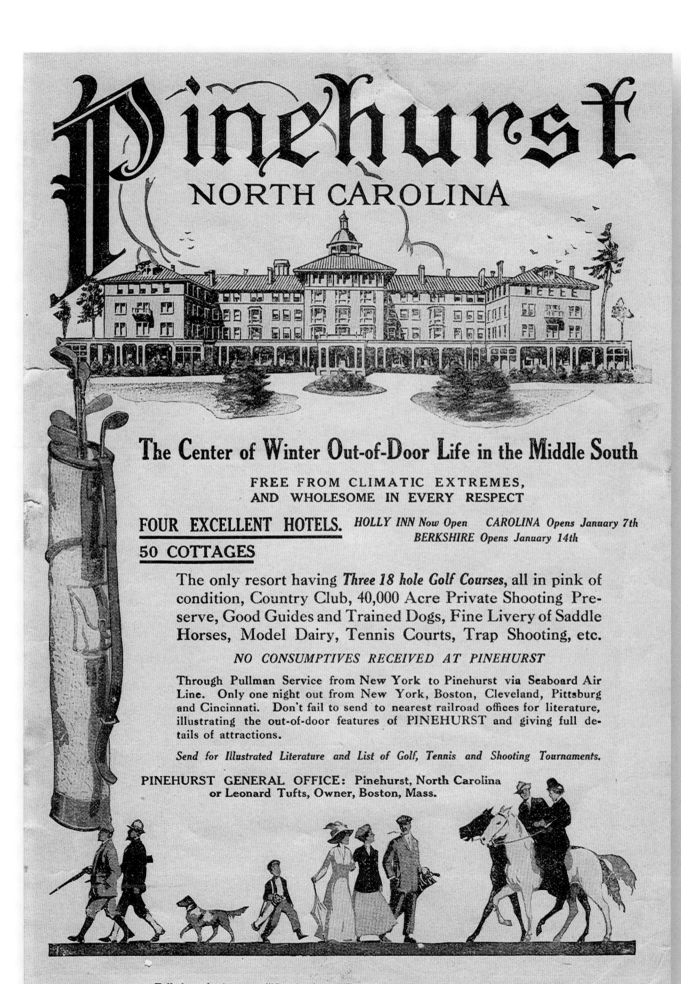

Pinehurst
NORTH CAROLINA

The Center of Winter Out-of-Door Life in the Middle South

**FREE FROM CLIMATIC EXTREMES,
AND WHOLESOME IN EVERY RESPECT**

FOUR EXCELLENT HOTELS. *HOLLY INN Now Open   CAROLINA Opens January 7th*
BERKSHIRE Opens January 14th

50 COTTAGES

The only resort having *Three 18 hole Golf Courses*, all in pink of condition, Country Club, 40,000 Acre Private Shooting Preserve, Good Guides and Trained Dogs, Fine Livery of Saddle Horses, Model Dairy, Tennis Courts, Trap Shooting, etc.

NO CONSUMPTIVES RECEIVED AT PINEHURST

Through Pullman Service from New York to Pinehurst via Seaboard Air Line. Only one night out from New York, Boston, Cleveland, Pittsburg and Cincinnati. Don't fail to send to nearest railroad offices for literature, illustrating the out-of-door features of PINEHURST and giving full details of attractions.

Send for Illustrated Literature and List of Golf, Tennis and Shooting Tournaments.

PINEHURST GENERAL OFFICE: Pinehurst, North Carolina or Leonard Tufts, Owner, Boston, Mass.

Tell the substitutor: "No, thank you, I want what I asked for.   Good-bye."

INDEX

N

O

P

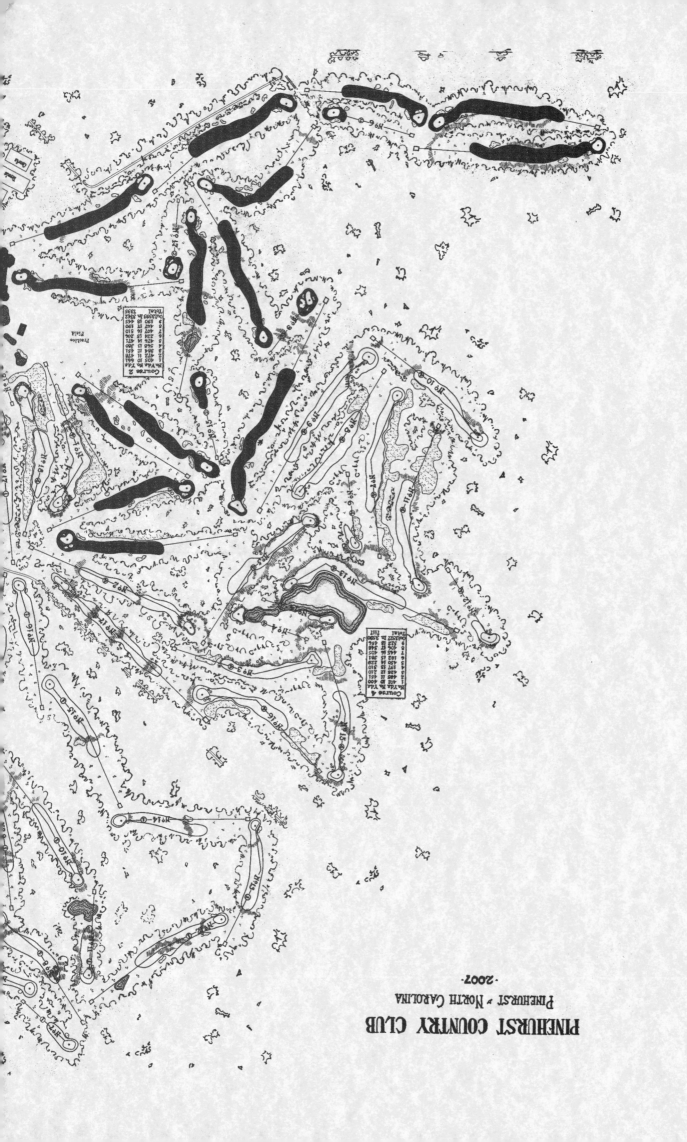

PINEHURST COUNTRY CLUB

PINEHURST ⚬ NORTH CAROLINA

· 2007 ·